America's Fi

America's First Interstate

The National Road, 1806–1853

✳✳✳

Roger Pickenpaugh

The Kent State University Press

KENT, OHIO

To Ken and Lena Williams

✳✳✳

© 2020 by The Kent State University Press, Kent, Ohio 44242
All rights reserved

Library of Congress Catalog Number 2019054934
ISBN 978-1-60635-397-4
Manufactured in the United States of America

Library of Congress Cataloging-in-Publication Data
Names: Pickenpaugh, Roger, author.
Title: America's first interstate : the National Road, 1806-1853 / Roger Pickenpaugh.
Description: Kent, Ohio : Kent State University Press, [2020] | Includes bibliographical
        references and index.
Identifiers: LCCN 2019054934 | ISBN 9781606353974 (cloth) | ISBN 9781631014055
        (epub) | ISBN 9781631014062 (pdf)
Subjects: LCSH: Cumberland Road--History--19th century. | Roads--United States--
        History--19th century. | United States Highway 40--History.
Classification: LCC HE356.C8 P48 2020 | DDC 388.10973--dc23
LC record available at https://lccn.loc.gov/2019054934

24 23 22 21 20   5 4 3 2 1

Contents

Acknowledgments

ONCE AGAIN, I MUST BEGIN with the time-worn, but true, observation that nobody produces a book alone. And once again, to my wife, Marion, goes my undying gratitude for proofreading, indexing, and putting up with me through yet another project. Thanks also to my mother, Fern Pickenpaugh, for proofreading and support.

Much of this book was written while caring for my stepdaughter, Anya Crum, who left us far too soon. I miss you, Punky! I also had the support of stepdaughter Jocelyn Brooks, her husband, Patrick, and grandchildren Parker and Harrison Brooks. It means more to me than they will ever know.

As always, librarians shared their expertise and made the research experience rewarding and enjoyable. Those who helped with this project included: Tutti Jackson, Melissa Dorsten, and Lily Birkhimer, Ohio Historical Society; Nicole Merriman, State Library of Ohio; Amy Welsh and Kelly Helm, U. Grant Miller Library, Washington and Jefferson College; MaryJo Price, Frostburg State University; Suzanne Hahn and Nadia Kousari, Indiana Historical Society; Laura Eliason and Lauren Patton, Indiana State Library; Natalie Fritz, Clark County, Ohio Historical Society; Allison Rein, Maryland State Archives; and numerous individuals at the National Archives and Records Administration.

I visited public libraries in almost every county through which the National Road passed. Almost without exception, I was treated kindly and professionally. Special thanks go to Beth Treaster of the Centerville-Center Township Public Library in Indiana. Beth not only guided me through the library's valuable collections regarding the road, but she also proofread most of the manuscript.

Professors Evan Kutzler of Georgia Southwestern State University and Angela Zombek of the University of North Carolina at Wilmington both read the entire manuscript. Although it is technically outside their area of expertise, one would not have guessed so from their incisive comments. Closer to home, Ken Williams read through it twice, catching, as usual, numerous errors. Thanks also to Agusta Daugherty and Ashley McCorkle, who provided invaluable assistance in producing the photographs, and Alex Secrest, who helped with indexing.

Thank you again to the folks at the Kent State University Press for their guidance and for putting up with someone who has to be their most computer illiterate writer.

Introduction

On December 19, 1805, Uriah Tracy, a Connecticut Federalist, rose to address the United States Senate. Tracy had been a member of a committee appointed to make recommendations for putting into effect certain provisions of the 1803 law granting statehood to Ohio. Specifically, the measure had set aside funds for building a road or roads connecting the seventeenth state with its eastern counterparts. Tracy's committee was given the assignment of, among other things, selecting a route.

"The committee have thought it expedient to recommend the laying out of a road from Cumberland, on the northerly bank of the Potomac and within the state of Maryland, to the river Ohio," Tracy reported. "To carry into effect the principles arising from the foregoing facts, the committee present herewith a bill for the consideration of the Senate," he continued. On behalf of his committee, the veteran lawmaker explained, "They suppose, that to take the proper measures for carrying into effect the section of the law respecting a road or roads to the state of Ohio is a duty imposed upon Congress by the law itself, and that a sense of duty will always be sufficient to insure the passage of the bill now offered to the Senate."[1]

Whether or not it felt a sense of duty, the Senate passed the measure the committee had recommended eight days later without debate. The House of Representatives took up the bill in March. There the debate was heated. Most opposition came from the Virginia and Pennsylvania delegations, both of which felt slighted in the choice of route. It was not enough, however, and on March 24, the House passed "an act to regulate the laying out and making a road from Cumberland in the state of Maryland to the state of Ohio" by a vote of 66–55. Five days later, President Thomas Jefferson signed it into law.[2]

The measure was unique in the Jefferson era. It was a time when the national government's domestic duties extended little beyond providing a meager defense, delivering the mail, and tending lighthouses. As an avowed strict constructionist on constitutional matters, Jefferson should have given the measure a resounding veto, as successors Madison, Monroe, and Jackson would to subsequent bills for funding the road. After all, the law would eventually involve the national government in running a road through six states; and the costs involved would not match up well with Jefferson's ideas regarding limited government spending.

Jefferson was not, however, one-dimensional. Although philosophy and principles were important to him, he was a practical and pragmatic politician. Three years earlier, he had put constitutional qualms aside when given the opportunity to purchase Louisiana and double the size of the United States. That transaction had suddenly and dramatically redefined the American frontier. It fit nicely with another important aspect of the Jeffersonian philosophy: an agrarian nation composed largely of yeoman farmers. To reach distant lands those pioneers would need good transportation. The same would be necessary for them to ship their produce to market. Politically, the majority of families heading westward would be headed by Republican voters. Politics was never far from Jefferson's mind, and there seems little doubt that the prospect of future Republican states entered into the president's thinking. The result was a presidential signature and the start of what was among the most significant projects taken on by the national government during the antebellum period.

The project offered arguments for both sides of the debate concerning ambitious government undertakings. On the positive side, the road served thousands of westward-moving emigrants, travelers, farmers, and businessmen. It seems very unlikely that the states could have completed such an undertaking, assuming they could have even agreed upon a route. At the same time, the project moved at a glacial pace—especially in the view of those communities waiting for the road's arrival. In doing so, it anticipated a twentieth-century stereotype of inefficient "government work." Even worse were the charges of corruption—many undeniable—that seemed to follow the road as it crept westward. In fairness, these charges grew more common after the road had been turned over to the states. They were, however, voiced from the earliest days of the project.

✳✳✳

Still, the National Road made a significant contribution to an expanding country. It filled a void that waterways could not fill. Cumberland was, realistically, the western terminus of the Potomac. The Ohio flowed several miles distant. In between were the Appalachians. That meant America had no choice but to build a road if it hoped to connect its eastern and western waterways—and its eastern and western citizens. It was a major, and a significant, undertaking. Despite that, the National Road has seldom attracted the interest of historians. Histories of the time period cover it briefly, if at all, and histories of the road itself are few in number.

The first history of the road was among the best. *The Old Pike: A History of the National Road with Incidents, Accidents, and Anecdotes Thereon* was published in 1894 by its author, Thomas B. Searight, and it was clearly a labor of love. Searight had grown up along the road in Pennsylvania, and "he saw it in the zenith of its glory, and with emotions of sadness witnessed its decline." Searight contacted former drivers of both stagecoaches and freight wagons as well as drovers and innkeepers. He also gathered numerous original government reports. The result is a book that is rich in detail, if sometimes uneven in presentation. It remains the starting point for anyone studying the road, and it likely will for many years to come.

The first work of modern scholarship was Archer Butler Hulbert, *The Old National Road: A Chapter of American Expansion.* Published in 1904, Hulbert's work was slim, drawing largely from government records and newspapers.

In 1902, Jeremiah Simeon Young published *A Political and Constitutional Study of the Cumberland Road.* Based on the author's PhD dissertation, it viewed the road through the lenses of "political influences" and "constitutional bearings and significances." Young added, "The attempt in this research is made to treat the Cumberland Road as a central thread running through the subject of internal improvements until 1856."[3]

The National Road, by Philip D. Jordan, was published in 1948 by Bobbs-Merrill as part of its American Trails Series. With over 400 pages of text, Jordan's work is thorough, covering the road through its early days and as US Route 40. It is also quite readable. The research far exceeds anything that came before, but it is nevertheless largely lacking in manuscript sources.

In 1996 the Johns Hopkins University Press published *The National Road.* Edited by Karl Raitz, the richly illustrated coffee-table book contains twelve essays by scholars representing a variety of disciplines. They cover various aspects of the road from concept to "The Interstate 70 Landscape."

✳✳✳

The goal of this work is to provide a solid narrative history of the National Road's earliest days. To accomplish this, I have attempted to dig more deeply into manuscript sources, particularly those at the National Archives, than previous historians of the road. Another goal was to offer more detail into the construction of the road through Indiana and Illinois. The highway tended to fade out as it attempted to cross the prairie, and historical accounts have tended to do so as well. Thanks to materials at the National Archives and reports in local newspapers, I feel I have made some strides toward filling in this gap in historiography. Finally, I attempted to uncover more details concerning state control of the road, another topic often overlooked. The level of success varied from state to state based upon the amount of surviving records, but I believe I was able in this area, too, to fill in significant gaps.

Although not meant to be an interpretive work, I did attempt to place the road within the political context of the time. Six presidents held office during the construction period. Only two, Jefferson and John Quincy Adams, gave the road their full support. James Madison and James Monroe, both Jeffersonians, vetoed bills providing construction funds, expressing constitutional concerns while at the same time asserting that they favored the project personally. Then as now, changing political tides affected the fate of a major government project.

Because of its nature, this book is definitely not meant to be the last word on the National Road. Instead, it has two goals. The first is to provide the historical background of this important road. Second, it is intended to be a starting point for future historians. My hope is that they will find the basic story interesting and build upon it, adding interpretive matter from their various specialties. It deserves no less.

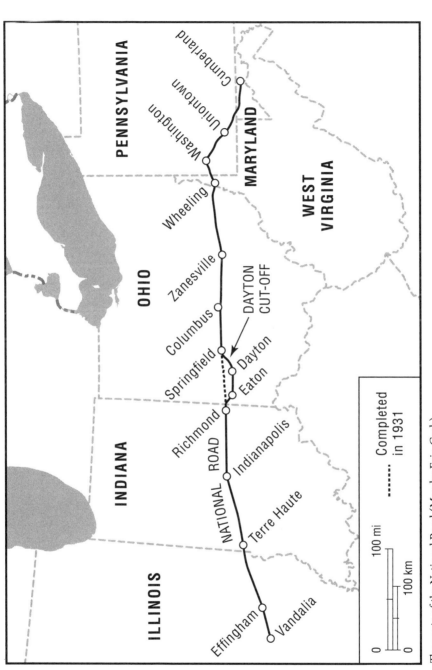

The route of the National Road (Map by Erin Greb)

CHAPTER ONE

"The touch of a feather"
The Highway Came with the Sun

To a great extent America's history has been the story of westward movement. From the Northwest Ordinance and the Louisiana Purchase to the Mexican "Cession," the California Gold Rush, and the Oregon Trail to "Seward's Folly" and Greeley's advice, this country's North Star has generally been the setting sun. For America's founding generation it was a continuation of the dreams that drew their ancestors across the Atlantic. For generations of immigrants who followed them it was a story of opportunity, if not for themselves then for their progeny. And for the native nations already here, long before either group arrived, it was almost always a tragic story of repression, relocation, and extermination.

To America's colonists, including the generation that led it to independence, the West meant the area beyond the Appalachians. For the generation that followed, the Louisiana Purchase redefined the parameters and heightened the mystique. Although the transmontaine West was not far distant in miles from America's original thirteen states, the barrier of the mountains made it, in practical terms, a world away.

Nobody was more aware of this geographical reality—or more concerned by it—than George Washington. The future father of his country was only sixteen years old when, in 1748, he made his first western venture. Crossing the Blue Ridge with his friend George William Fairfax, Washington helped survey the vast landholdings of Fairfax's father, Col. William Fairfax. At first put off by the lack of creature comforts, he came to embrace the rugged life of a frontier surveyor.[1]

In 1753 Washington made the first of six expeditions to the trans-Allegheny region. It marked his debut as an actor on the international stage and his introduction to the challenges of travel beyond the mountains.

He went at the behest of Robert Dinwiddie, the Virginia colony's lieutenant governor, whose motives in dispatching the youthful surveyor were both patriotic and pecuniary. As British colonists began to push west of the Appalachians, the French were entering the Ohio Valley from their colonies along the St. Lawrence River. In retrospect, a clash seemed inevitable. Dinwiddie's instructions to his emissary, approved by King George II, were to demand that the French leave the Ohio Valley country and to scout out locations for fortifications in the likely event that they refused. Much was at stake for the lieutenant governor. In addition to protecting the interests of the crown, Dinwiddie was also interested in protecting the interests of the Ohio Land Company. He was a major investor in the company, which had acquired title to half a million acres of land beyond the mountains.[2]

Washington left Williamsburg on October 31, late in the season for a mission across the mountains. Six men accompanied him. Most notable among them was Christopher Gist, a noted frontiersman and surveyor, who was well acquainted with the native people of the western country. Two years earlier Gist had scouted a trail from Cumberland, Maryland, to the Monongahela River, and on Washington's expedition he rode at the head of the column. Despite his expert guidance, the journey was not easy. Winter came early to the Appalachians; heavy rain turned to snow, and ice soon clogged waterways. It was, the normally stoic Washington complained, "as fatiguing a journey as it is possible to conceive." The route carried the party over the Alleghenies, across the Youghiogheny River, over Negro Mountain and Laurel Hill, before delivering them to the Monongahela, which they reached on November 22.[3]

After examining a site for a potential British fort, Washington spent the next few days parleying with Indian leaders, attempting to discern their intentions and win the wary over to his side. Then, traveling through still more rain and snow, he headed for Fort Le Boeuf. He reached the crude fortification on December 11 and presented Dinwiddie's ultimatum to the commander, Capt. Jacques Legardeur de St. Pierre. The Frenchman's reply was blunt, if quaintly elegant: "As to the summons you send me to retire, I do not think myself obliged to obey it." The response was not what Washington desired, but it was likely what he expected. He had fulfilled his instructions, and he headed for home, firmly convinced that British hopes for military success in the Ohio Valley would largely depend upon a serviceable road to deliver men and matériel to the likely scene of conflict.[4]

The following April Washington and a force of 160 started out for what would soon become an actual scene of conflict. Dinwiddie had received word that the French were dispatching a raiding party to the forks of the Ohio. He ordered Washington, then headquartered in Alexandria, to proceed in that direction. Hacking out a road as they advanced, it took the small army three weeks to reach Cumberland. From there the going was just as slow as the axmen did battle with the mountainous wilderness of Maryland and Pennsylvania.

They labored under the watchful eyes of Indians loyal to the French. On May 24, Washington learned that a French force commanded by one Joseph Coulon de Villiers, Sieur de Jumonville, had crossed the Youghiogheny and was fewer than eighteen miles away. The colonial officer decided to make his stand at Great Meadows, near present-day Uniontown, Pennsylvania, carving out what he termed "a charming field for an encounter." Despite that assessment, Washington went on the hunt of his enemy. On the twenty-eighth he found them, a detachment of thirty-five men. The colonial force surprised them, and in a fifteen-minute skirmish killed ten and captured twenty-one. Jumonville was among the dead, his comrades insisting his mission was diplomatic, the delivery of a warning message to the British similar to the one Washington had transmitted one year earlier.[5]

Washington's impetuous attack would win him praise from Dinwiddie and condemnation from officials in London, who saw it as confirmation of their view that American officers were recklessly impulsive. In the moment, the Virginia colonel did not have time to worry about the reviews. Instead he prepared for the retaliatory French attack he knew would be coming. He erected a crude fortification on the Great Meadows, which he aptly named Fort Necessity, had trenches dug and breastworks put up, and awaited the inevitable onslaught. It came on July 3. Attacking in overwhelming numbers, the French and their Indian allies killed or wounded a third of Washington's force before the Americans surrendered. French chicanery and a translator's laxness made things even worse. The young commander signed a paper "confessing" that the French attack came in response to the "assassination" of Jumonville, not his death in honorable combat. Harshly criticized in London, Washington managed largely to hold on to his good reputation in Virginia. Right or wrong, Washington's actions had brought on the French and Indian War, although it would have started with or without him.[6]

Washington's role in the conflict was not yet over. On February 20, 1755, Maj. Gen. Edward Braddock, along with two regiments of British regulars, arrived at Hampton Roads. Sixty years old, Braddock had spent forty-three years in the army. Charged with ridding the Ohio Valley of the French "invaders," he arrived with a sterling reputation and a dearth of knowledge or experience regarding frontier warfare.

Braddock apparently sensed his weaknesses. Learning that Washington had more knowledge of the area into which he would be venturing than anyone else, the British veteran asked the young officer to serve as an aide-de-camp. Despite any misgivings he may have harbored because of the debacle at Fort Necessity, Braddock treated Washington with kindness and respect. Still, the self-assured veteran did not always follow his youthful subordinate's counsel. This proved unfortunate when he dismissed Washington's suggestion to leave behind his wagons and heavy siege guns, instead taking only what could be carried on packhorses. It was a curious bit of obstinacy because Braddock had already become painfully familiar with the challenges of transportation in the colonies. It had taken his procession twenty-seven days to cover the 180 miles from Alexandria to Fort Cumberland, which the general attributed in part to "the Badness of the Roads."[7]

On May 30 Braddock dispatched a force of six hundred men to begin opening a road from Fort Cumberland to Little Meadows, a distance of twenty miles. The result of the first day's effort was two miles cleared and three wagons destroyed. Part of the problem was that the general's engineers and axmen had never encountered a mountainous wilderness such as this. Both men and horses fell dead from exertion as they challenged the rugged terrain. Washington chafed as his commanding officer insisted on "halting to level every Mold Hill" along the route. As a result, the column continued to creep along at a rate of two miles a day. It was enough finally to convince Braddock of the wisdom of his subordinate's advice. The general ordered his officers to send back to Fort Cumberland wagons, artillery, and all unnecessary baggage. He also accepted Washington's proposal that a lightly armed detachment of eight hundred be sent ahead, with supplies and artillery to follow.[8]

On July 9 this advance force, now nearly fourteen hundred strong, crossed the Monongahela. The French were waiting on the other side, along with their

Native American allies. Their attack seemed to come from out of nowhere, punctuated by piercing war whoops that totally unnerved the trained and disciplined British regulars. Braddock, combining courage with foolishness, rushed forward to the sounds of gunfire, forming his men into compact ranks that made them an easy target for their foes. His bravery cost him his life, an ignoble end to an honorable career as a soldier. Braddock's campaign, however, led to an unexpected legacy. The road that his men had hewn out of the wilderness would parallel, but not trace exactly, the route of the National Road. It seems unlikely that the British general, fiercely loyal to his homeland, would appreciate his unintended contribution to the soon-to-be rebellious Americans. Still, that contribution was real and lasting, and for those who to this day traverse US 40 across western Maryland and Pennsylvania, it is an ongoing legacy.[9]

Washington's next major western foray was a nine-week expedition begun in October 1770. Its purpose was to scout lands to be allotted to him and his officers for their wartime service. Accompanied by Dr. James Craik and three servants, he followed familiar terrain to Pittsburgh before thoroughly exploring the Ohio to the mouth of the Great Kanawha. There was a certain sense of urgency to the effort. Settlers were venturing over the mountains, and Washington wanted to ensure that the best lands ended up with the right purchasers, himself included. He had also learned of a British investment plan to secure 2.5 million acres of prime western land. As he sought out the best real estate, Washington also tried to discern the best routes for overland roads and to determine which waterways might be navigable. The effort would become a passion, one born of difficult wartime experience.[10]

Washington would soon return to war, leading recalcitrant colonists against his recent allies. During that time his Mount Vernon estate was largely neglected, and he returned home financially strapped. At the same time, his frontier tenants fell behind on their rent, and squatters occupied other sections of his western holdings. In September 1784, Washington made his last expedition over the mountains. One of his goals for the trip was to collect delinquent rents, an attempt that produced mixed results.[11]

More significant was Washington's thorough exploration of the western territory and his detailed observations on the potential for transportation both by roads and waterways. Once again traveling from Fort Cumberland, Washington made no nostalgic comment on scenes of past conflict but limited his remarks to the practical. Writing in his diary at Great Meadows, he did not mention Fort Necessity, instead noting that the spot seemed a good location for raising hay and grain and was "a very good stand for a tavern." Along the way he had found the road to be "upon the whole indifferent." The Little Youghiogheny, he believed, could "be improved into a valuable navigation."[12]

Continuing west, Washington interrogated virtually everyone he encountered about potential navigation of rivers and creeks and of "the Nature of the Country." Near Uniontown, Pennsylvania, Washington met in a one-room log cabin with a group of local landowners. He asked for their assistance in discerning the best location for a road over the Alleghenies. As Washington questioned those in attendance, an impetuous young surveyor and budding politician named Albert Gallatin reportedly inserted himself into the discussion. Gesturing at a map, Gallatin pointed out what he considered the obvious best route. His impertinence earned the young man a piercing stare from the general. Then, after studying Gallatin's path, Washington concluded, "You are right, sir." Washington did not mention the incident in his diary, but it has become a staple of Gallatin biographies. It received some corroboration from Sir Augustus Foster, who worked at the British embassy when Gallatin was secretary of the treasury. Foster recorded the following conversation: "Mr. Gallatin told me he once met him [Washington] when he (Gallatin) was quite a young man, in the back country, and that he thought him heavy and rather stupid. He was in a small room questioning some hunters about roads and distances." Foster added that Gallatin had since changed his opinion of the first president.[13]

Washington had planned to revisit the Kanawha Valley, but "reports of the discontented temper of the Indians and the Mischiefs done by some parties of them" changed his mind. Instead he headed south to explore the Cheat River, returning to Mount Vernon on October 4.[14]

Six days later Washington put his thoughts to paper in a lengthy letter to Virginia Governor Benjamin Harrison. He began by stating the problem as he saw it:

> I need not remark to you Sir, that the flanks and rear of the United States are possessed by other powers, and formidable ones too; nor how necessary it is to apply the cement of interest, to bind all parts of the Union together by indissoluble bonds, especially that part of it, which lies immediately west of us, with the middle States. For, what ties, let me ask, shou'd we have upon these people? How entirely unconnected with them shall we be, and what troubles may we not apprehend, if the Spaniards on their right, and Gt. Britain on their left, instead of throwing stumbling blocks in their way as they now do, should hold out lures for their trade and alliance?

The western settlers, Washington believed, "stand as it were upon a pivot; the touch of a feather, would turn them any way." It might have already happened, he continued, had Spain not made the impolitic mistake of closing the Mississippi to American trade, the "stumbling block" to which he had referred. At the same time, all that attracted trade eastward was "a long Land transportation and unimproved roads."[15]

Blending altruism with parochialism, Washington observed, "A combination of circumstances makes the present conjucture more favorable for Virginia, than for any other State in the Union to fix these matters." He called for the appointment of commissioners to survey the James and the Potomac, as well as "the streams capable of improvement which run into the Ohio." He concluded, "Upon the whole, the object, in my estimation is of vast commercial and political importance: in these lights I think posterity will consider it, and regret (if our conduct should give them cause) that the present favourable moment to secure so great a blessing for them, was neglected."[16]

When Washington wrote his letter, the Constitutional Convention was three years away. With the government laboring under the Articles of Confederation, the United States were united more in theory than in fact. Therefore his call to state action was less selfish and more pragmatic than it may appear today. It was also written at a time when the American Revolution—which was fought to restrain centralized power—was fresh in people's minds. Washington was painfully aware of this as he wrote, knowing he was facing an uncomfortable paradox. Ultimately, for American liberty to survive, the Union that grew out of the revolution had to survive as well. At the same time, internal improvements necessary to connect this vast Union, despite Washington's proposals, would require the involvement of a central government clothed in the powers to make them possible. The question of the national government's authority to do so would eventually hang over congressional debates concerning the funding of the National Road for more than three decades.[17]

During his presidency Washington would see some of his fears of disunity materialize. In 1794 farmers in western Pennsylvania rose up in revolt against an oppressive federal tax on whiskey. The law establishing the excise had given government inspectors wide latitude in searching barns and cellars. This appalled the independent-minded westerners, who showed their displeasure by shooting at the inspectors and setting fire to their homes.

At the heart of the problem were the transportation woes Washington had long decried. A lack of good roads prompted the farmers to distill grain into whiskey, making it much easier to transport. It was sold or bartered for needed goods, becoming a medium of exchange on the frontier. The president may have sympathized with their plight, but he was more concerned over the threat "so daring and unwarrantable a spirit" posed to the infant government. Egged on by Secretary of the Treasury Alexander Hamilton, the mastermind of the tax, Washington called upon governors in Pennsylvania, New Jersey, and Virginia to raise a militia force of 13,000 men to put down the uprising. This was more soldiers than Washington had led at any one time during the revolution. The president rode at the head of the column much of the way, the only time an American commander-in-chief ever led troops in the field.

His heart, however, seemed not to be in the effort. One observer in Carlisle, Pennsylvania, wrote that Washington appeared to be more interested in "roads, distances, etc." than he was in the military campaign. After the president turned back for the comfort of Philadelphia, Hamilton eagerly assumed command of the troops. As the overwhelming force approached, the rebellion evaporated, and the treasury secretary returned to the capital with some 150 prisoners. Two were later sentenced to death for their part in the uprising. Washington pardoned them both.[18]

Rogue frontiersmen were not the only ones threatening to tilt Washington's metaphorical pivot. James Wilkinson had served as an officer in the American Revolution. His chicanery while acting as the army's clothier general led to an investigation that discovered "gross irregularities in his accounts." After the war he moved to Kentucky, where his gift for graft leapt to a much more sinister level. Following a 1787 trip down the Mississippi, he informed Spanish officials that he was "transferring my allegiance from the United States to his Catholic Majesty." Of course he did not make the American government aware of his change of heart. Instead he worked behind the scenes in a failed attempt to thwart Kentucky statehood.[19]

In 1791, following Indian raids along the Ohio-Kentucky frontier, Wilkinson reentered the army as a colonel. At that point, it might have seemed reasonable for him to sever his ties with Spain. Instead he asked the Spanish for a raise, asserting that his new position would place him in a position to provide more valuable information. Later he played an unclear role in Aaron Burr's even murkier expedition to the American Southwest.[20]

In 1803 the United States purchased the Louisiana Territory from France, extending the United States well into the trans-Mississippi. The "pivot" about which Washington was justifiably concerned was thus removed. The need for roads and waterways may have become less critical on a geopolitical level. On a practical level, the need to link the East Coast with the ever-expanding frontier was just as important as ever.

One individual had already tried to link the East and the West. In 1796, seven years before the Louisiana Purchase, Ebenezer Zane made the first notable attempt to pierce the Ohio wilderness. Zane's Trace, as the road was known, also marked the national government's first serious, albeit somewhat detached, involvement in such an effort.

Zane was born on October 7, 1747, along the South Fork of the Potomac River, near present-day Moorefield, West Virginia. In the spring of 1768, he and either two or three of his brothers, along with some of the family's slaves, moved to Brownsville, Pennsylvania. Two years later the group continued westward, likely on or near the route of the future National Road. Their path took them to the mouth of Wheeling Creek, where they became the founders of Wheeling, Virginia. More family members arrived the following year. Zane quickly acquired all the land the present city of Wheeling comprises, including Wheeling Island, as well as substantial holdings up the river and on its opposite bank. At the same time, he became the de facto leader of the settlement, although he was only in his twenties.[21]

Events soon made him the area's military leader as well. In 1774 hostilities broke out in the region south of the Ohio as settlers encroached upon Indian lands. The murder of several members of Mingo Chief Logan's family further fueled the discontent. In June Virginia's governor, John Murray, 4th Earl of Dunmore, called out the militia. The brief clash that ensued was known as Lord Dunmore's War. Zane became Wheeling's disbursing agent of the militia, making him "practically the commander" of the settlement's Fort Finncastle.

The fort saw no action during the conflict, but that changed when the American Revolution came to the Ohio Valley. The renamed Fort Henry became a safe haven for Wheeling's residents. On August 31, 1777, four hundred Indians, led by Simon Girty, attacked and laid siege to the fortification. Only a dozen men and boys were on hand to defend it, but they held out for twenty-three hours before reinforcements arrived. Five years later, in the waning days of the war, Fort Henry repulsed four attacks launched by forty British regulars and 260 Indians. Zane's leadership was eclipsed, at least in the eyes of the public, by the exploits of his sister, Elizabeth "Betty" Zane, who made a sixty-yard sprint through enemy fire, returning with badly needed gunpowder. Poet John S. Adams would immortalize her with an ode, which began:

This dauntless pioneer maiden's name
Is inscribed in gold on the scroll of fame
She was the lassie who knew no fear
When the tomahawk gleamed on the far frontier.[22]

If his sister upstaged him at Fort Henry, Ebenezer would find his own historic fame in the area of frontier transportation. On March 25, 1796, during the last year of the Washington administration, Zane sent a memorial to Congress. He wrote that "the public as well as individuals would derive great advantage" by the opening of a road from Wheeling to the Scioto, then on to Limestone, now Maysville, Kentucky, along the Ohio. Using the third person, Zane reported, "He Hath at his own expense employ'd a number of labourers, and hath actually made progress in marking and opening the same in such manner as to be passable to travellers on Horseback." As an incentive to Congress, he pointed out that the road would result in a significant reduction in the cost of transporting the mail. He further noted, "The advantages which must result to Travellers, particularly emigrants are too numerous to be detailed." In return for this public service, Zane asked for grants of land, not exceeding one square mile each, where the Trace would cross the Muskingum, Hocking, and Scioto Rivers. This would come at no direct cost to Congress, but Zane would be acquiring property certain to increase significantly in value with the coming of his trail. He promised to establish ferries at each of the three river crossings.[23]

On May 17, 1796, Congress approved a bill "authorizing Ebenezer Zane to locate certain lands in the Northwestern Territory." By then, as Zane noted in his memorial to Congress, he had already begun blazing his Trace through the wilderness. The size of the work parties was generally eight to a dozen men. Zane's most trusted subordinate was his brother Jonathan, who had explored eastern Ohio extensively. He was largely responsible for determining the route of the trail. John McIntire, Ebenezer's son-in-law, was also a part of the expedition. A shoemaker by trade, he did not participate in clearing the route. Instead he kept the party supplied with game. Following a long day of blazing trees, cutting out branches and undergrowth, and clearing the path of logs and limbs, members of the party likely appreciated his efforts. Two men stood watch each night, insurance against an Indian attack, which was not likely. A blazing campfire deterred wolves, a more probable menace.[24]

Leaving the Ohio River opposite Wheeling, Zane's Trace followed Wheeling

Creek for seven miles, then continued west along ridges and through valleys. Along the way the road passed through what was or would become St. Clairsville, Morristown, Fairview, Old Washington, Cambridge, and New Concord. West of Cambridge the Trace at first paralleled "the old Mingo Indian trail." This would have carried it to Duncan's Falls, where it would have crossed the Muskingum at a point ten miles below what was to become Zanesville. However, after some reconnoitering, Jonathan recommended crossing where the Licking River flows into the Muskingum. That site, he believed, provided superior water power for mills. It was here that the city of Zanesville would be founded.[25]

Until this point, Zane's road followed the same route that the National Road later would. This changed beyond Zanesville. From there the Trace turned to the southwest. The communities of Fultonham and Somerset would eventually be located along the road. It crossed the Hocking, where Zane's second land grant would grow into the city of Lancaster. The next major crossing was at the Scioto. Here pioneers had first platted Chillicothe in 1796, as Zane was beginning his work. In 1803 the community would become Ohio's first capital. West of the Scioto, the road followed Paint Creek for five miles before continuing on to the southwest. Its last leg was along Big Three Mile Creek, which it followed to the Ohio opposite Limestone.[26]

Although Zane completed his Trace in 1797, he did not receive his three land grants until 1800. On February 5 Rufus Putnam, one of the Northwest Territory's three federally appointed judges, informed Secretary of the Treasury Oliver Wolcott, "Col. Ebenezer Zane has in the course of the last year, caused the road from Wheeling to Limestone to be straightened, and other wise improved by bridges &c." In Putnam's opinion this put Zane in compliance with the bill authorizing him to build the road. On February 18 President John Adams approved the transfer. Zane then deeded over the Muskingum River tract to Jonathan Zane and McIntire for their assistance in opening the road.[27]

Despite Putnam's endorsement, the road was still little more than a path through the wilderness, not yet wide enough for wagon traffic. Trains of packhorses, tied together, bore their loads in single-file caravans of ten to twelve. It did not take long for this situation to change. Drivers, armed with axes and eager to gain the benefits of a wagon road, gradually widened the Trace. By the time Ohio achieved statehood in 1803, they had completed the task. At the same time, crude taverns and inns began to spring up along the route, although they remained widely spaced for several years. The traffic became heavy as thousands of emigrants packed up a few belongings and headed west. Their wagon wheels and their horses' hooves left deep ruts in places, some so bad that those who followed had to detour around them.[28]

It is doubtful that many of the individuals who crossed the river at Wheeling and headed into the woods gave much thought to politics. But those who found a home before they reached the Ohio a second time became part of a political movement by their very presence. As Zane completed his Trace, the Northwest Territory was turning ten years old. The law that established it detailed a path to statehood for its various sections. Politically astute or not, most of the settlers were anxious to see Ohio enter the Union. Their territorial governor, not anxious to lose a large portion of his domain, led the opposition to statehood. The tide of emigration—not to mention the tide of history—was working against him. Congress would soon welcome Ohio as the seventeenth state with legislation that would also offer funding for the construction of a highway that would connect the new state with those east of the mountains.

CHAPTER TWO

"The most effectual cement of union"

Planning the Road

IF THERE WAS A "Father of the National Road," it was Albert Gallatin—at least that was Albert Gallatin's opinion. The impetuous young man who had pushed his views on George Washington in 1784 had gone on to serve in both houses of Congress. In 1801 Thomas Jefferson named him secretary of the treasury, a post he would hold longer than any other individual. Perhaps his encounter with Washington had spurred an interest in a western road. More likely travels from western Pennsylvania to Philadelphia prompted a personal desire for such a project. Whatever the motivation, in 1791 Gallatin joined the Philadelphia Society for Promoting the Improvements of Roads and Inland Navigation.[1]

As treasury secretary he had the opportunity to turn his plans into policy, and he wasted little time. The Northwest Ordinance, which the Congress passed under the Articles of Confederation in 1787, had set a number of criteria by which three to five states could be carved out of the Northwest Territory. As the nineteenth century dawned, Ohio had met those terms, and its people were clamoring for statehood. The Federalist governor of the entire territory, Arthur St. Clair, did not wish to see the most populous portion of his domain lopped off. Hoping to avoid being the governor of virtually nothing but wilderness, he fought the Republicans, who supported statehood, tenaciously. However, with a Republican in the White House and a Republican Congress on the way, the governor could do little to delay the inevitable. In 1802 Congress passed the Enabling Act, allowing Ohioans to draw up a state constitution. Jefferson signed the bill on April 30.[2]

In these events Gallatin saw an opportunity to accomplish much more. Early in 1802 he had a conversation with William B. Giles, the Virginia congressman who chaired the House committee that would consider Ohio statehood. The treasury secretary followed up their chat with a letter on February 18. In it he proposed: "That one-tenth part of the net proceeds of the lands hereafter sold by Congress shall, after deducting all expenses incident to the same, be applied towards laying out and making turnpike or other roads, first from the navigable waters emptying into the Atlantic to the Ohio, and afterwards continued through the new States; such roads to be laid out under the authority of Congress, with the consent of the several states through which the same shall pass." He predicted, "The roads will be as beneficial to the parts of the Atlantic States through which they are to pass, and nearly as much so to a considerable portion of the Union, as to the North-West Territory itself." They would, he added, "contribute towards cementing the bonds of the Union between those parts of the United States whose local interests have been considered as most dissimilar." Sometime later Gallatin endorsed this letter, "Origin of the National Road."[3]

The Enabling Act contained Gallatin's proposal, but it reduced the amount of land sale funds set aside to 5 percent. Even with this change, the plan provoked opposition. The most vocal of the dissenters was Roger Griswold, a Federalist representative from Connecticut. He pointed out that Congress, in 1790, had earmarked proceeds from land sales to paying down the national debt. This Federalist deficit hawk also grumbled that the proposed road would only benefit Virginia and Pennsylvania, adding that the idea originated with a western Pennsylvanian. To all that, Giles replied that Griswold had never spoken out against lighthouses erected along the Connecticut shore by the national government to benefit local fishers. "We have waters running to the East—they to the West," he noted, "and the committee thought it was desirable to connect these by good roads."[4]

Leaders in the proposed state also raised a concern with the legislation. Ohio politicians desired that three-fifths of the 5 percent of land sale monies be used for roads exclusively within the borders of the state. The remaining two-fifths could be used for roads passing through the Buckeye State from beyond its borders. Congress agreed, meaning Gallatin's 10 percent had been chopped down to just 2 percent. Still, the Congress of the United States and the soon-to-be state of Ohio had tacitly recognized the national government's authority to construct highways through the several states. By signing the Enabling Act, so, too, had the strict constructionist president. This is not really surprising. Jefferson would soon approve the purchase of the vast Louisiana Territory, practical concerns overwhelming constitutional qualms. Writing to Gallatin on the subject of internal improvements in general, he observed, "By these operations, new channels of communication will be opened to the states; the lines of separation will disappear, their interests will be identified, and their union cemented by new and indissoluble ties." Once again Jefferson felt he was justified in setting aside theory to promote the general welfare.[5]

Ohio was now a state, but the question of a road to join it with the rest of the Union lay dormant for over two years. Then, on December 19, 1805, Sen. Uriah Tracy of Connecticut, chairman of the chamber's Committee on Ohio Statehood, reported on potential routes for the government road. The senate, particularly members representing states with possible starting points, listened intently as he spoke.

First, Tracy addressed the practical. Land sales in Ohio from 1802 through September 1805 amounted to $632,604.27. Two percent of this was just $12,652. By the time construction began, this amount might rise to $18,000 or $20,000, he explained. Still, the sum would be so small that there would be only enough money available to build one road. That route, the senator continued, should be one that "will be most accommodating to the citizens of the State of Ohio." To strike the river and continue through the state, the road needed to commence at Philadelphia, Baltimore, Washington, or Richmond. The distance from Philadelphia to a point between Steubenville and the mouth of Grave Creek, south of Wheeling, was 360 miles "by the usual route." From Richmond it was 377 miles, and from either Baltimore or Washington it was 275. "The mercantile intercourse of the citizens of Ohio with those of the Atlantic States is chiefly in Philadelphia and Baltimore," Tracy observed. The Richmond route, he went on, would approach Ohio "in a part thinly inhabited" and was so "hilly and rough" that roads could not be "conveniently made."[6]

Tracy also pointed out that both Pennsylvania and Maryland had been pushing roads westward. If the national government were to parallel those efforts, "it would, probably, so far interfere with the operations of the respective States, as to produce mischief instead of benefit." Maryland, he pointed out, had no plans to extend its road projects over the Alleghenies. Therefore, the committee recommended Cumberland, Maryland, as the starting point for the highway. By commencing there, the proposed road would be an extension of the roads leading from Baltimore and the District of Columbia. Cumberland's location on the Potomac River offered further incentive. Tracy then offered a bill on the subject with the goal of "cementing the Union of our citizens located on the Western waters with those of the Atlantic States." He concluded: "In the present case, to make the crooked ways straight, and the rough ways smooth, will, in effect remove the intervening mountains, and, by facilitating the intercourse of our Western brethren with those on the Atlantic, substantially unite them in interest, which, the committee believe, is the most effectual cement of union applicable to the human race."[7]

The bill passed the Senate on December 27, 1805. The House took up the measure on March 22. Michael Leib of Pennsylvania immediately moved to postpone it indefinitely. Christopher Clark of Virginia supported the motion, favoring instead the construction of three roads, commencing in Pennsylvania, Maryland, and Virginia. John Jackson, Clark's fellow Virginian, joined the fray. Since the Ohio statehood bill called for laying out "turnpike or other roads"—plural—he believed the construction of just one highway would violate its terms. To this Roger Nelson of Maryland responded that the construction of one road would not preclude others in the future. Pennsylvania Representative William Findley favored postponement so "disinterested Commissioners" could be appointed to study potential routes. Findley said he had traveled along the proposed route, and he believed a better one could be located. George Bedinger of Kentucky disagreed, saying he considered the route "the shortest and best for the general interests of the Union." Although pointed at times, the debate was brief. When it ended, the House voted against postponement 59–51.[8]

Two days later, after another motion to postpone failed, the House approved "An act to regulate the laying out and making a road from Cumberland, in the state of Maryland to the state of Ohio." The senate concurred, and President Jefferson signed it into law five days later. In the final vote, only three states cast a majority against the measure. Virginia congressmen rejected it 16–2, Pennsylvania 13–4, and South Carolina 4–2.[9]

The bill was brief, consisting of seven one-paragraph sections. The first empowered the president to appoint three "discreet and disinterested citizens" to lay out the route from Cumberland to the Ohio. The right-of-way was to be sixty-six feet wide with trees cleared the entire width. It could have "no deviation above five degrees from the horizon" and was to be raised in the middle. A "ditch or water-course" was to be placed on both sides. Beyond those stipulations, the president held full discretion in the manner of making the road.[10]

The law charged the president with securing permission from the states through which the highway would pass. It authorized him to take "prompt and effectual measures to cause said road to be made through the whole distance, or any part or parts of the same as he shall judge most conducive to the public good." It also called upon him to report to Congress at the start of each session the progress made on the road. The bill made an initial appropriation of $30,000.[11]

Jefferson selected Elie Williams and Thomas Moore of Maryland and Joseph Kerr of Ohio to serve as commissioners. All had spent time in public service. Kerr would represent his state in the US Senate. Williams was named president of the commission. His detailed diary of the trio's first expedition provides a vivid account of three serious individuals dispatched on a daunting expedition.[12]

Williams, Moore, and Kerr left Cumberland on the morning of September 4, 1806, accompanied by a number of curious local residents. Also working with the party, though not always in the same location, was Josias Thompson, "a surveyor of professional merit." Accompanying Thompson were two chain carriers, a vaneman, a marker, and "a packhorse man." The commissioners headed west believing they had ample time to locate their route to the Ohio. They soon came to realize that their assignment was "a work of greater magnitude, and a task much more arduous, than was conceived before entering upon it." As a result, severe winter weather forced them to retreat back to Cumberland in late November. They had made it to the Ohio by then, but the trio would return believing they had not studied the entire route as carefully as they had desired.[13]

The commissioners first trudged along Wills Creek, then up Braddock's Run. The next day they followed "the present road," which they found to be steep. Over the course of the next week the group continued their explorations of Braddock's Run and examined their first major impediments, Wills Mountain and Savage Mountain. For the first several days they returned to Cumberland each evening. Then, on November 13, they sent their baggage ahead. The same day the party encountered a number of residents from Washington, Brownsville, and Uniontown, Pennsylvania, bearing a memorial recommending that the road pass through their communities. It was the first of many such encounters. The commissioners later conceded that they paid "due attention" to the "comparative merits of towns, establishments, and settlements already made." They also reported that their "task [was] rendered still more incumbent by the solicitude and importunities of the inhabitants of every part of the district, who severally conceived their grounds entitled to a preference."[14]

On the sixteenth, after twelve days in the field, the men examined Turkey Foot Road in western Maryland to the top of Negro Mountain, at an elevation of over two thousand feet. They were still fewer than thirty miles from Cumberland. The commissioners remained in that vicinity for the next three days, considering various paths from the mountain to the Youghiogheny River. At one point Williams separated from the other two, allowing them to pursue more options. This would become a common practice. Meanwhile Thompson and his party had been working eastward from Wheeling, trying to locate a straight route from there to Braddock's Road. They met him on the evening of the 20th. The next day the commissioners dispatched their surveyor to Cumberland with instructions to study various lines from there to Savage Mountain. At the same time, they retained a few members of Thompson's crew "to run lines of reference & experiment on the way to the Ohio."[15]

Williams and party arrived at Uniontown on September 23. Rainy weather kept them there the next day, but they used the time to study maps and gather information from the community's inhabitants. On the 25th, each accompanied by a local guide, the commissioners again split up to explore different routes over Laurel Mountain and on to the Monongahela. On October 1 they reunited in Brownsville.[16]

The commissioners remained in the community, located on the banks of the Monongahela, the next four days, tramping up and down the river to locate crossing points and examine potential routes to the west. Occasionally citizens of Brownsville, likely eager to assist, but equally as likely to get in the way, accompanied them. They left the town on the morning of October 6 and arrived in Washington, Pennsylvania, after dark. Like Brownsville, Washington became their base for several days as the commissioners, either together or separately, explored potential routes to the Ohio, a matter that would eventually become a major bone of contention.[17]

In the days that followed, they examined ground at the northern limits of their instructions, terminating either opposite Steubenville, Ohio, or at Wellsburg (then Charlestown), Virginia. After again dividing on October 8, Williams followed routes farther south via West Liberty, Virginia. Four days later, after being joined by the other commissioners, he wrote that a ravine between the community and the river was prone to flooding, forming "weighty objections to the adoption of this as a crossing place for the great thoroughfare."[18]

Wheeling, where the commissioners arrived on the twenty-third, also presented problems. The path along Wheeling Creek to the river was flood prone.

A separate route, one hewn out by local residents, was well beyond the 5 percent incline and was poorly drained, making it susceptible to slips. Williams concluded that the makeshift road "serves rather to the enterprising spirit of the inhabitants than their prudence & caution." Also troublesome was Wheeling Island, which bisects the Ohio adjacent to the city. Although it offered two easy fords at low water, it forced travelers to pay twice for ferriage when the river was high. This, Williams concluded, was "a tax which a great proportion of the [westward] emigrants can ill bear." More problems awaited on the opposite banks of the Ohio. A road already existed from Bridgeport (then Canton), Ohio, to Zanesville, but Williams concluded that it required so much improvement that he believed an alternate route might prove cheaper and more practical.[19]

The commissioners made Wheeling their headquarters for the next two weeks, but they made numerous side trips. Sojourns east took them as far as Waynesburg, Pennsylvania. On the Ohio side of the river, they ventured south to Pipe and Captina Creeks, taking them beyond the geographical limits of their instructions. On November 7 Moore and Williams boarded a riverboat to ascertain how impediments in the river from Steubenville downward might affect a decision as to where the road should strike the river. On November 13, 1806, after over two months in the field, the party started back east for Cumberland, reexamining old ground and exploring still more potential routes.[20]

On November 27 the commissioners returned to Cumberland. They remained until December 6, comparing their notes in an attempt to reach a consensus on the best route. They reported to President Jefferson on December 30. The report was dominated by geographical markers and references to property owners, as opposed to place names, a measure of the remoteness of much of the country through which the highway would pass. Williams, Moore, and Kerr recommended the following route:

> From a stone at the corner of lot No. 1, in Cumberland, near the confluence of Will's Creek and the north branch of the Potomac river; thence extending along the street westwardly, to cross the hill lying between Cumberland and Gwynn's, at the gap where Braddock's road passes it; thence near Gwynn's and Jesse Tomlinson's to cross the Big [Youghiogheny] near the mouth of Rogers' run, between the crossing of Braddock's road and the confluence of the streams which form the Turkey foot; thence to cross Laurel Hill near the forks of Dunbar's run, to the west foot of that hill, at a point near where Braddock's old road reached it, near Guest's old place, now Colonel Isaac Mason's; thence through Brownsville and Bridgeport, to cross the

Monongahela river below Josias Crawford's ferry; and thence on as straight a course as the country will admit to the Ohio, at a point between the mouth of Wheelen creek and the lower part of Wheelen island.[21]

Commissioners Williams and Moore returned twice to study the route, Kerr remaining behind to attend to unnamed "domestic concerns." Their first sojourn occurred during the fall of 1807, the second in May 1808. On their first expedition, they made a survey of a new route through Uniontown. They also ruled out making use of "the road now traveled [Braddock's Road]" with minor exceptions amounting to less than a mile. The road's "crooked and hilly course" was their stated reason. Following the May expedition, they informed Jefferson that stone (referred to as "metal" by the road builders) for the road was plentiful between Cumberland and Brownsville and adequate on west to Wheeling. They recommended stone arch bridges for all streams along the route except the Big and Little Youghiogheny, where they believed wooden bridges were more advisable because of the width of those rivers. As for the Monongahela, even wider and flood prone, they considered bridging to be "a work of too much magnitude to encourage the attempt at this time."[22]

By then politics intervened. On April 9, 1807, Pennsylvania's state legislature voted to allow Congress to build the road through the Keystone State—with one stipulation. Their approval was contingent on the route being altered to pass through Uniontown and Washington. This condition was not unreasonable. The legislature's proposal would take the road through two important communities without adding materially to its distance. Gallatin, the former Washington County resident, supported the realignment. He reminded the president that his one-time home county "gives a uniform majority of about 2000 votes in our favor." Jefferson groused, decrying the necessity "to barter away . . . a public trust committed to me." Sanctimony notwithstanding, Jefferson was a political creature, and a two thousand–vote majority in a key county of a key state was something not to be ignored. The same day he wrote to Gallatin expressing righteous indignation, he also wrote the commissioners, asking them to make an examination "of the best route through Washington to Wheeling."[23]

The commissioners had filed their reports, and the politicians had had their say. Then, as the West waited, the government delayed. The reason was finances. On February 16, 1808, in response to a request from the House of Representatives, Gallatin reported that the fund for the construction of the road contained $27,951. At a rate of 2 percent, he predicted that it would grow by just $9,000 a year.[24]

It was apparent that if the road were to be built, Congress would have to make appropriations beyond the monies realized from the sale of Ohio lands. Four months after receiving the treasury secretary's report, a bill appropriating $60,000 for the road cleared the Senate. When it reached the House, the going was tougher. Acting as a committee of the whole, the legislators considered an amendment offered by Representative Jackson of Virginia, who remained a foe of the project. He contended that it would cost in excess of $1 million to "complete the turnpike road originally and now contemplated." He offered an amendment, "That the president be authorized to apply the moneys to the improvement of the road as may be most expedient, without contemplating a turnpike road." Jackson offered no details, but presumably his intent was to construct a road not paved with stone, somewhat narrower, and with fewer bridges. The amendment failed, its opponents pointing out that the law bound the government to construct a "turnpike road." At the same time, the House tabled the appropriation. There the matter remained until December, when Congress again considered the measure. Once again the Senate acted quickly. The House did not, but on February 14, 1810, they approved the bill. With the necessary funds appropriated, work could finally begin on the National Road.[25]

✳✳✳

CHAPTER THREE

"Entirely in the woods"
Construction to the Ohio

ON NOVEMBER 6, 1810, the Treasury Department announced that it would receive proposals until February 1, 1811, for the first eight sections of the National Road, a distance of twenty-one miles. Contractors were to clear trees for a width of sixty feet, grub the stumps, and level the roadbed for thirty feet. In addition, "The hills [were] to be cut down, the earth, rocks and stones to be removed, the hollows and valleys and the abutments of all the bridges, and culverts to be filled, so that the whole of the road . . . be reduced in such manner that there shall not in any instance be an elevation in said road, when finished, greater than an angle of five degrees with the horizon." Stone, twelve inches in depth, was to cover twenty feet of the road's width. Each piece had to fit through a three-inch ring.[1]

The notice, published in several newspapers, attracted a number of responses, most of them expressing concerns. Henry McKinley, a veteran road builder, was awarded the contract for the first section, just over two miles. Soon after receiving the contract, he asked for more money. He would have to move his family to the site, the contractor explained, as well as tools, horses, and laborers, and McKinley believed if he had two or three contracts he could "start a good company on each of them." James Cochran, who got the contracts on the third and fourth sections, wrote in a similar vein. He wanted his work extended to sections five through eight.[2]

The man in charge of sorting out all of this was David Shriver Jr., who accepted the post of "Superintendent of the U. States western road" in late February 1811. The job paid $1,800 annually. A member of a prominent Maryland family, Shriver had served briefly in the state's House of Delegates as Frederick County's representative. He had also been in charge of the construction of a turnpike road from Hagerstown to Westminster. He faced a daunting challenge, particularly as the project grew and many sections required maintenance while others were under construction. Capricious weather and contractors who could be unruly or incompetent added to the challenge. Shriver served faithfully, but not always selflessly. During his tenure he employed at least two close relatives as assistants. He also could be prickly if his feelings were hurt, and he possessed a flair for the dramatic, frequently referring to the project as "our road" in communications with Gallatin and other officials.[3]

If surviving documents are any indication, the treasury secretary offered Shriver little advice as the superintendent began his duties. In a March letter Gallatin suggested that stone be secured from people who owned land along the route. He felt they should be willing to supply it without charge but informed Shriver he could allow "a moderate compensation." Although the law gave the president authority to deviate from the surveyed route, Gallatin stressed that this should apply to "small deviations in the details of the road." In any event, Shriver should not make any alteration unless it was "absolutely necessary."[4]

Less than a month after receiving Gallatin's instructions, the superintendent recommended two major alterations. After viewing a portion of Cochran's third section, he suggested that "seventy or eighty perches or more" be changed. The commissioners had located the road on a mountainside with a descent of between twenty and forty-five degrees. Shriver proposed moving it to the adjacent bottom and raising the roadbed two feet above the high water mark. He also recommended a change to the first section based on "the exstream rufness of the ground." He had attempted to locate a better route, and by his own words, "succeeded beyond expectation." Shriver bolstered his case to Gallatin by enclosing an endorsement of the new route penned by contractor McKinley. The treasury secretary approved the change to section one. His decision on section three is not known.[5]

On April 22 Shriver announced that McKinley was at work in Cumberland with about twenty men. C. Randle had five hands and was hoping to begin work on the second section. He had been at the site since March 25, had erected houses and stables, and was waiting to sign his contract with the government.

Meanwhile, no work meant no payment. "I am sufering," he informed Gallatin on the thirtieth.[6]

The contract came through, and soon all three contractors were at work. Their crews felled trees, and oxen attached to chains removed the stumps. Then laborers cut away hills, leveled the roadbed, and broke stone to the required three inches or less. Meanwhile other workers dug ditches on both sides of the road. In the wake of these labors, wagons hauled away earth and rocks.[7]

Often the contractors did not see eye-to-eye with Shriver and his surveyors. For example, they did not understand why side slopes could not exceed thirty degrees. They cut corners, often failing to meet the standard, forcing costly and time consuming regradings. Although generally pleased with McKinley's work, on one occasion Shriver reprimanded him over the failure of his workers to break stone to three inches. The superintendent threatened to withhold payment until the work was done right. Cochran simply disappeared for over three months while the work was going on.[8]

Shriver's biggest headaches came from Randle, who worked "unkindly and improperly." His credit was so poor that he had difficulty finding laborers. Once, the superintendent reported, Randle "threatened . . . to drag me off my horse and beat me to death." When he later bid for a section in Pennsylvania, Shriver informed the Treasury Department, "Persons frequently are the bidders, and sometimes are the lowest, who we at the time have good reason to believe would never complete the work." Randle, he feared, was in that category. Shriver explained, "This man has now failed a second time, once here and once on the Baltimore to Frederick Road." As a result, his credit was "entirely destroyed," and he would not be able to secure hands or supplies. Employing a higher bidder, Shriver contended, would be cheaper than replacing shoddy work. The question of employing Randle became moot, at least temporarily, in June 1813, when the troublesome contractor ended up in jail for debt.[9]

Randle was not the only contractor who disappointed, a fact made clear in Shriver's correspondence with Gallatin. On one occasion a man the superintendent considered "honest and generally well disposed" was low bidder for a section of road. Unfortunately he was "a poor man, has never made any road, and of course knows little of road making." Even the normally reliable Cochran, after completing four sections, found himself broke and unable to pay his workers. He had bid on six more, which it appeared he would be unable to begin. Shriver regretted the situation. "He is very prudent and honourable," the superintendent wrote, adding that he had "undergone in this wilderness what but very few persons would have sufficient resolution to have gone through." The contracting firm of Adams and McKinney successfully completed two sections and bid on two more. Then "a misunderstanding" arose between the pair, and each told Shriver not to pay the other. After thoroughly explaining the complicated situation to Alexander J. Dallas, who had succeeded Gallatin at the Treasury, Shriver asked for advice. Since Adams had left and gone home, Dallas wrote, McKinney should receive the payment.[10]

Problems with contractors were not temporary. As late as 1834 an official of the road prepared a list of "the frauds practiced heretofore" in both construction and repair:

1st   Diminishing the size and altering the angle of the guage

2nd   Concealing or covering up in the pile of metal large masses of stone or other matter

3rd   Loosening the pile of metal just before measurement to increase its bulk

4th   Breaking stone of a softer and otherwise inferior quality than the sample agreed upon

5th   Breaking the metal to a larger size than that agreed upon

6th   Removing the prepared metal from one point to another after it has been measured

7th   Taking metal from the face of the Road of the first or second Stratum to make it appear the desired quantity has been broken to fill the Guage

8th   On parts of the Road where limestone has already been delivered waggoners with a partial load passing from the quarries to the point of delivery have been detected in stealing a piece from several piles, thus making a full load from what has been already paid for[11]

Despite the lack of reliability—and sometimes honesty—on the part of many of the contractors, the work went on, albeit slowly at times. On May 13, 1811, Shriver reported that McKinley had completed nearly sixty perches, all still within the limits of Cumberland. By the following January 14 he was able to inform Gallatin that about five miles of roadbed were finished. Four of them were stoned and nearly completed. On December 31 the superintendent announced that the first ten miles of the road were completed. He added that the contractors were making "considerable progress" on the second letting of contracts, sections five through eight of the highway, but offered no details. He did note that those sections were "entirely in the woods."[12]

On December 19, 1814, Shriver was able to report that, despite an unusually wet summer, the second letting was completed and being used by travelers. The third letting, comprising nine sections covering nearly eighteen miles, was under contract. Some eight miles were "in great forwardness and nearly completed, and on ten but little progress is made." The contracts that had been made would carry the road thirty-nine miles to the east bank of the Big Youghiogheny.[13]

At the time this report arrived, the War of 1812 was nearly at a close. The work went on during the conflict, but the war may have contributed to a shortage of manpower. In December 1813 Cochran placed an advertisement in Cumberland newspapers seeking laborers for the following spring. He assured potential workers that he had always made prompt payments to hands and asserted that, "No doubt is entertained of the work progressing much further and consequently continuing many years to come." Another contractor offered a dollar a day in wages and informed men that their families "can live very cheap; provisions being plenty, and housement comparatively nothing." An ad apparently placed by a group of contractors asked for "ONE THOUSAND GOOD HANDS." They did not limit their appeal to Americans. "DESERTERS FROM OUR ENEMY," the notice contended, "might here find a comfortable retreat, with an employ that will yield them fourfold the income which labor produces in Europe, whilst they enjoy the most perfect freedom and happiness." As the work advanced into southwestern Pennsylvania, labor shortages became more acute. Workers did not come forward as enthusiastically, Shriver explained, because of "the distance they have to travel, the wilderness they will have to live in, [and] the prevailing bad weather, which shortens the period of labor."[14]

Bad weather during the winter of 1815 reduced work to a point that wages fell by over 50 percent. This, the superintendent reported, "produced a disorder among the men." About one-fourth left, and the apparent fear of potential violence arising from the situation led travelers nearly to desert the road.[15]

Labor was not all that was in short supply. In the spring of 1812, Shriver informed the Treasury Department that, unless more quarries were found, stone would have to be hauled two miles. He predicted that the shortage would increase the cost of the sixth and seventh sections by nearly five dollars per perch. Cochran appealed directly to Gallatin for extra pay after he inspected the route of the seventh section and found he would need twenty-three horses for hauling stone. The following spring a group of quarry owners took advantage of the situation when they "colluded to obtain better prices."[16]

As the road snaked westward, a new problem emerged. Sections that had been completed were being used, and they were rapidly falling into disrepair. Shriver had anticipated this situation. As early as January 1812, he had written, "I would respectfully suggest the propriety of demanding such a toll as will be sufficient to keep [the road] in good and perfect order." One year later he added that provisions for keeping the work in repair "are every day becoming more necessary." Five months after that he reported that a slip on a section of the road that he did not identify would require repairs amounting to $1,000 or $2,000. In early 1815 another slip carried away half the road for a distance of five to six perches, sinking it some five feet. Not all the problems were the fault of Mother Nature. Late in 1816 Shriver wrote, "Frequent abuses take place upon the road, such as throwing down the walls, digging down the banks, felling trees . . . locking of wagon wheels, placing fences within the sixty-six feet, and many other improper acts." He urged that stern measures be adopted to prevent this. Shriver also suggested that "an honest and industrious man [with] a cart horse and tools" be employed, along with a laborer, to roam the highway and make repairs as needed.[17]

Shriver further recommended abandoning the contract system. He contended that it caused men with good intentions but limited resources to offer bids that were unreasonably low. "The consequences are," the superintendent continued, "the retarding of work by the failure of the contractor; the hands lose their wages, and are thus deterred from labor, and in a manner driven from the road." Instead he proposed the work be done as day labor. This, he believed, would increase both the quality and the speed of the work. In addition, "All inducements to fraud or deception would be done away." Despite Shriver's pleas—and the numerous problems with contractors—the system remained in place.[18]

At the end of 1816, Shriver reported that sections one through eight were finished, as was eleven. Nine, twelve, thirteen, and fourteen were so near completion that they were open to travel. Work was going forward on ten, fifteen, sixteen, and seventeen. Soon, he predicted, the road from Cumberland to the Big Youghiogheny would be complete. One year later the superintendent announced that forty-five miles had been built, ending about fifteen miles from Uniontown. Contracts to take the road to the Pennsylvania community had already been let, as had contracts to carry it thirty miles west of the Monongahela.[19]

As the road advanced, streams large and small had to be bridged. During the early stages, James Kinkead built most—if not all—of the bridges along the road. In part this was because Shriver considered him "a stout able bodied man" who had "always acquited himself much to the satisfaction of his imploy-ers." Another factor was that he was the only contractor in the area qualified and willing to take on the task. His first major project was the bridge across Clinton's Fork of Braddock's Run. He agreed to build the bridge, which had a twenty-five-foot span, for $1,100.[20]

Despite Shriver's esteem, Kinkead was not involved in the first significant bridge along the National Road. The firm of Abraham Kerns and John Bryson constructed the bridge over the Casselman River, then known as the Little Yough-iogheny. They began the project in 1813. On November 17, 1814, the contractors proudly informed Shriver, "It gives us pleasure to inform you that we succeeded beyond our most sanguine expectations in turning the largest and we think the most permanent stone arch [bridge] in the United States." This was not hyper-bole. With a 354-foot span, the bridge was the largest stone arch structure built in the United States to that point. As to permanency, the bridge carried vehicular traffic until 1933 and still stands as part of a Maryland state park. Local lore holds that Shriver, on the night before the bridge's public dedication, stood under the structure and ordered that the supporting timbers be removed, preferring death to a ruined reputation. The contractors' letter suggests otherwise. "Yesterday," they wrote to Shriver, "we lowered the centers sufficiently to give the arch its full bearing. The rings have only settled four and a half inches." Some finishing work remained, but they believed 95 percent of the work was done. Like other contractors, Kerns and Bryson wrote that they were in debt to their "industrious laboring men" and asked for a prompt payment of the money due to them.[21]

That proved problematic. Under the strict terms of the contract, the pair could not be paid until the work was 100 percent completed. This was standard procedure in nineteenth-century government contracts. Shriver nevertheless pleaded their case to the Treasury Department. "I believe they are distressed for want of money," he wrote. "I have received the bridge since the centers have been removed, every part of the building firm, without any perceivable giving in any part, and I believe the work to be permanent." Dallas agreed, and in June 1815 Shriver settled with the pair.[22]

The next major bridge project on the road was at the Big Youghiogheny River near Somerfield, Pennsylvania. A House committee first considered such a bridge in 1812. They opposed it largely because the route to the river was still uncertain, leaving open the question of where exactly the structure would be. Two years later Shriver endorsed the project, citing the successful completion of the bridge across the Little Youghiogheny. He later added that the Big Youghiogheny was "a large stream, and is frequently too high to be crossed."[23]

Dallas and Congress approved the project, and on July 21, 1815, Shriver reported that James Beck and Evan Evans were the low bidders. "There can be no objection to them," Shriver wrote," noting that Evans had been involved in constructing the bridge over the Little Youghiogheny. Beck he esteemed as a "first rate work man." They began their work in the fall of 1816. Shriver had proposed a bridge with three spans, one ninety feet, another seventy-five feet, and the third sixty feet. Dallas believed four spans would be "firmer, stronger, and more likely to stand," but he left the decision to his superintendent. Shriver stuck to his original plan. The work went quickly, and as 1817 ended, Shriver reported that the bridge was virtually completed, with only the parapet walls to be finished. In early 1818 it was opened to traffic.[24]

As the road extended westward, maintenance and repair needs commanded more and more of the superintendent's attention. As early as June 1812 he appealed to Gallatin for permission to employ an assistant. He recommended the trusted bridge builder Kinkead, who received the position and held it for three years before resigning. Shriver felt the loss, lamenting, "I know of no person qualified to fill his place, none can be found that possesses the experience he does." The job went to James Shriver, the superintendent's nephew. "This young man is qualified in an emanant degree," he wrote to Dallas. James was less certain. Writing his mother the same day, he confided, "I am fearful I will labor under some [sort] of disability on account of my deficiency in the knowledge of road making." He was pleased to report, however, that "Uncle David" and Kinkead were both "much disposed to aid me and establish me."[25]

In April 1816 Congress appropriated $300,000, by far the largest sum voted upon to that point, to complete the road to the Ohio River. Desiring to spend it as efficiently as possible, Dallas divided the administrative responsibilities. Shriver remained the "General Superintendent" and would also be the "local agent" for contracts between Cumberland and Brownsville. Josias Thompson, who had served as surveyor for the original three commissioners, was placed in charge of contracts between Brownsville and Washington. John Connell held the same position for the area between Washington and the 113-mile mark, and Moses Shepherd was responsible for contracts between the latter point and the Ohio River. Elie Williams, one of the original commissioners, was employed as a "Commissioner to divide the road into convenient sections, and to prepare contracts in concert with the Superintendent."[26]

Although the arrangement called for Williams and Shriver to cooperate, their egos soon clashed. It began in August. Shriver, according to his account, wanted to fix specific sections for contracts, but Williams refused, saying the exact route was not yet determined. The matter escalated when Shriver proposed to change a portion of the commissioners' original route east of Uniontown. Both men appealed to Dallas, who turned the mess over to the president. James Madison, acting the part of Solomon, recommended that a surveyor agreed upon by both men study the respective routes and deliver a final decision. Thomas Wilson received the assignment, and the following April he announced that he favored Shriver's "Southern route." Meanwhile Williams received an appointment as superintendent of the road for the area west of the Monongahela and a pay raise from $1,800 to $2,500 annually. He also received assurances that he would be "in all respects independent of the present Superintendent," meaning Shriver, who remained in charge of things east of the Monongahela and got the same pay raise.[27]

As construction advanced through Pennsylvania, expenses shot up dramatically. From Cumberland to Uniontown, including some very mountainous country, the road had cost $9,745 per mile. West of Uniontown and on to Wheeling the figure rose to nearly $13,000 a mile. Overly generous contracts were the suspected culprits, and Col. John Cox was dispatched to investigate the dealings of Williams and Thompson. On August 7, 1818, he sent letters to a number of potential witnesses who might be able to "implicate or exculpate these gentlemen." At least nine responses supported the pair. One came from Moses Shepherd, one of Wheeling's most prominent residents. He defended both men, taking on the charge that the final route gave "great advantage to the farm on which Mr. Thompson now resides." This, Shepherd asserted, was not true. Cox apparently agreed. On September 25 he informed William Crawford, who had succeeded Dallas at the Treasury Department, that there was "no evidence to . . . justify a belief that the agents have otherwise than faithfully discharged the duties of the appointment."[28]

Unfortunately for Thompson, the matter did not end there. On November 30, 1819, Crawford sent Alexander LaCock, Thomas Wilson, and Thomas McGiffen to investigate alleged "unnecessary expenditures" in bridge and masonry work and in the construction of sidewalls. They reported their findings the following January 3. The trio found Thompson to be cooperative, "even solicitous." Despite that, they concluded, "We are decidedly of the opinion that unnecessary expense to a large amount has been incurred in the erection of bridges, when culverts would have been sufficient; side walls, when fillings of earth would have been less expensive [and] more permanent." Solicitous or not, Thompson's work on the road was at an end. Shriver assumed his duties.[29]

Another area of controversy involved the route to the Ohio River. The question appeared to have been long settled. In their report of December 30, 1806, Commissioners Williams, Moore, and Kerr determined that there was "a decided preference to Wheeling" if the government's goal was "to give such direction to the road as would best secure a certainty of navigation on the Ohio at all seasons." They pointed out that the worst obstructions in the river were north of the city. In addition, Wheeling was on a straight line from Brownsville to the center of Ohio.[30]

Wheeling's upriver rivals saw things differently. One of them was Wellsburg, Virginia, then known as Charlestown. Its leading citizens dispatched letters, petitions, and delegations to Washington, DC, to plead the community's case. A road along the route to Wheeling, they insisted, would cost the government at least $80,000 more and would be eight miles longer. They denied the commissioners' claim that there were serious obstructions upstream, supporting their assertion with statements from "several of our most experienced Pilots and Boatmen." A group of seven petitioners suggested the more northern route could later be used as the first part of "a great military highway, from the Ohio River to [Lake Erie]." One even observed that two of three original commissioners hailed from Maryland, suggesting that their selection of a route to Wheeling was made with Baltimore's interests in mind.[31]

Steubenville, located across the river just north of Wellsburg, supported these claims, hoping to become the highway's first stop in Ohio. Wellsburg also gained strong support from Pittsburgh interests, who had long viewed Wheeling warily as a potential commercial rival. On July 17, 1816, twenty members of Pennsylvania's congressional delegation sent a letter to President Madison stating their case. The route to Wellsburg, they argued, was shorter, was located on better ground for road making, and would pass through "a much more populous and productive country."[32]

Wheeling boosters disputed the claims advanced in support of the Wellsburg route. Since both paths remained within six miles of each other for twenty-five miles, they noted, their opponents' claims as to cost and ruggedness seemed dubious. At the same time, a route to Wheeling would save about ten miles as the road advanced westward toward Zanesville. Their response was likely unnecessary. In June 1816, early in the controversy, Dallas assured the three original commissioners that President Madison had "confirmed" their route to Wheeling. There is no evidence that the government ever seriously considered a change. Despite this, Wheeling residents credited Henry Clay, a staunch advocate of the road, with steering it through their community. They felt so strongly about the politician's alleged assistance that they erected a statue in his honor.[33]

Controversies concerning personnel and route did not deter the laboring men who were pushing the highway westward. In the fall of 1816 Williams announced plans to let a number of contracts. Proposals, he informed the public via local newspapers, would be received at Brownsville on December 16 for one-mile sections east and west of the Monongahela. Two days after that, contractors could bid at Washington, Pennsylvania, for sections stretching two miles east and ten miles west of that point. On the twenty-first they could submit proposals at Alexandria, Pennsylvania, to complete the road from that community to the Virginia line, a distance of some six miles. Finally, two days later, proposals for the sections from the Virginia line to the confluence of Big and Little Wheeling Creeks and from there to the Ohio River would be accepted.[34]

The contractors showed up at the designated points and submitted their proposals. The successful ones, crews in tow, then headed into the wilderness to start work on their respective sections. Some of the names were familiar, while others were new to the effort. Kinkead, Beck, and Evans received most of the contracts for the portions east of Uniontown. By then John Kennedy and John Miller were also associated with the firm. From Washington to the Virginia border, Thomas McGiffin, Thomas H. Baird, and Parker Campbell were the successful bidders. Col. Moses Shepherd and Daniel Steenrod were the primary contractors across the Virginia panhandle. In other areas, Mordecai and James Cochran, Thompson McKean, and Thomas and Matthew Blakely built significant sections.[35]

It still proved difficult for the contractors to remain solvent. In February 1817 the otherwise reliable James Cochran found himself in need of a two-thousand-dollar advance. He wrote to Shriver, who urged Crawford to authorize the funds. "He has completed eleven miles of our road," the superintendent wrote, "and has now nearly twelve miles more nearly done." Shriver again pointed out that few contractors would have had "sufficient resolution" to labor under the conditions he did. Shriver also supported his contractors in July 1819 when the redoubtable Kinkead, Beck, and Evans requested an advance of $33,000. He noted that their conduct "has been highly honorable." In neither case is the secretary's decision known.[36]

Then there was Jesse Lincoln, who in late 1817 submitted a claim to the Treasury Department for labor allegedly performed. Crawford sent the claim to Thompson, who was then still superintendent for the western section. Thompson reported that "Mr. Lincoln did abandon the work of that section with out having done or finished any part of it." He added, "Mr. Lincoln did work some time with considerable force but more like a deranged man than any thing else paying no regard to course or grade." All of his work, Thompson added, had to be redone. The disposition of this case is also not known.[37]

In the autumn of 1818 the road was completed to Uniontown except for some masonry east of the town. This came as a relief to the residents. Not only did they have a connection with Cumberland, but the construction project had torn up Front Street, causing a great deal of inconvenience.[38]

At least one traveler was also pleased with the work. In 1816 Uria Brown, a Baltimore resident, started out on a trip to Ohio. The road was then completed to Brownsville, and he wrote glowingly of the project. It was, Brown observed, "far superior to any of the Turnpike roads in Baltimore County for Masterly Workmanship," adding, "the Bridges & Culverts actually do credit to the Executors of the same." The bridge over the Little Youghiogheny, he went on, "is possitively a Superb Bridge." A devout Quaker, Brown believed, "The goodness of God must have been in Congress unbeknownst to them." As a result they had approved a "great Turnpike road which is the Salvation of those Mountains or Western Countrys & more benefit to the human family than Congress have any knowledge."[39]

Meanwhile, the miles through Virginia were not coming easily. The problem was Wheeling Hill, which descended steeply to the Ohio River. In the late fall of 1817, soon after contractor John McClure had cut the road bed to six feet, wet weather caused much of it to slip. A number of accidents followed, and on one occasion a wagon driver narrowly escaped serious injury. Thompson discussed the problem with President Monroe, who passed through Wheeling in 1817 as part of an extensive tour. The chief executive felt a wall was necessary, but McClure demurred, saying his contract did not cover the added expense. More slips occurred the following year, and in 1819 McClure finally received a contract to erect side walls.[40]

In the spring of 1819, Shriver advertised for proposals to complete the road from Uniontown to Washington. The contract went to Kinkead, Evans, and Beck. They worked quickly, and on December 19, 1820, a local newspaper announced that the project had been completed. By then the Virginia contractors had also finished their work. The construction project had been going on for nine years, but as 1820 came to a close, the dream of joining the Atlantic with the Ohio had been realized.[41]

At the same time, Shriver was repeating his call for repairs to the sections already completed. On April 28, 1817, he again proposed dividing the highway into ten-mile sections and employing a man with a horse and a cart for each. This system, he believed, would result in a competition between the various contractors and lead them to work more efficiently. They could construct cabins for their families, and additional structures for their employees, along the government's sixty-six-foot right-of-way. Shriver proposed paying them $500 a year, which the superintendent believed would be cheaper than day labor. Shriver concluded, "Our road must be repaired, the work ought to have been commenced early in the season."[42]

Shriver issued yet another call for "an ample provision for repairs" in December. He also recommended a tax on narrow wagon wheels, which caused more damage to the roadbed. The superintendent repeated his pleas the following June. He reported that banks had slid in several places and covered the road. Trees had fallen across it, and standing water covered it in places. By March 1819 his messages conveyed a tone of desperation. "If repairs are not made without loss of time," he direly predicted, "the road between [Cumberland] and Union Town will be destroyed." In December he sent the Treasury Department a piece of legislation to submit to Congress. Three months after that, Shriver conceded that he had "frequently written on the subject of repairs." He was doing so again, the superintendent asserted, because "unless continual repairs are made, the road will in a short time go to destruction."[43]

In March 1819 Congress appropriated $285,000 for completing the road. Apparently Shriver used some of these funds for repairs. On August 5 he reported that he had between fifteen and twenty men at work with six or seven carts. "Should I be enabled to increase to advantages the number of Labourers, it certainly would be to the interest of the government," he added. The superintendent also wrote that he was "preparing a house to be moved on wheels so that the workmen can be lodged and boarded without [a] loss of time." It is the only known reference to such a structure. On Christmas Eve Shriver informed Crawford that some sixty-two miles of road had been repaired between Cumberland and Uniontown. Congress had appropriated $10,000 for the purpose, not enough to "place it in its original perfect state." This goal, he estimated, would require an additional $10,000.[44]

In March 1823, Crawford informed Shriver that Congress had approved a $25,000 appropriation for repairs to the road. On July 12 a much-relieved superintendent announced that all of the contractors had commenced work. One had nearly 130 hands "and is yet engaging every labourer that offers." Following an inspection tour in September, Shriver reported, "The progress made is considerable, yet much remains to be done." The work continued in 1824. On September 8 Shriver informed Crawford that some 150 hands were at work between Cumberland and Brownsville. Apparently Shriver had problems with one of the contractors working in the vicinity of Brownsville. As a result he had been "obliged" to employ sixty day laborers, a system he had long advocated. The rate of pay was 62½ cents a day. In thinly populated mountainous sections, he had to raise the rate to 75 cents per day to secure enough workers.[45]

One contractor who caused Shriver major problems was William Hoblitzell. In October 1823 Hoblitzell discharged two-thirds of his workers, who were engaged somewhere in the vicinity of Uniontown. He then took off to the east with two of his teams and most of his tools. The superintendent overtook him at a tavern twenty-nine miles west of Cumberland. Hoblitzell said he could not complete his contract for graveling at the agreed-upon price of $2,000. Shriver started back west, learning along the way that a western Pennsylvania sheriff had placed writs of attachment on the contractor's horses, carts, and tools.

Meanwhile James Bradley, described as Hoblitzell's "principal over seer," fearing arrest for debt, had "marched his men through Union Town in Military order Eastwardly." A constable, accompanied by a posse of citizens, pursued and overtook Bradley and the men in Monroeville, two miles east of Uniontown. Bradley and his party gave battle with stones, and the pursuers returned fire with the same weapons. The fray went on for some time. When it was over some seven or eight individuals lay on the ground wounded. The constable and his contingent were forced to retreat, but he returned with a larger force, again caught up with Bradley, and this time prevailed. Between twenty and thirty prisoners ended up in the Uniontown jail. Shriver concluded, "So you see we are going on in rather a different way to what we used to."[46]

Shriver had endured many headaches, but through it all he had guided "our road" through the wilderness, across streams, and over mountains to the Ohio. He had also fought for the repairs needed to keep it in operation. Now it was time to continue the highway west across Ohio, Indiana, and Illinois—and possibly farther. This goal, however, was about to be delayed by a president who supported the project personally but had grave concerns about its constitutionality.

CHAPTER FOUR

✳ ✳ ✳

"A scene of zeal and industry"

Construction through Ohio

IN HIS LAST ANNUAL MESSAGE to Congress, delivered December 3, 1816, President James Madison called for the creation of "a comprehensive system of roads and canals, such as will have the effect of drawing more closely together every part of our country by promoting intercourse and improvements and by increasing the share of every part in the common stock of national prosperity." Earlier the president had signed a bill that chartered the Second Bank of the United States, the type of institution he had vehemently opposed as a congressman when proposed by Alexander Hamilton in 1790.[1]

His words and his support of the bank suggested that Madison had dramatically moderated the strict constructionist ideas he had firmly held for nearly three decades. John C. Calhoun certainly thought so. On December 16, 1816, the South Carolinian, then a passionate nationalist, called for the creation of a special congressional committee. It would be charged with studying the expediency of setting aside the $1.5 million "bonus" the national bank was to pay the government, in return for its charter, to finance a system of roads and canals. Future dividends from the institution would be earmarked for the same purpose. On February 4, 1817, in the waning days of the Fourteenth Congress, the bill was called up by the House Committee of the Whole. Calhoun's plea anticipated what Henry Clay, two years later, would label the "American System," and it was impassioned. "We are under the most imperious obligations to counteract every tendency to disunion," the future sectionalist declared. "Let us bind the republic together with a perfect system of roads and canals. Let us conquer space." Calhoun's eloquence may have made the difference in the outcome. The bill passed the House by just two votes before clearing the Senate. The president, however, had not entirely abandoned strict construction, and he vetoed the measure. The legislative powers, he wrote, did not include "the powers to be exercised by the bill."[2]

Madison, to his credit, informed Calhoun of his decision in advance. This prompted Clay to appeal to the president, who would leave office in days, to leave the decision to his successor, James Monroe. It likely would not have mattered. In his inaugural address, the new president called for "the improvement of our country by roads and canals, proceeding always with a constitutional sanction." At the time he offered no details about what was constitutionally sanctioned. Nine months later, in his first Annual Message, he was very specific, asserting that there was "a settled conviction in my mind that Congress do not possess the right" to fund highway projects. He called for the adoption of a constitutional amendment granting the power to Congress.[3]

If Monroe's position seemed definite, his subsequent words and actions proved inconsistent. Two years after expressing his settled conviction, the president seemed to relax his views. Projects of a truly "national character," he wrote, could be sanctioned under the Constitution's General Welfare Clause. At the same time, bills for continuing construction and repairs to the National Road managed to avoid a presidential veto. "Surely if they had the right to appropriate money to make the road they have the right to appropriate it to preserve it from ruin," he explained in 1822.[4]

That same year Congress passed a bill to repair the road. It appropriated $9,000 and called for the erection of tollgates to pay for future maintenance. The House considered an amendment to turn the highway over to the states through which it passed. The amendment failed by a vote of 103–50, but the bill passed. Monroe vetoed the measure "with deep regret, approving as I do the policy." His message was brief, but he followed it with a 25,000-word opus, titled "Views on the Subject of Internal Improvements." In the former he explained, "A power to establish turnpikes with gates and tolls, and to enforce the collection of tolls by penalties, implies a power to adopt and execute a complete system of internal improvement." Echoing his earlier Annual Message, the president wrote, "I am of [the] opinion that Congress do not possess this power." His reasoning, put forth in the latter document, was convoluted.

The president asserted that Congress could appropriate funds for roads and canals but added that it lacked the authority to construct them. If nothing else it was a constitutional nicety that justified Jefferson's support of the original measure and Madison's and his own approval of repair bills. The House made a weak attempt to override the veto. Far from mustering the needed two-thirds majority, the lower chamber now voted it down 72–68.[5]

A change of administration soon brought a change of policy. In 1824 a four-way race for president did not produce a winner in the Electoral College, where a majority vote is required. On February 9, 1825, the House of Representatives selected John Quincy Adams to be president after Clay, who had also been a candidate, urged his colleagues to vote for the New Englander. Clay became secretary of state, in those days a stepping-stone to the presidency, and Andrew Jackson, who had garnered a plurality in the Electoral College, accused the pair of engineering a "corrupt bargain." The maneuverings, if any, remain unclear, but one thing was certain. The new chief executive and his top cabinet officer were staunch nationalists who had no constitutional qualms about internal improvements. On March 3, 1825, one day before the inauguration, Congress voted to appropriate $150,000 to extend the National Road from the Ohio River to Zanesville and to survey a route through Indiana and Illinois and on into Missouri.[6]

Congress had already voted for funds to pay for a survey of a route through Ohio. Superintendent Shriver, Alexander LaCock, and William McRee were appointed in 1821 to serve as commissioners. Because funding was in question, they chose to go only from Bridgeport to Zanesville with the monies available to them. On January 2, 1822, they submitted their report to Secretary Crawford. The men found the ground to be "very hilly and broken." Streams were numerous, and the commissioners predicted that the expense for bridges and causeways would be large. In addition, a substratum of the ground, especially on hillsides, was "generally a lime, or rotten slate stone," making slides a likely problem. "The necessity of avoiding ground of this nature is obvious," they wrote. The men recommended abandoning the road then used between Bridgeport and Zanesville, noting that their proposed route saved five miles. They also reported that stone was plentiful along the way.[7]

On July 4, 1825, ground was broken at St. Clairsville, Ohio, for the westward extension of the National Road. The ceremony included a reading of the Declaration of Independence, appropriate for the day, a volley by the Belmont County Light Cavalry, and various addresses by local politicians. Following a pause of six years, work was about to begin in Ohio.[8]

It would proceed under a new cast of characters. On April 30, 1824, Congress approved a bill authorizing the president to utilize the Army Corps of Engineers for internal improvement projects. The following March President Adams transferred responsibility for construction of the National Road from the Treasury Department to the Corps of Engineers. Caspar Wever, a native of Frederick County, Maryland, was named superintendent of the road in Ohio. Wever, who had dabbled in local politics and was involved in the planning of the Chesapeake & Ohio Canal, had most recently served as an engineering superintendent at the Treasury. Shriver remained east of the Ohio, having been named superintendent for repairs in 1823. Wever established an office in St. Clairsville and reported to Maj. Gen. Alexander Macomb.[9]

On April 25, 1825, the superintendent announced that he would receive proposals at his office between June 15 and 30 for construction of the road from Bridgeport to Zanesville. On June 20 he made a similar call to bridge builders. Apparently his first notice did not produce satisfactory results because he made a second appeal for the same sections on July 13. In both cases Wever noted, "Testimonials of character will be expected to accompany proposals for the road."[10]

Although the Corps of Engineers conducted surveying and often supervised projects, the work continued under the contract system that Shriver had decried. The Ohio contractors, as far as existing records show, were all new to the project, and none of them received more than one section. This was not true of the more specialized masonry work, for which many bidders received from two to six sections. Among them was Shriver's favorite, James Kinkead.[11]

On March 28, 1825, James Barbour, the secretary of war, announced, "After the most mature consideration, I have determined that the road shall be made on the McAdams plan." By then Scotsman John Loudon McAdam was the internationally recognized authority on road construction. He rejected the idea of a crowned highway, preferring a flat surface. McAdam also suggested that the number of layers of stone should be determined by local conditions, the paramount consideration being a road surface that was impervious to water.[12]

As in Pennsylvania, local interests haggled over the route the road would follow. Before construction began, a group of landowners petitioned for a more southern route, which would have carried the project through the community of Barnesville. Macomb sent Jonathan Knight, a respected surveyor and future politician, from Washington County, Pennsylvania, to examine both routes and make a recommendation. Knight arrived in May, and the following month he reported in favor of the commissioners' original route.[13]

With the latest controversy as to route settled, St. Clairsville enjoyed its ceremony, and the work began. Some twenty-eight miles were contracted for construction in 1825, which officials believed to be as far as the most recent congressional appropriation would take them. In late August the *St. Clairsville Gazette* reported that the first of the project's three divisions, extending about ten miles from the Ohio, was under contract and being graded. The government had also let contracts for bridges. Unlike what the *Gazette* termed "gentlemen contractors" east of the river, those in Ohio were hands-on. "The contractors of the different sections now under contract," the paper explained, "perform as much work as any of their hands and are constantly upon the spot to direct the manner of its execution." It further reported that labor was cheap. Six dollars a month was the top wage paid to "common laborers," and many worked for less. The paper added, "They come in great numbers from different sections of the country to find employment, but at least nine-tenths of them are disappointed."[14]

The *Gazette* went on to explain the manner of construction under the McAdam system:

> The bed of the road is to be formed thirty feet in width, the hills cut down and the valleys filled up so that no elevation, shall in any part of the road, when finished, be greater than an angle of four and a half with the horizon. The road is to be covered twenty feet in width with stone, to be broken in pieces weighing not more than four ounces; the bed first to be formed nearly flat. When the stone is inspected and passed by the superintendent, they are to be sown or scattered upon the road with a shovel.[15]

Laborers wearing metal goggles with slits and wielding round-headed hammers received six dollars a month to break the stone to the required size. Local folklore holds that farmers and their families would on occasion charge the government twice for the same pile, prompting officials to pour whitewash over them at the time of purchase. Once it was broken, the stone was shoveled onto the roadbed and leveled to a depth of three inches. In keeping with the McAdam process, a heavy roller then passed over it. The Scotsman's goal was to have the stone "unite by its own angles so as to form a solid, hard surface." The crews repeated the process once, and twice when necessary.[16]

On September 17 the *Gazette* reported that the second and third divisions, carrying the road to Fairview, on the Belmont-Guernsey County line, were under contract, with a large number of hands at work. Their labors would carry the highway the planned twenty-eight miles. Six weeks later the paper observed that the road "presents a scene of zeal and industry, seldom witnessed." On November 21 Macomb reported to Congress that the workers had made "very satisfactory progress." Nearly the entire route to Fairview had been cleared, cut, and graded, making it ready for stone. That would occur the following spring.[17]

The deadline for completion of the first division in Ohio was July 1, 1826. For the second and third it was September 1. On June 21 the *Gazette* reported that 826 men were at work on the three divisions, and the paper predicted a timely completion. This was not to be the case. It is not clear when the road reached Fairview, but in December 1826 Wever informed his superiors that it would take two more months to finish the work. He blamed wet weather in June and July, which made it difficult to haul stone and at times shut down work altogether. He also blamed the contractors, who he said underestimated the number of workers they would need to reduce the stone. Still, like Shriver before him, Wever felt not paying contractors the full amount due them, late or not, was "rather oppressive."[18]

It was not all work for the laborers. On July 1 the *Gazette* reported that the previous Thursday had been payday, and the superintendent had disbursed $19,000. The paper observed, "Our streets are always crowded on pay day; for most of the laborers, and many of the citizens on the margin of the road, come to town on that occasion, as well as the contractors, in order to share more liberally in the amount received by their employers for their work." Sadly, little more was recorded about the lives of these laboring men, mainly Irish, who made the National Road a reality. Largely illiterate, they left virtually no record of their efforts. One man who grew up along the route in Licking County, Ohio, later recalled tales of the workers related by his mother: "She would tell us how the camp-fires of the workmen lighted up the night all along the line; about the bustle, the teams coming and going, and on Sundays the drunken carousals and rioting." Leaders of what would become the Whig Party complained that the laboring men tended to vote for the emerging Jackson party. One Adams newspaper in Zanesville observed in 1828, "Their predilections, generally, are in favor of the 'hero.'" Adams supporters believed that road and canal workers added five thousand or more votes to Jackson's tally that year.[19]

As the work advanced from Bridgeport to Fairview, plans were under way to carry it further west. On April 27, 1826, Macomb instructed Knight to examine the proposed route between Fairview and Zanesville. "It has been suggested that some considerable improvements may be made in the location of the road," he explained. Macomb suggested that Wever accompany Knight whenever possible to familiarize himself with the course of the road. The two men visited Cambridge on May 24, and they impressed the editor of the *Guernsey Times*. He wrote, "They evince by their indefatigable industry a disposition to arrive at the best information and most correct conclusions on the subject." Knight completed his work on July 22, and Wever reported that his route, covering forty-four miles, was "a very eligible one." The superintendent divided it into four divisions and on July 25 placed advertisements in local newspapers for road and bridge builders. To the latter he promised, "There will be several Bridges of considerable size and many small ones."[20]

On June 1, 1827, the *Guernsey Times* reported that work between Fairview and Cambridge was "progressing with great rapidity." The newspaper credited "the zeal, industry and skill of Mr. Wever, for the expedition and permanency of the work." Some sections, the *Times* continued, had already been opened to travelers. The following month crews had completed the grading to a point three miles west of Cambridge. The entire distance was open to traffic, although the "metal" would not go on until the following spring. All that was left to be done was the bridge over Wills Creek, near Cambridge, a large stream subject to "very high freshets." Wever explained that a lack of funds had forced choices upon him, and since a private toll bridge crossed the creek, he had delayed the project. That changed in 1828, when Joseph P. Shannon received the contract to erect a bridge with stone abutments and a 150-foot wooden span.[21]

As the limestone went on from Fairview to Cambridge, grading was under way to Zanesville, just over twenty miles west of Cambridge. Wever let the contracts in July 1827. At Jonathan Knight's suggestion, the work was suspended so an alternate route could be surveyed. It proved to reduce grades, and Wever approved the change. By June 1828, despite heavy rains, workers had graded and bridged the entire section. The Corps of Engineers allowed traffic on July 15. James Hampson, who succeeded Wever as superintendent in 1829, informed Washington that the work was complete, with nine inches of stone in place, in April 1829. However, the *Zanesville Messenger* reported in August that only six inches covered the road and that plans were under way for the remaining three.[22]

In addition to the wooden bridge over Wills Creek, there were forty-two stone arched bridges between the Ohio and the Muskingum. Many were the famous "S" bridges, some of which still stand alongside US Route 40. They got their name because their curved approaches meet the arch at opposite angles, forming the shape of an "S." Numerous tales emerged concerning the origins of these serpentine spans, ranging from drunken designers to a desire to stop runaway horses. In reality, they were simply easier to build because it is far less complicated to cross streams with a straight arch as opposed to a skewed one.[23]

✳✳✳

Wever's removal and Hampson's appointment came at the hands of Andrew Jackson. It was part of what the newly inaugurated president termed "rotation in office" and his opponents considered a cynical use of the "spoils system." The new superintendent, a Zanesville resident, had reportedly been "violently for Jackson" as early as May 1827. Wever's Frederick supporters did not accept the dismissal with good grace. According to a pair of local historians, "The bitterness of the Whig newspaper knew no bounds and the leading articles each week [were] about 'King Andrew I.'"[24]

Hampson soon became a figure of controversy. In December the War Department nullified one of his contracts because it extended farther than he was then authorized to take the road and because it exceeded congressional appropriations. Soon reports of questionable financial dealings reached Washington. The War Department sent an inspector, Captain A. Talcott, to investigate. His report was damning. Hampson, the captain reported, was in the habit of taking the signatures of contractors on blank receipts. "Signatures thus obtained," the report went on, "have in some instances been used as vouchers for payments that were not made, and in others have been filled up for a greater amount than was paid upon them." Contracts furnished the War Department, Talcott charged, were "in some instances fictitious." He cited a number of examples. In one case, "Thomas Monaghan was the ostensible contractor for the 18 section; Hugh McGinnis the real one." Allegedly, Monaghan had signed the receipts and left the state. McGinnis then carried on the work, receiving payment on Monaghan's receipts. When Monaghan's contract was finally declared abandoned, McGinnis reportedly received a new contract, with an advance pay of nearly 60 percent.[25]

It was enough to get Hampson suspended pending a formal investigation. The result was that Hampson returned to his post on January 18, 1832. It is not clear whether Talcott was unable to make his case or political pressure from Jackson and his good friend, Secretary of War John Eaton, made the difference.

In any event, the political press fell along predictable lines. The *St. Clairsville Gazette,* a Jackson paper, pointed out that during his first year Hampson had overseen fifty-two miles of repairs, finished twenty miles of construction, and contracted for and begun work on an additional twenty-six miles. When

Zanesville's *Ohio Republican,* an opposition sheet, ran a letter from "A CON-TRACTOR," accusing Hampson of being absent from his duties, the *Gazette* leapt to his defense. The paper produced a missive signed by nearly fifty contractors refuting the charge. The *Republican* then turned to sarcasm, observing, "The question has been repeatedly asked us, whether James Hampson is still retained on the National Road and under pay from Government? We cannot inform our readers whether he is or not, but have heard that he is, and that his salary has been increased, whether by an actual advance, or whether by his doing nothing and receiving his usual salary we can not say."[26]

Upon his return to office, Hampson promptly fired David Scott, his assistant superintendent, whom Hampson blamed for most of his problems. Writing to Gen. Charles Gratiot, chief of engineers, the superintendent claimed that a cabal, including the bridge builder James Kinkead, had formed "a combination to rule the road." Scott, he asserted, was in league with them. Hampson further charged that the *Ohio Republican,* one of his tormentors, had turned Scott's head when the paper suggested that Scott replace him as superintendent. Hampson also claimed that Scott had helped circulate a pamphlet "issued against me." When Captain Talcott was conducting his investigation, Hampson added, Scott lined up contractors to offer negative testimony. Scott denied the charges, telling Hampson he was "indignant at the liberties some people calling themselves your friends take in falsely representing me to you." He also produced a letter from a third party denying that he had ever heard Scott "make use of . . . any language vilifying or abusing Capt Hampson." Fifty-two residents of Zanesville also supported Scott by sending a petition to the War Department. What actually transpired will never be known, but his superiors ordered Hampson to reinstate his assistant, which he did on March 31 in a brief, tersely worded letter.[27]

In April 1828 Jonathan Knight left the road to accept a similar position with the Baltimore & Ohio Railroad. He brought with him the recently discharged Caspar Wever, securing him the position of superintendent of construction. Joseph Shriver succeeded Knight. The following April Shriver met with Hampson in Zanesville and directed the superintendent to trace the line of Knight's 1825 survey from Zanesville to Columbus, fifty-two miles. He finished the task on June 12. Notices had already gone into area newspapers announcing that Hampson would receive bids between June 23 and 30 for work on the one-mile sections into which the project would be divided. He let the contracts for the first twenty-six miles, the limit of congressional appropriations, on July 1, and construction began the following month. Fall rains, which stretched into winter, slowed the work, but when the wet weather abated, Hampson increased the number of workers to make up for lost time. He opened the division during the summer of 1830 "to produce that compactness requisite in the body of the road."[28]

In making their 1822 survey, Commissioners LaCock, Shriver, and McRee had predicted that the "difficulty of making a location [for the road] will considerably diminish" as work progressed west of the Muskingum. Hampson confirmed their prediction, reporting that the first twenty-one miles west of the river were "rough and hilly," marked by "deep excavations and heavy embankments." West of that point, workers found occasional depressions, but the terrain leveled out and the soil proved easy to drain and "favorable for the formation of the road." Stone, he reported, was abundant. The only negative was the number of streams to be crossed. Five, Hampson reported, would require bridges with 50- to 180-foot spans, and there were numerous smaller ones.[29]

✳✳✳

As road building conditions grew better, another, more ominous, threat emerged. In advertising for contracts between Zanesville and Columbus in 1829, Hampson added, "This part of the road passes through a very healthy country." The following year, after inspecting the route, Capt. Richard Delafield observed that "the prevailing sickness on the line of the road" had shut down construction operations in places. In 1833 Secretary Eaton was more specific about the threat. Crews had not replaced faulty masonry west of Columbus because of "the existence of cholera" in the area. The disease, and the shortage of labor that it produced, also delayed construction between Zanesville and Columbus. The next year Lt. Henry Brewerton, who was put in charge of construction in 1832, reported that "the appearance of cholera" had "operated against the advancement of the work the present year."[30]

Although Eaton and Brewerton were understated in their reports, the cholera outbreak that struck America in 1832 and did not fully abate until 1834 was anything but subtle. When the disease advanced from Russia to Great Britain in 1831, Americans knew its arrival was inevitable. On June 6, 1832, Montreal reported the first case in North America. It took only eight days to reach upstate New York, and on June 26 an Irish immigrant became New York City's first victim. Eventually cholera struck virtually every section of the country, killing some five thousand in New Orleans alone. So terrifying was the disease that in Illinois, where the Black Hawk War was raging, Chicago residents fled the city, risking the wrath of the Sauk tribe rather than facing the scourge. Although not spread by human contact, cholera tended to follow America's system of internal improvements, starting with the Erie Canal. Later it attacked construction crews on both the Chesapeake & Ohio Canal and the Baltimore & Ohio Railroad. It traveled the country's rivers and plagued communities—and work parties—on the National Road from Cumberland to Columbus.[31]

※※※

Controversies over the adopted route—and the adamancy of those who wanted it changed—added to the Corps of Engineers' headaches. The military men's straight-arrow policy carried the road some seven miles south of Newark, seat of Licking County, the next county west of Zanesville. This did not sit well with Newark's civic leaders, particularly because the highway would pass through a community they had long viewed as a rival. In 1826, long before the road reached Zanesville, they contacted Knight, who invited them to conduct him along what was, in their view, the best route to Newark. They accepted his offer, and the surveyor filed his report. He concluded that carrying the road through Newark would add two miles to the distance from Zanesville to Columbus. It would also require more bridging. At the same time, stone would be easier to obtain along the Newark route, including extensive deposits of flint. In addition, a state road went on from Newark to Columbus, meaning less clearing of timber if crews chose to follow it. Knight concluded that the government would save $2,740 by altering the route to pass through the courthouse community. This left much to consider, but in the end the War Department informed Newark's leaders that it did not have "the power to change the route of the road from its original location."[32]

Civic leaders in Dayton were also eager to have the road pass through their city, and their battle to secure it lasted nearly a decade. They began lobbying in 1826, at a time when the road had not yet reached Zanesville. Their effort attracted enough attention that the Corps of Engineers instructed the redoubt- able Knight to examine the proposed diversion. He reported in early 1827, concluding that the Dayton route, which continued through the courthouse village of Eaton, in Preble County, had much to recommend it, despite the fact that it would add nearly four miles.

While workers would have to erect a 360-foot bridge across the Miami River at Dayton, the route would avoid two large branches of that river. The net savings to the government, Knight estimated, would be about $3,000.

Because a road was already in place from Dayton to Eaton, the cost of clearing timber along the alternate route would be more than $10,000 less. Good gravel was also abundant, resulting in additional savings of nearly $8,000. At a time when Congress was becoming more dubious about appropriating funds for the road, these findings were not insignificant. Knight added, almost as an afterthought, that legislation passed in 1820 did not allow for a deviation from a straight line, even for "the accommodation of towns, villages, or settlements." Wishing to avoid the politics of the matter, he concluded, "I have, under a conviction of imperious duty, located and reported the direct route, leaving the final determination of the question to the Government."[33]

Unlike Knight, the Ohio General Assembly was not bound by "imperious duty," and in 1830 they petitioned Congress to adopt the change. Much of their appeal cited Knight's report and the cost savings it mentioned. The state legislators also observed that the Dayton and Eaton route passed through a populous and rapidly growing area. Dayton was home to five thousand souls, and Eaton was "a flourishing town" of 630. Finally they reminded the congressmen that "a primary object" of the road was "to facilitate the transportation of the public mail." That object, they contended, could not be achieved by pursuing a route that "does not strike a single town or village."[34]

In 1835 Congress directed the War Department to examine the conflicting routes again. The Corps of Engineers sent Capt. A. Canfield to western Ohio, and on April 10 he began his work. Canfield believed carrying the road through Dayton would add three miles, and this, he felt, was reason enough not to pursue it. The captain dismissed arguments relating to mail delivery, suggesting that "the principal mails will be carried over the shortest road." He concluded, "It seems evident that 'the public convenience and interest' will be best promoted by adopting the direct route as now located."[35]

Canfield's report only prompted advocates of the Dayton-Eaton route to redouble their efforts. During the winter of 1836–37, they made their feelings known in a series of letters and petitions. Rep. Taylor Webster, whose district included the area in question, supported the change primarily because it would "meet the wishes of a majority of my constituents." D. F. Heaton, a "special delegate" sent from Preble County to lobby for the change, was much more adamant. In a lengthy missive, he attempted to place history on his side, going back to the Ohio statehood bill and noting that land sales in the Buckeye State had funded much of the project. He then quoted a message written by Thomas Jefferson, which stated, "Material interest shall be had to the interests and wishes of the populous part of Ohio." Heaton next reminded Congress that Pennsylvania had secured the changes of route that it had desired. On a pragmatic level, he cited the Knight report and explained that people had laid out lots in Preble County in anticipation of the road's arrival. Returning to the Ohio statehood bill, he concluded, "Ohio has done much in the construction of this road, not only in her own territory, but also in those of Maryland, Pennsylvania, and Virginia; therefore, she ought to have a strong voice in its permanent location."[36]

By this time Ohio had passed legislation, approved by Congress, to assume ownership of its portion of the road as it became completed. A trio of lobbyists sent from the Dayton area noted that fact and suggested that the state should have a significant say over the route of a road for which it would soon be responsible. Samuel Forrer, a member of Ohio's Board of Canal Commissioners, pointed out that Canfield had conceded that surfacing the road along the Dayton route would be cheaper because of an abundance of stone. This being the case, he argued, future repairs would also cost less. These and other points persuaded the House Committee on Roads and Canals, which recommended that the route be changed. It did not matter. By the time the committee issued its report, some fifteen miles of the direct route had been cleared and grubbed, and a portion had been graded. Likely more important was the obsessive tunnel vision of the Corps of Engineers. The military men had received orders to plot a straight line. They had done so, and they were going to stick to it, local interests and politics notwithstanding.[37]

✳✳✳

Dayton and Eaton likely did not appreciate this adherence to discipline, but it did keep the road moving westward. So, too, did favorable congressional action. For four years, beginning in 1829, Congress overcame its doubts and voted annual appropriations of $100,000 for construction in Ohio. In 1833 they increased the amount to $130,000, and in each of the following three years they approved $200,000 for the work. In 1837 the amount was $190,000. The next year, following a long and contentious debate on the issue, Congress approved its last appropriation for work on the National Road. Ohio's share was $150,000.[38]

In 1830 work focused on the first twenty-seven miles west of Zanesville, on which most of the grading was already complete. This carried the road to the crossing of the Ohio & Erie Canal at Hebron and connected it with a state road that continued on to Columbus. By the end of August workers had completed all of the bridging along this section. Except for a ninety-five-foot wooden span over the South Fork of the Licking River, all were made of stone. At Hebron the road crossed the canal over a "slight and inconvenient" bridge hastily erected by the canal company. A more substantial structure replaced it in 1835.[39]

Work slowed during the next three years, despite the arrival in 1832 of Lieutenant Brewerton, an energetic officer. The cholera epidemic was a factor. So too were unreliable contractors, some of whom abandoned their work. In some cases culverts gave way because of "bad material and workmanship" and had to be rebuilt.[40]

Still, the work got done. In 1832 two strata of stone went down for twenty-one miles west of Zanesville. That same year the Corps of Engineers contracted for all bridges and culverts on the twenty-seven miles between Hebron and Columbus. The longest was to be a 203-foot wooden span crossing Big Walnut Creek. They also awarded contracts for clearing and grubbing much of the same stretch of highway.

In 1834 the road's famous triangular milestones went up between Zanesville and Columbus, despite the fact that they dotted a section of highway that had not yet reached the Ohio capital. Those milestones were different from the markers east of the Ohio. Those placed from Cumberland to Wheeling were made of cast iron. The mileposts between Cumberland and Brownsville came from the James Francis foundry in Connellsville, Pennsylvania. John Snowden's foundry in Brownsville produced those placed from Brownsville west to Wheeling. Ohio's mile markers were five feet tall and usually made of sandstone, although limestone and an experimental type of cement were occasionally used. Workers buried them two feet in the ground. They were rounded at the top, a section that always gave the number of miles to Cumberland. Below were mileages to important communities lying ahead for both eastbound and westbound travelers.[41]

The Engineers reached Columbus in 1836 as the last strata of stone went down between there and Zanesville. This did not come easily. About ten miles west of Zanesville, limestone deposits faded. This forced the road builders to transport limestone on the Ohio & Erie Canal to Hebron and haul it for several miles along the roadbed. There were problems in Columbus as well. In July 1834 a flood carried away a bridge over the Scioto River that had been privately built eight years earlier. Lieutenant Brewerton made sure the new bridge was built above the level of the Scioto's highest known flood. Workers finished it in 1836. There was also the predictable squabble over route, this time involving the city's northern and southern sections. The military men averted this potential civil war with a compromise. The road entered Columbus on Main (then Friend) Street, appeasing the south side. It then turned due north on High Street before exiting the city along Broad Street.[42]

Long before the road was completed from Zanesville to Columbus, workers were clearing, grading, and bridging west of the city. From there it was ninety-six miles to the Indiana border. In July 1830 the Engineers advertised for clearing, grubbing, and grading the roadbed and for building bridges and culverts for fourteen miles west of Columbus, carrying the project to Big Darby Creek. The work got under way in August, and it was soon beset by problems that delayed its completion. First, Columbus residents and individuals living west of the city petitioned to have the route changed to "a more eligible location." The outcome is not known, but the investigation their action prompted resulted in very little being done during 1830 and 1831.[43]

Once the crews got started on the project, the flat terrain west of Columbus posed a problem. The area was susceptible to high water, forcing the men to raise the roadbed between one and two feet and to dig an extensive series of ditches. Shoddy work also plagued the effort. In 1832 Brewerton reported that virtually all the masonry was "of a very inferior character, and altogether disreputable to the great national work of which it forms a part." Most of the grading was done, he added, but several stumps remained in the roadbed. Workers had not properly screened the stone they had put down, and many of the stones weighed between one and six pounds. It was, the lieutenant concluded, "of greater harm than service to the surface of the road." If human error did not produce enough problems, flooding had done damage to the roadbed, bridges, and culverts.[44]

In 1834 workers removed about two hundred stumps and finished clearing the section of timber. Yet another flood had produced damage just west of Columbus. To address the problem, crews reduced the embankments, forming "long and gentle curves, which would pass the water in time of a freshet." Two years later the project was finally completed, carrying the road to the community of Jefferson (now West Jefferson). Ohio received the fourteen-mile section on March 25, 1827. Included were a 168-foot wooden bridge over Big Darby Creek and a 146-foot span over Little Darby.[45]

In 1836 Lt. George Dutton arrived to take control of the project in Ohio. A no-nonsense officer, he would be promoted to captain during his tenure on the highway. Dutton annoyed residents along the route, instructing them to take down fences and other barriers so the work could proceed apace. He also dispatched inspectors to check minutely the work of contractors, empowering them to insist upon changes if the work was not done according to the terms of their agreements.[46]

Continuing west, the next section of road was the twenty-nine miles from Jefferson to Springfield, the last large community through which it would pass in Ohio. Work crews began in 1834, completing the clearing and grubbing and starting construction on bridges and culverts. Within two years they had completed the grading on all but ten miles of the section. Bridging was complete from Springfield to a point eleven miles east. Stone became a problem as the work extended westward. It was plentiful in the Scioto Valley and in the valley of the Miami River west of Springfield, but in the area between the two streams it was not to be found. This necessitated lengthy and expensive hauling operations. Getting stone where it was needed produced so much wagon traffic that Captain Dutton had two rakers constantly employed along certain sections of the project so the loads could pass easily.

Workers began putting stone on the roadbed in 1837. The same year work began on an eighty-foot bridge over Buck Creek and a 150-foot bridge over the Mad River. Workers completed an eighty-seven-foot span over Deer Creek that same year. Two years later the Engineers and their contractors finished the road to Springfield. Dutton proudly announced that a continuous 302-mile highway connected the western Ohio city with Cumberland. "The gentle grades adopted west of Zanesville," he boasted, "together with the hard and smooth surface of the road . . . allows the space and burden of the four horses customarily employed to be very considerably enlarged beyond their usual magnitude." He added, "For the same reason, the transportation, in wagons, of heavy loads of merchandise or produce may be effected with fewer horses, and greater ease and safety, on the finished Macadamized road."[47]

From Springfield the highway had fifty-three more miles to go to reach the Indiana border. It would take nearly a century for the road to achieve that goal. The end of funding in 1838 brought an end to the Engineers' work. On October 15, 1839, Dutton reported that all they had accomplished that year was the completion of contracts let in 1838. This allowed them to finish the highway from Columbus to Springfield, the last segment receiving stone in June. West of Springfield workers had graded four miles and grubbed nine more.[48]

With no further appropriations coming from Congress, the project limped along with what remaining funds were available. On July 24, 1840, Dutton was informed that "it becomes necessary to bring the operations to a close." Chief

Engineer Joseph Totten instructed his subordinate, "You will bear in mind that these closing operations must be as complete as if they were final, although it is hoped they may not prove so." All public property was to be sold, and the proceeds applied to finishing as much of the road as possible. Dutton's priorities were to be: "1st. to the preservation of the road; 2d. To its good condition; and 3d. To its extension." The work went on for the remainder of the summer. When it was finished, thirty-nine miles had been grubbed west of Springfield, but only four miles had been graded, and less than a mile had stone. Workers had also completed 80- and 150-foot bridges "in the valley of the Mad river," and three spans of 50 feet each between Springfield and the Miami River. This was all the Corps of Engineers would do in Ohio.[49]

Some travelers learned the fate of the road in Ohio through hard experience. Among them were Jane Voorhees and her family, who decided to emigrate from New Jersey to Illinois in 1841 after neighbors who preceded them sent back positive reports. At Springfield they had a choice of continuing on along the National Road or taking an alternate route through Dayton. The family chose the former after being told that "movers go that way." Jane estimated that they went six miles before the highway became "nothing but a foot path . . . and that ended the National road." Fortunately another road carried them from there to Dayton where a turnpike took them on to Richmond, Indiana.[50]

That turnpike was part of the Dayton Cutoff, a pair of roads built by private interests when they came to realize that the National Road would not extend beyond Springfield. Two companies were involved in the effort. The Dayton-Springfield Turnpike Company constructed the road between those two communities. The Dayton-Western Turnpike Company carried it on through Eaton and thence to the National Road just east of Richmond. Both companies erected milestones that closely resembled those along the National Road, giving travelers the impression that they never left that highway.

On January 20, 1853, Congress passed "An Act to surrender to the State of Ohio the unfinished portion of the Cumberland Road in said State." By then the Dayton Cutoff had become the primary route for National Road travelers, giving by default to city leaders that for which they had lobbied so strenuously. It would remain so until 1931, when the last two miles of the Engineers' preferred straight-line route were paved, becoming part of US Route 40.[51]

CHAPTER FIVE

✳✳✳

"Embarrassments and difficulties from the beginning"

Construction through Indiana and Illinois

WORK ON THE NATIONAL ROAD in Indiana began in 1827 when the Corps of Engineers dispatched Jonathan Knight to the Hoosier State to survey the route. He divided the task into two sections. On June 11 Knight began working from the Ohio state line to Indianapolis. On September 10 he started west from the capital, bound for the Illinois border.[1]

"The location is very direct," he wrote of the former section, "meeting with comparatively few impediments sufficient to justify material deviations from a straight line." In places the "basin-like form of the ground" created a permanent swampy condition, forcing Knight to stray a bit from his and the Engineers' desired direct line. Although limestone was abundant in places, there were lengthy stretches where it could not be found. So great were the shortages that the surveyor reported that he could not form a reasonable estimate of the cost of procuring stone. Some sections, he feared, could not be macadamized. The route was also very thinly settled. There were no towns between Centerville, only ten miles west of the Ohio border, and Indianapolis, and few homes. Trees, by necessity, became the surveying crew's benchmark.[2]

The section west of Indianapolis was even more remote, and it was heavily timbered. Although Knight reported, "The country is settling rapidly," there were no communities between the capital and Terre Haute, a distance of nearly eighty miles. The party discovered extensive low grounds, which were "liable to frequent and great inundations." There were also several ravines, which abruptly broke the otherwise generally flat landscape. The crew encountered a hilly area in the vicinity of the Eel River, about forty-five miles west of Indianapolis. The Wabash, Knight reported, was prone to extensive flooding, covering bottomlands up to three miles in width. He recommended bridging the river at Terre Haute, where a ferry crossing was already in place. Knight did not remark as to the availability of stone along the western section except to note that it was plentiful in the vicinity of the Wabash.[3]

All told, Knight reported, the road would stretch for nearly 150 miles across the state. From the Ohio line to Indianapolis it would continue the virtually due west course that carried it through Ohio. Beyond the capital it would turn southwest, placing it on a direct path to Vandalia, then the capital of Illinois. Knight observed, "I have never passed through a greater extent of uniformly rich land than on the route through Indiana." He further reported that the national government still owned all the land along the Hoosier State route for fifteen miles east of Indianapolis and thirty-five miles west of the capital. If these lands were sold, he predicted, they would bring in more than enough money to clear the timber to eighty feet wide the entire distance of the state.[4]

When Knight left the road to work for the B&O in 1828, Joseph Shriver succeeded him. On July 3 he began surveying the route through Illinois, making a second reconnaissance in August that continued on to the Mississippi opposite St. Louis. From the Indiana line to Vandalia, Shriver divided the route into thirteen sections, ranging from five to eight miles in length. He reported that stone and gravel were scarce, although reports on the individual sections often mentioned the presence of limestone or "sandstone of a good quality." The landscape alternated between prairie and stands of timber. The latter were mainly located along streams, making material for bridges readily available. As in Indiana, the route through Illinois was thinly settled. Besides Vandalia, the only settlement was located at Big Creek, a short distance east of the capital, where the surveyors found a number of farms.[5]

✳✳✳

Through Maryland, Pennsylvania, and Ohio, although individual sections were put under contract at different times, the National Road generally progressed from east to west. That changed in Indiana. When officials let the first bridging and grading contracts in 1830, they extended eleven miles west and twelve miles east of Indianapolis.[6]

Work had actually begun a year earlier. On December 24, 1829, Homer Johnson and John Milroy, superintendents of the road through Indiana, submitted a report to the Speaker of the State House of Representatives. They informed the Speaker that they had divided the state into five roughly equal sections and let contracts for the cutting of timber and grubbing. Although they did not state how many sections they had let, the pair wrote, "The work has progressed beyond our most sanguine expectations." About two-thirds of the cutting and one-eighth of the grubbing were done. They urged travelers not to use the uncompleted thoroughfare. Grubbing, they explained, had left deep holes, and "many low and swampy places must be raised and ditched before it can be made a tolerably good or even passable road."[7]

The following June Gratiot informed the superintendents that Congress had appropriated $100,000 for grading and bridging in Indiana. "This act," he wrote, "contemplates the completion of the road, except in covering it with stone or gravel, to as great a distance on each side of Indianapolis as the means will allow." Specific instructions followed. Thirty feet in the center of the roadbed were to be graded. That roadway, Gratiot insisted, must be virtually flat, having a slope of only one inch in three feet from the center. He urged Milroy and Johnson to be very careful in the construction of ditches and drains so all water would be carried away efficiently. "The chief requisite of the masonry being strength," he insisted, "no expense must be lavished in dressing or finishing the work with a view merely to ornament—let it be plain and strong." Gratiot likely recalled previous experiences with contractors when he wrote that inspections should be thorough before the superintendents made any payments. He also instructed them to withhold at least one-fourth of the amount due at each payment as a security that the entire contract would be completed.[8]

In July ads began appearing for clearing the route east and west of the capital and for the construction of bridges and culverts. Bridges, potential contractors were informed, would be built of brick or stone if they were a span of twenty feet or less. If greater than twenty feet, they would have brick or stone abutments "and superstructures of wood, covered and painted." In a rare display of bipartisanship, both the *Indiana Journal,* a Whig newspaper, and the *Indiana Democrat* agreed that contractors were numerous and enthusiastic. "Many gentlemen are already here awaiting the result of their bids," the *Democrat* enthused on August 11, "and we are pleased to say that there is a prospect of an energetic commencement of this great work." A few days later, the *Journal,* somewhat more subtly, observed, "A considerable crowd of people have been drawn to this place by the prospect of obtaining contracts on this road."[9]

At first Johnson and Milroy awarded separate contracts for felling trees and grubbing stumps. They combined the two after determining "that more labor was necessary to grub a stump than a tree." The strategy apparently worked. By the end of 1830 the superintendents were able to report that the entire 149 miles across Indiana were cleared to the required eighty-foot width and grubbed to thirty. In 1831 Johnson and Milroy's duties changed when Congress voted to divide their responsibilities. Johnson took charge of the road west of Indianapolis, Milroy east of the city, each working independently of the other. Both men let contracts for grading and masonry that summer.[10]

In July 1831 Lewis Wernwag and Walter M. Blake & Co. received an $18,000 contract to construct a bridge over the White River on the west side of Indianapolis. At 320 feet it was easily the longest bridge along the road in the state. The *Indiana Democrat* termed Wernwag "a celebrated bridge builder," while the *Journal* wrote that he was "said to be one of the first bridge builders in the United States." A steam mill soon went up at the site to furnish lumber for the project. When a steamboat laden with stone for the bridge arrived, most of the city's 1,100 residents turned out to greet it, and the local artillery company fired a salute. Their enthusiasm waned somewhat when the vessel ran aground on an island, which became its home for several months. The stone was transported the rest of the way on a flatboat. The contractors finished the project in 1834, and the bridge remained in service for sixty years.[11]

✳✳✳

In late 1832 vague accusations began to appear "relative to the conduct and official character of the Superintendents of the Cumberland Road in Indiana." The *Indiana Democrat* leapt to their defense, suggesting that there was a partisan slant to the charges. The paper's editor made a personal reconnaissance of the route east of Indianapolis in September 1833. He reported that bridges and grading were complete for thirty miles, "making one of the finest roads in the west." He gave the credit to "the able and efficient superintendent, General John Milroy." In December the *Democrat* printed a letter from a group of travelers who had just arrived in Indianapolis from Terre Haute. "We were quite astonished, but highly gratified," they wrote, "to find that so much work had been done during the last summer and fall." They saluted Johnson "for his untiring exertions, in hastening the progress of this road." These endorsements were not enough to convince the War Department, which sent Lt. T. S. Brown to make a minute inspection of the road in Indiana. He submitted his report on December 23, 1833. All grading, masonry, and bridging, he wrote, were completed for twenty-five miles east of Indianapolis and twenty-eight miles west, except for the then unfinished White River Bridge. The masonry, Brown reported, "already exhibits decided symptoms of dilapidation." Much of the stone used was what local residents gave the name "nigger-heads," an unfortunate term that sadly reflected the national racism of the Jackson era (and a few eras that followed). Largely sandstone, these rocks proved to be of inferior quality, and the lieutenant predicted that many bridges would have to be rebuilt.[12]

By then the superintendent in Illinois was also under scrutiny, and Congress decided to act. On June 24, 1834, they passed a law allowing the War Department to place an officer from the Corps of Engineers in charge of the road in both states. The next month the department selected Capt. Cornelius Ogden, who established headquarters in Terre Haute. Following his own inspection of the road, he concluded, "There are but very few of the bridges or culverts on any part of the road that will not have to be rebuilt." With the sandstone crumbling badly, Ogden redoubled the effort to locate limestone quarries, an effort that proved successful. The laborers he described as "citizens of the country [who] seem anxious for the success of the operations."[13]

The captain ran the project with military precision. He appointed two superintendents of grading, each with an assistant, in Indiana, and one superintendent with two assistants in Illinois. Each state had two inspectors of carpentry and two of masonry. Ogden divided the entire route through both states into ten-mile sections. If any section had more than two parties at work on the road, he appointed a superintendent. An overseer supervised every group of workers. Laborers were employed by the day. Wages were sixty-two cents a day east of the Wabash and seventy cents a day west of the river, where labor was more scarce. Workers who "served faithfully" for three months received raises. The workday was from sunrise to sunset. From October through March the men got an hour off at noon. In April, May, and September they received an additional break from 7:00 to 7:30. During the summer months, the idle periods were from noon until 2:00 and from 6:00 to 6:30. Ogden gave instructions that laborers were to be "able bodied white men." If this was not clear enough, he added, "No negroes nor mulattos will be employed." Finally, "Intemperance; bringing ardent spirits to the place of labor; forming combinations for effecting any object whatever; insulting travelers, or quarrelling and fighting, will, either of these, be a cause for immediate dismissal."[14]

Despite the accusations lodged against him, Johnson apparently remained in charge of the work in western Indiana, albeit under Ogden's supervision. He submitted monthly reports to his new superior at least through July 1835. Although there were occasional disputes between laborers and superintendents, he generally wrote that the work was progressing "very well."[15]

On July 2, 1836, Congress voted $250,000 for continuing the road in Indiana. The legislators also attached conditions to this generous appropriation, which curtailed Ogden's flexibility in directing the operation. First, the legislation called for the work to be limited to "the greatest possible continuous portion of said road." Congress had begun turning the highway over to the states through which it passed, and they wished to surrender more significant chunks as quickly as possible. As a result, Ogden decided to focus his attention on three areas. In and around Richmond, he proposed to work on ten-mile sections, grading one at a time, then stoning the graded portions as the work advanced. At Indianapolis he planned to utilize the same method to continue the effort east and west of the city. Finally Ogden planned to grade and stone from the Illinois line eastward to a point ten miles east of the Wabash River.[16]

Another provision of the law rendered his goals impossible. It required that "an officer of the Corps of Engineers . . . be charged with the disbursements of the moneys appropriated for the construction of the Cumberland Road through the States of Indiana and Illinois." The legislation was apparently designed to prevent fraud. At the same time, it made Ogden responsible for 240 miles of payroll. "It is hardly necessary," he protested, "for me to state the impossibility of complying with the requirements of this law." Previously, he added, from two to six officers had assisted him with disbursements. Attorney General Benjamin F. Butler offered an opinion that the superintendent could delegate the disbursements, but he would still be "personally accountable" for every penny.[17]

The legislation changed Ogden's plans. He refused to be responsible for funds in six figures strung out over two states, and he informed Gratiot of his decision. The general supported his superintendent, acceding to Ogden's decision to limit his work in 1836 to a section stretching from the Illinois border to a point twenty miles east of Terre Haute. This, he reasoned, would give him an area small enough to be easily supervised while also allowing him to direct construction efforts in Illinois.[18]

The people of Indianapolis did not appreciate the superintendent's reasoning. Facing the loss of a year's labor in the vicinity of their city, a group of citizens met at the Marion County Courthouse on August 6. They had already put pressure on a local bank, and they adopted a resolution offering assurance that "abundant security can be given in Marion county, in favor of any honorable appointment that may be made, for disbursing any amount of money." They also appointed George L. Kinnard, their representative in Congress, as their spokesman to communicate their feelings to Ogden and Gratiot. Writing to the general, Kinnard asserted that, "There is, perhaps, no part of the line of the road west of Wheeling which receives more travel than the three or four ten-mile sections west of Indianapolis." If those sections were ignored, he feared that work already finished might "become comparatively useless." Ogden stood his ground, and Gratiot continued to support him publicly. However, Gratiot privately informed the superintendent that the secretary of war had given him authority to move his headquarters to Indianapolis. Ogden replied that the work had been "pushed to the utmost" for twenty-seven miles east of the Illinois line. To interrupt it now, he argued, would be "unwarrantably expensive." There the matter rested.[19]

On March 3, 1837, Congress voted another $100,000 for the road in Indiana. The legislators also repealed the portions of the 1836 law that required Ogden to be the sole disbursing agent and that called for the Engineers to build only continuous sections of road. At the same time the legislation mandated the abandonment of day labor and the reinstatement of the contract system, which had produced so many problems in the past. On April 11 a party of engineers, followed by Ogden, arrived in Richmond to make surveys and estimates and to put the work under contract. In June the group moved on to Indianapolis, repeating the process. After venturing to Vandalia to see about work in Illinois, Ogden and the engineers went to Terre Haute, arriving in early September. There they put under contract a section starting about three miles east of the community and continuing east for three and one-half miles.

On October 19 Ogden reported that the road had been cleared and grubbed the entire distance through Indiana. Workers had graded about two-thirds of the road. Unfortunately, "a considerable portion of it," done before the superintendent arrived, had not been raised sufficiently above the adjacent ground. The result was a muddy roadbed, which, combined with heavy travel, "cut the road in pieces." It was a similar story with culverts and bridges. Inferior sandstone had "disintegrated," and many had to be repaired or rebuilt.[20]

To prominent residents of the Hoosier State, the work seemed to be proceeding at a glacial pace. In the spring of 1837 James Whitcomb, an Indiana state senator, wrote to Joel Poinsett, Martin Van Buren's secretary of war, to ask what the problem was. Poinsett forwarded the missive to the Engineers, and their response came from one of Gratiot's young engineers, Lt. Robert E. Lee. He explained the problem with disbursements in 1836 and reported that Ogden had recently visited both Richmond and Terre Haute to push the work forward. Finally, Lee reminded Whitcomb that the most recent congressional appropriation had required that day labor give way to contract work. In the understated style that would become one of his trademarks, he explained, "It will necessarily take time to prepare and arrange this mode of operating."[21]

Late in 1838 General Gratiot, who had supervised work on the National Road for ten years, was dismissed from the Corps of Engineers. He was accused of misusing government funds, although it is likely he was the victim of political machinations. Totten replaced him. Gratiot had been a father figure to Lee, and the lieutenant wrote of his superior's fall from grace, "Nothing has distressed me so much for many years."[22]

Gratiot's dismissal had little effect on the National Road. With the final congressional appropriation in 1838, the Engineers' days on the project were numbered. Among the victims of the end of funding was the proposed bridge over the Wabash. This had been a pet project for Ogden. On November 4, 1835, he had reported that the river was a capricious stream. For most of the year it was "small and clear, the current gentle, the deepest point where the road crosses not being more than nine feet." But in the rainy season it became "a turbid and rapid stream, floating down immense trees and other drift." During that time, he added, the river inundated the surrounding bottom for several miles. He placed the total cost of the bridge at almost a quarter of a million dollars. In addition workers would have to erect at least ten spans of one hundred feet between the main bridge and the adjacent western bluffs.[23]

The superintendent threw himself into the work. In June 1837 he entered into a contract for the delivery of eight thousand perches of stone to be towed fifteen miles to Terre Haute on a steamboat constructed just for that effort. The quarry was kept in constant operation that summer. Ogden ordered the construction of a "wooden railway, three quarters of a mile in length," to deliver the stone the rest of the way to the riverbank. There a steam-powered "stone-breaking machine," prepared it for use at the bridge site.[24]

It was all for naught. Although Ogden termed the river "by far the greatest obstruction on the whole road," the end of funding meant the end of the

Wabash River bridge. Instead, a ferry continued to deliver travelers across the stream. As for the huge pile of stone delivered for the project, local residents appropriated it for personal, if less impressive, purposes.[25]

As 1839 ended, Ogden reported that the road had been opened through its entire extent in Indiana. About four-fifths had been graded, but rain and travel had badly injured much of it. Those sections not graded were in locations where culverts needed to be either built or rebuilt before the work could be continued. Only about nine miles of the road were macadamized. Included were portions running through Richmond, Centerville, Terre Haute, and Indianapolis. In Centerville residents took the initiative to pave four blocks of the road along Main Street. Twenty-eight residents paid half of the $7,500 cost, and the national government paid the other half. The stones came from nearby Lick Creek. They remained in service for over seventy-five years, one bright spot along a largely unfinished 149-mile section of the National Road.[26]

On May 31, 1830, Congress appropriated $40,000 to begin construction on the National Road in Illinois. Specifically, the legislators voted the funds to carry the project ninety miles from the Indiana line to Vandalia. The Corps of Engineers appointed William C. Greenup as superintendent. He arrived in late June and soon realized that the effort would not be easy. "The country traversed by that part of the road," he later observed, "was uninhabited [and] wild, the settlements of the country were new, spare and considerably remote, supplies were uncertain and difficult to procure, the people, although well disposed and interprizing, were without the requisite means to undertake work of much magnitude."[27]

In August the superintendent placed ads in newspapers, announcing that he would receive bids for clearing and grubbing the route. As in Indiana, the job of potential contractors would be to clear the roadway to a width of eighty feet and grub thirty feet in the center. They were required to offer a certificate of "good moral character" signed by a government official. Their workers could not "commit depredations" in the areas where they were employed, nor could they insult travelers. The work progressed quickly. On January 16, 1831, Greenup announced that the entire ninety miles had been cleared.[28]

In 1831 Greenup put under contract sixteen bridges and nearly one hundred culverts. Most were completed by November 1832, and many others were near- ing completion by that time. Many of the longest spans were "Jackson Bridges," wooden structures based on a design developed by Col. Stephen H. Long. One of the largest crossed the Little Wabash, where pioneer residents formed Effing-ham County in February 1831. The new county had a permanent population of three hundred, with an additional three hundred made up of men working on the road. Shanties and a small supply store went up to serve the latter.[29]

After that the work slowed considerably as a number of factors combined to retard the effort. Among them were "countless swarms of blood-sucking prai-rie flies," described as "green and about twice the size as the . . . horse fly." Wet weather slowed the project in 1832, as did early frosts, which made it difficult for contractors to provision their men. The same year the Black Hawk War also hindered construction. The brief conflict was fought miles away, in the northern part of the state, but it cost workers, many of whom were called away for militia duty. Even Greenup's assistant engineer was required to take part in the fight.[30]

Officials soon came to believe that much of the fault lay with Greenup him-self as reports reached Washington accusing him of everything from incom-petence to intemperance. General Gratiot suspended the superintendent and sent Lieutenant Brown, who had already been his troubleshooter in Indiana, "to make a minute and thorough inspection of the national road in the State of Illinois." Brown conceded that Greenup labored under many difficulties. Workers, particularly skilled road builders, had been nearly impossible to obtain. Stone was also scarce. Success, Brown concluded, would have required "the greatest zeal and industry joined to professional attainments, practical and theoretical, of an elevated order."[31]

Greenup fell short of the qualities the inspector enumerated. The result was shoddy work all along the route. This was particularly true of the masonry. The superintendent had let contracts at rates below estimates. What he got as a result were walls that were too weak, mortar that was often nothing more than clay or mud, and bridges in danger of collapsing. "Throughout the whole line," Brown reported, "evidences appear of a want of supervision and attention." He added, "A capital error has consisted in endeavoring to do more, along the whole line of the road, than the assistance he has had would warrant him in attempting." With the work scattered over ninety miles, contractors were largely "left to themselves." Some deliberately cut corners to reduce expenses, while others did wrong "because they know not what is right." Brown con-cluded that if Greenup was returned to the post, "he should be furnished by the department with very explicit instructions for his future government."[32]

That did not happen. Instead Ogden arrived in August 1834 to find the work "in a very dilapidated state." The superstructures of many bridges were giving way so rapidly that they required immediate trestling. It came too late for the bridge across the Little Wabash, a 125-foot span. Before workers could place all the necessary supports beneath it, the western abutments gave way and the superstructure ended up in the river.[33]

Ogden worked diligently, but the story of the work continued to be what one of his assistants termed "one of embarrassments and difficulties from the beginning." On November 18, 1835, Ogden reported that no bridges had been built since he arrived. Instead carpentry work had been limited to the construction of tools and machinery and the preservation of bridges already in place. Rainy weather during the spring and early summer, combined with a shortage of labor, limited the amount of grading done. Masons and stonecutters were also in short supply. On a more positive note, Ogden reported that there were nine quarries in operation, "all yielding fine stone." A large quantity of stone had been delivered for the bridge over the Kaskaskia River at Vandalia, but it had to be hauled twelve miles, making the cost great.[34]

Like David Shriver before him, Ogden abandoned the contract system and instituted day labor. As one of his assistants observed, "If those employed were not diligent and faithful, the discovery was soon made." In some sections virtually the only workers available were local farmers. Many had little or no experience in road building. In addition many left the work during plowing, planting, and harvesting seasons. Ogden tried to lure them back with pay raises, but few accepted the offer. In 1835 he attempted to continue the project through the winter months, but bad weather kept away most laborers who did not live in the immediate vicinity of the work.[35]

By 1837 crews had rebuilt every bridge constructed during Greenup's tenure as superintendent. That summer Ogden put twenty-one sections of road under contract, including ten bridges with spans ranging from twenty to three hundred feet. Despite the ongoing work, he also announced that the entire ninety miles of roadway in Illinois were open to travel. He added, "During the greater portion of the year the road may be traveled with comparative ease; but during the thaws of the spring and the seasons of heavy rains it cannot be passed without great fatigue and difficulty."[36]

In October 1839 Ogden announced for a second time, "The road in Illinois has been opened to Vandalia . . . and with a few exceptions (where by-roads are followed) is traveled on throughout its whole extent." Only a few streams remained that required "bridges of any magnitude." Already in place was a significant span that crossed the Kaskaskia River at Vandalia. None of the route through Illinois was macadamized, nor would it be. Lack of funding was a factor in this decision, as was Shriver's observation following his original survey that the prairie clay could suffice as a roadbed. By the time Ogden penned his report, it had been over a year since Congress passed what would prove to be its final appropriation for construction of the road. Lobbying for additional funds, the superintendent wrote:

> The importance of this work, its general utility, and its purely national character, are no longer, if indeed they were, questions of doubtful import. The United States mail is transported over this road, in four-horse post-coaches, daily in Indiana, and triweekly in Illinois. Travelers and emigrants are thronging this road, literally in thousands. Already it passes through portions of no less than six States of this confederacy. It unites the Atlantic with the Ohio, approaches near the banks of the Mississippi, and seems destined, ere long, to embrace, in its ample span, the half of a mighty continent. And will it still be insisted, that this is a work of a local character, and that it is unworthy of a national construction?[37]

The answer from Congress was not the one for which the superintendent had hoped; nor did it sit well with the citizens of Indiana and Illinois. Although railroads and canals appeared to be supplanting roads in the public imagination, the people of those two states still wanted their highway completed. In the end, it did them no good, but they made their feelings known.

The movement may have begun with a letter from "A Subscriber" that appeared in April 1839 in the *Visitor*, a newspaper published in Greencastle, Indiana. "The slow progress of the Road," he wrote, "and the increased opposition arising from various quarters, together with the indifference and reluctance so manifest in making appropriations, are full cause of alarm, and in the opinion of many, call for public attention." Toward that end, he recommended that those who agreed with him hold a convention that summer in Terre Haute. Delegates from Ohio, Indiana, and Illinois, he suggested, should gather "for the purpose of recommending to the next Congress some more certain and efficient mode of prosecuting this great National Thoroughfare to final completion at an early day."[38]

Aided by newspapers, which reprinted the letter, the idea spread quickly. The citizens of Effingham held a public meeting at their courthouse on April 9. They listened to addresses from the Illinois attorney general, Wickliffe Kitchell, and from the Illinois Secretary of State, A. P. Field. The group then adopted a variety of resolutions before selecting two delegates to send to Terre Haute as Effingham County's representatives. Fayette County, Illinois, where Vandalia is located, was the next to hold a meeting. On May 6 a gathering at Greencastle, Indiana named six delegates. Citizens of Greenfield, Indiana met at the Hancock County Courthouse on June 1 and chose two representatives to travel the National Road to Terre Haute. Indianapolis waited until the twenty-sixth. Their meeting passed four resolutions, the first of which stated, "That from the great importance of the National Road to Indianapolis, and to the State in general, this meeting will send ten delegates to Terre-Haute, to meet in convention with such delegates as may be sent from the States interested in the work."[39]

The delegates met in the western Indiana community on July 8–9. Indiana sent seven county delegations, Illinois five, and Ohio one. The lone Buckeye contingent came from Miami County, where the road remained unfinished west of Springfield. In all some eighty men attended. They chose William Lee D. Ewing as president of the convention. A veteran politician, Ewing had served in both houses of the Illinois state legislature, had spent three years in the United States Senate, and had served as governor for two weeks in 1834 after his predecessor resigned to accept a US House seat.

The delegates appointed a committee, including at least one member from each county represented, to draft a memorial to be sent to Congress. They gave the committee two specific instructions. First, they were to "treat the completion of the Cumberland Road as an act of strict justice which the People of the Northwestern States have a right to claim of their fellow-citizens of the Union." Second, the committee members were "instructed to enquire into the expediency of adopting some new means of prosecuting the work upon the Cumberland Road . . . which may promise more efficiency and economy."[40]

The convention then adjourned, and the committee went to work. When they presented their memorial the following day, the delegates approved it unanimously, apparently with little discussion. The message, which covered just over two newspaper columns, began with a brief legislative history of the road. The committee noted that the project was "originally designed as a National Work." To complete it they called for annual appropriations of $300,000 apiece for Ohio, Indiana, Illinois, and Missouri. "This sum," they observed, "within a short period, could not fail to place the Road in that condition originally designed by Congress." They repeated the argument that western votes in Congress had helped fund harbor improvements and lighthouses. The committee regretted what it termed "in some instances a total lack of every thing like reciprocal good feeling manifested by the favored [eastern] Representatives, in regard to our cherished interests."[41]

Nothing came of the efforts, nor of those that followed. As late as November 1841 the citizens of Fayette County, Illinois met and passed a series of resolutions. As at earlier gatherings, they termed the road "a great national work." The failure of Congress to vote further appropriations was "a violation . . . of a solemn compact." In bizarre language, they added, "That the West can no longer, in honor and justice to herself, tamely submit to the step-mother policy hitherto exercised toward her."[42]

The West, in reality, could do little more than complain. It lacked the political clout to achieve its goals. Besides, the alleged grievances of the South were beginning to attract more attention in the halls of Congress. On July 24, 1840, Totten informed Ogden that operations in Indiana and Illinois would be brought to a close. As he had instructed Dutton in Ohio, the chief engineer informed the superintendent that he must operate as if the decision was permanent. Ogden reported that he had about eleven thousand remaining dollars available for work in the state. He planned to spend six thousand on grading east of Richmond, which would connect the road with the Dayton Cutoff. Another four thousand would be devoted to putting the road "in the best condition the means will admit of" throughout the state. He planned to use the small amount remaining to collect materials and shut down the abortive Wabash bridge project. In Illinois Ogden had only four thousand dollars to spend on the road. Most of this he would need to pay contractors for extra work they had already performed. The rest he proposed to apply "to placing the road in a proper state to await further operations."[43]

The following year Ogden reported that "finished portions of the road in Indiana" totaled just nine miles. The bulk was four miles in and around Indianapolis. There were shorter completed sections in and around Richmond, Terre Haute, and Centerville. In Illinois he reported thirty miles of the road as being finished. These included thirteen miles west from the Indiana line and seventeen miles from Vandalia east. As 1842 ended, Totten reported that "the operations have been entirely suspended, the business closed, and the officers ordered to other stations." He added, "Much of the road being left in an unfinished state, it is liable to be worn away; unfinished structures upon the road are exposed to destruction; and the longer the resumption of operations is deferred, the greater must be the cost of final completion." Congress remained unmoved. No further appropriations would be voted for the National Road.[44]

The result was a road that never would be completed through Indiana and Illinois. William Oliver, an Englishman, who ventured over the road one year later, was blunt in his assessment. Describing the highway east of Vandalia, he wrote, "Most part of this road is nothing more than a track." His opinion did not improve in Indiana. East of Indianapolis, he repeated, "The National Road was still, in many places, no more than a track winding its way among boulders and the stumps of the trees which had been cut on surveying the line." One section of it passed through "a marshy bottom . . . across which were a most insufficient bridge and corduroy road." A stage coach his party encountered had gotten stuck, although with much effort the driver was able to extricate it. If these conditions were to improve, the people of Indiana and Illinois and their state representatives would have to institute the changes. Congress had ceased to fund the road, and that decision would prove to be permanent.[45]

CHAPTER SIX

✳✳✳

"An instructive admonition"

The States Take Control

THE ELEVATION OF John Quincy Adams to the presidency in 1825 had given proponents of the National Road reason to hope. For the first time since Jefferson left office in 1809, sixteen years earlier, it appeared that a firm friend of the project would occupy the White House. The new president's inaugural address seemed to confirm their optimism. While dutifully noting, "To respect the rights of the State governments is the inviolable duty of . . . the Union," the speech in general was a nationalistic one. As to internal improvements, Adams diplomatically observed that those who questioned the national government's authority to finance them did so from "pure patriotism." Then he added, "But twenty years have passed since the construction of the first national road was commenced. The authority for its construction was then unquestioned. To how many thousands of our countrymen has it proved a benefit? To what single individual has it ever proved an injury?" Adams echoed that sentiment in his first Annual Message. After detailing a number of internal improvement projects, he noted, "The continuation of the Cumberland road, the most important of them all, after surmounting no inconsiderable difficulty in fixing upon the direction of the road, has commenced under the most promising auspices."[1]

A friendly president, however, did not guarantee favorable legislation. Adams, after all, arrived as a minority chief executive, having not even secured a plurality in the Electoral College. The perceived "Corrupt Bargain," which

Jackson and his followers made sure was not forgotten, weakened him further. It represented the embryonic stage of the Second American Party System, which would coalesce over the next few years, and as politicians began taking sides, it made Congress a volatile and unpredictable body. Adams did not help his cause with his first Annual Message to Congress. In addition to internal improvements, he called for a federal university, a national astronomical observatory, a new cabinet department to administer "home affairs," and monies for expeditions to explore both American territory and points overseas. The message was magisterial in its goals, soaring in its rhetoric, and totally inept in its politics. One example was his injunction to the legislators, elected by citizens in the House, not to be "palsied by the will of our constituents." His timing could not have been worse. Most states had extended the voting franchise to those who did not own property (although it was still necessary to be white and male); and in those same states, legislators were ceding to voters the privilege of selecting presidential electors. Adams was appealing to a generation that wore powdered wigs, but, for good or ill, buckskin was the wave of the political future. Like his father before him, this president did not care. And like the second president, this improbable politician placed what he believed was right far above what was politically expedient. In a new, more democratic, America, this made his chances for success much slimmer.[2]

Bills to fund ongoing construction and repairs on the road almost always passed the Congress, but seldom without considerable debate. Then, in January 1828, the tone of the discussion changed. At issue was a bill to complete the road from Bridgeport to Zanesville and to survey the route from Zanesville into Missouri. Debating the issue on January 22, Benjamin Ruggles, a senator from Ohio, argued that because the work had gone beyond the Ohio, to stop now would be "out of the question." Other senators agreed. Samuel Smith of Maryland termed the road "a great national work," and asked, "Are we to stop short?" As the discussion continued the next day, Sen. John Eaton, ironically a Tennessee protégé of Andrew Jackson, asserted that, if the work was halted before reaching Zanesville, "all that had been done on the remaining portion would have been thrown away."[3]

Thomas Willis Cobb of Georgia turned the proponents' argument around. "If what had been done already required so large a sum for repairs," he asked, "was it not incumbent on the senate to consider what the repairs of the road, when extended to the Seat of Government of Missouri, would cost?" He further inquired, "Why do not the friends of the whole system establish toll gates, and make those who travel upon the road pay for it?" South Carolina Senator William Smith pursued the same line of reasoning. "They argue as if our having gone thus far entailed upon us the obligation of still proceeding ad infinitum." He also injected a note of humor. "Poets have sung to us that bolts and bars cannot confine true love," Smith waxed. "And yet, forsooth, our modern lovers must have a smooth road paved with 'metal of a good quality' to bring them together."[4]

The measure, which had already cleared the House, passed in the Senate 25–18. Then Nathaniel Macon offered a resolution that threatened to change the nature of the project. He called on the Judiciary Committee to "inquire into the expediency of relinquishing to the States through which the Cumberland road passes to the Ohio river, whatever claim, if any, the United States may have to the same." After more than two decades of debate, often heated, concerning the National Road, this was the first formal resolution to suggest that the national government abandon it. The resolution passed, but the Judiciary Committee did nothing.[5]

In 1828, aided by the trend toward greater democracy, Andrew Jackson gained the revenge he had craved, handily defeating Adams in a one-on-one rematch for the presidency. Supporters of the National Road knew they had lost a friend and suspected they had gained an enemy. The president's first Annual Message seemed to confirm their fears. "Every member of the Union, in peace and war, will be benefited by the improvement of inland navigation and the construction of highways in the several States," he wrote. He then added, "The great mass of legislation relating to our internal affairs was intended to be left where the Federal Convention found it—in the State governments." Legislation on the issue, Jackson observed, had often come "at the expense of harmony in the legislative councils." To avoid this, he recommended that surplus federal revenues be apportioned to the states according to their populations to be used for internal improvement projects. Jackson appeared to make his views more clear on May 27, 1830, when he vetoed a measure to build a road from Maysville, Kentucky, to Lexington. The project would have been an extension of Zane's Trace, but as Jackson noted, it was to be "exclusively within the limits of [one] State." Although dubious of the government's power to support any internal improvements, he pointed out that when such legislation had been passed, it came "under the control of the general principle that the works which may be aided should be 'of a general, not local, national, not State,' character." He went on, "A disregard for this distinction would of necessity lead to the subversion of the federal system." Jackson cited Madison's and Monroe's vetoes as precedents for his action and repeated the latter's call for a constitutional amendment to confer and define the rights of Congress in the area of internal improvements. He also passed along an observation concerning the National Road: "The Cumberland road should be an instructive admonition of the consequences of acting without this right. Year after year contests are witnessed, growing out of efforts to obtain the necessary appropriations for completing this useful work. Whilst one Congress may claim and exercise the power, a succeeding one may deny it; and this fluctuation of opinion must be unavoidably fatal to any scheme which from its extent would promote the interests and elevate the character of the country."[6]

With Jackson the political was never far from the personal. The Maysville Road would have terminated about two miles from Ashland, Henry Clay's estate, and sticking it to his hated political rival may have been as much a factor in Jackson's veto as were any constitutional qualms. (Later that year he would also veto bills to construct the Washington turnpike, and use the pocket veto to kill legislation to construct lighthouses and dredge harbors.) His views on the capriciousness of Congress, however, were beyond doubt. Advocates of the road realized this. They also realized that, whatever his motives, the president was not a supporter of federally funded internal improvements. As one biographer of the road observed, "Only die-hards failed to recognize that the period of Federal control of the National Road was about over."[7]

The Ohio General Assembly recognized the reality of the situation, and on February 4, 1831, the Buckeye legislators acted. They passed a bill authorizing the governor, once Congress gave its consent to the measure, to "take under his care . . . so much of the road commonly called the National Road, within the limits of this State." It empowered him to appoint a superintendent to contract for repairs and to set up tollbooths at distances of twenty miles or greater to pay for them. Toll rates would be ten cents for every score of sheep, twenty cents for every score of cattle, three cents for every led horse, mule, or ass, and six and one-half cents for a horse and rider. The fee was twelve and one-half cents for a one-horse sleigh, sled, sulky, chair, or chaise. A chariot, coach, stage, or phaeton pulled by two horses would pay a toll of eighteen and three-fourth cents and an extra six and one-fourth cents for every additional horse. The rate for carts and wagons if their wheels did not exceed two and one-half inches was twelve and one-half cents. If they were two and a half to four inches, the toll would be six and one-half cents. Wagons and carts with four- to five-inch-wide wheels would pay four cents, while those with wider wheels could pass for free. People attending worship services or funerals were exempt from tolls. So were individuals conducting business on their farms or at mills or markets. Stages or horses carrying the US mails also did not have to pay tolls (a provision stage lines would later exploit), nor did US soldiers or state militia members.[8]

The legislators left no account of any debates they may have held concerning the bill, simply noting in their journal how the members voted. In the House, the measure passed 53–16. Nine of those voting in the negative represented counties along the Ohio River, suggesting they did not want the state subsidizing a rival transportation artery. Most of the other no votes came from counties that were a considerable distance from the highway. The only ones representing a county along the route of the National Road were the two legislators from Muskingum County, which includes the city of Zanesville. There is no record of their motives, but a likely explanation is that the county was lobbying for a project to canalize the Muskingum River, which flows south from Zanesville to the Ohio.[9]

The Ohio law reached Congress on February 17. It remained on the table until March 1, when a vigorous debate began in the House. Joseph Duncan, an Illinois representative, expressed concern over how the measure would affect construction in his state and Indiana. He also objected to the numerous exemptions, which he claimed, in effect, would allow Ohioans to use the road virtually toll-free while residents of other states would bear the burden. Even Ohio's representatives were not unanimous in supporting their state's law. As at the state level, geography was generally the deciding factor. Echoing Duncan's sentiment, Joseph Vance, whose district was located well north of the road, complained that Buckeye State residents who lived along the route gained all the benefits, while residents from other parts of the state had to pay the tolls. Despite these objections, the House gave its assent by a vote of 89–60. The Senate approved Ohio's action 29–7.[10]

Once Ohio acted, other states followed suit. On April 4 Pennsylvania's state legislature passed its own act. Its law was more specific than Ohio's, naming the five commissioners who would be responsible for erecting six or more tollhouses at fourteen-mile intervals within the Keystone State. The toll for a score of sheep or hogs would be six cents, twelve cents for a score of cattle. Led or driven horses would pass at three cents, horse and riders at four cents. The toll for one-horse sleighs or sleds was three cents. For dearborns, sulkies, chairs, or chaises, it was six cents. Vehicles with four wheels, pulled by two horses, would incur a toll of twelve cents. If there were four horses, the rate was eighteen cents. As in Ohio, the fee for carts and wagons depended upon the width of the wheels. If they were two and one-half to four inches, the toll was four cents. If four to five inches in width, it was three cents, and the toll was two cents for wagons or carts with six- to eight-inch wheels. Those with wheels exceeding eight inches could pass for free. The Pennsylvania law offered the same exemptions as Ohio's. It also exempted students going to or from school and witnesses going to or from court.[11]

Maryland passed a similar measure on July 3, 1832, and Virginia did so the following March 2. Pennsylvania and Maryland included stipulations in their laws that they would only accept their portions of the road after Congress had put them in proper repair. Congress agreed, voting in July 1832 to appropriate $150,000 for the work. They voted an additional $125,000 the following year, and in 1834 earmarked $300,000 more "for the entire completion of repairs east of Ohio." All three pieces of legislation also included funds for construction of the road in Ohio, Indiana, and Illinois.[12]

On July 23, 1832, Gratiot dispatched Lt. Joseph K. F. Mansfield to superintend repairs of the road east of the Ohio. The assignment was a temporary one. Capt. Richard Delafield was slated to succeed him in October. Nevertheless, the twenty-eight-year-old Mansfield, who would fall mortally wounded thirty years later at the Battle of Antietam, received strict instructions. At first he would limit his responsibilities to Pennsylvania, which he was to divide into six sections, and Maryland, to be split into two sections. Gratiot informed his youthful subordinate that he must adhere strictly to the McAdam system: "The pavement of the old road must be entirely broken up, and the stones removed from the road; the bed of which must then be raked smooth, and made nearly flat, having a rise of no more than three inches from the side to the centre." Workers must spread the stone, reduced to four inches or less, with shovels and rake it smooth in strata of three inches. "None but limestone, flint, or granite, should be used for covering," when possible, Gratiot insisted. The chief engineer also sent detailed instructions for bridges, culverts, side walls, and ditches.[13]

Mansfield got quickly to work, but he did not like what he discovered. On August 1, following an inspection of the road in Maryland, he wrote, "I find it in a shocking condition, every rod of it will require great repair. Some of it, is almost impassable." At the direction of his superiors, Mansfield employed Valentine Giesy, a well-known Brownsville contractor, to be his assistant at a rate of four dollars a day. The appointment came despite a report from Mansfield stating that repairs made by Giesy two years earlier had not been done well. The lieutenant first instructed his new assistant to determine where limestone could be procured. At the same time, Mansfield was making repair contracts. By September 29 he had signed forty-two. They included what he considered the worst section in Maryland and the two worst in Pennsylvania, the three forming "a continuous line" east of Uniontown.[14]

Like Shriver before them, Mansfield and Delafield soon realized that a large percentage of the contractors did not fully grasp their responsibilities for resurfacing the road. In addition to spreading stone on the roadbed, Mansfield observed in October that many had "thrown on dirt and all the fine stuff." Delafield found the work so inferior that he planned to print "a manual or primer with a few lithographic sections" to instruct the contractors. They soon taxed the limits of the captain's patience. When a local resident interceded on behalf of a pair of Pennsylvania contractors, asking that they be granted "another extension" for the completion of their work, the military man's response was blunt. "You must be fully aware," he replied, "that all their promises have to this date had but little influence in convincing me either of their ability or fidelity in the execution of their work." He continued, "They are without exception not only the worst road makers on the whole route but have shown a perverseness and determination not to listen or conform to the requisites of the superintendent charged with that section of the road." If that headache was not enough, mail contractors complained to Delafield that road contractors left large rocks and other obstructions in the roadbed, making nighttime travel especially dangerous.[15]

After winter shut down operations, work resumed in the spring of 1833. As Mansfield had done the previous summer, Delafield focused his efforts on the eastern sections, which were most in need of repairs, rather than spreading the limited monies appropriated across the entire route. An exception was a small amount of work conducted across the Virginia panhandle. The captain abandoned the contract system in favor of day work, and on May 11, after inspecting the entire route, wrote that he was "highly gratified with the appearance and results." The editor of the *Wheeling Gazette* agreed, at least about the work being done in his neighborhood. "In a short excursion on the National Road," he reported, "we were pleased to perceive that the repairs by the general government are progressing rapidly." The newsman announced that the road was now wider in places and would soon have "a much better appearance than it has ever had." He termed Lt. J. C. Vance, who was in charge of the local project, "indefatigable."[16]

Still, there were problems. One of the biggest was stone. For much of the route, sandstone rested at the highest stratum. When reduced to four-ounce pieces it quickly dissolved. Limestone was not only rare, but where it was available, it was generally located beneath the sandstone, making it both difficult and expensive to procure. Delafield solved the problem, at least in part, by persuading Gratiot to allow him to reuse the "substantial yet rough pavement" whenever possible. The situation eased the following year when, redoubling their efforts, the captain and his crews located additional quarries.[17]

As work got under way in the spring of 1834, Delafield was able to report that the highway was "a very excellent turnpike" between Frostburg and Brownsville. At the same time, Gratiot informed the House of Representatives that $645,000 was needed to complete repairs east of the Ohio. The $300,000 he received forced Delafield to make difficult decisions. Many involved cutting corners. Instead of spreading the "metal" to a width of twenty feet, the amount was reduced to between twelve and fifteen. The leftover limestone went to areas that had not been previously supplied. Wooden bridges instead of stone structures spanned a number of streams. At other crossings Delafield indefinitely suspended bridge projects. One thing that was not in short supply was labor, where the captain enjoyed a buyer's market. Every section, Delafield reported, attracted at least six bidders, and some drew as many as thirty-six.[18]

The budget constraints, along with qualms over jurisdiction, threatened one of Delafield's pet projects, a bridge over Dunlap's Creek near Brownsville. It had its genesis in 1832, when Mansfield first assumed his duties, and a number of local residents asked him to examine the bridge then in place and offer an assessment. He concluded that the structure would not survive another year and so reported to his superiors. At first Secretary of War Lewis Cass rejected the proposal, pointing out that the span was a county bridge. The law for repairs, he observed, only applied to the route originally laid out by the commissioners and approved following their survey by President Jefferson.

Cass changed his mind the following May, approving the project so long as the new bridge was "in the line of the Cumberland Road." It was again nixed in 1834, following the action of Congress appropriating only $300,000 for repairs. Then, about seven weeks later, after Delafield pleaded the case for the bridge, the secretary once again gave his approval, this time for good. Brownsville and vicinity was home to a number of iron foundries, leading Delafield to propose building America's first cast-iron bridge. It was to have an eighty-foot span with an eight-foot rise and five arched ribs at intervals of 5.77 feet.

Delafield purchased 140 tons of pig iron from southern Ohio's Hanging Rock region, shipping it by river to Brownsville's foundries. He hoped to finish the project in 1836, but wet weather delayed the start of the work and plagued it throughout the summer. By then rising iron prices forced further delays. As 1837 ended Delafield was compelled to place iron castings and other parts in storage as he waited for additional funding. The bridge was finally completed on July 4, 1839. By then Delafield was serving as superintendent of the United States Military Academy. His successor, Capt. George Dutton, boasted, "The bridge now presents a handsome and substantial appearance."[19]

The other major project undertaken as part of the 1830s repair process was a six-mile relocation of the road immediately west of Cumberland. Soon after taking charge of the program, Delafield ordered surveys "for turning Wills' mountain by the valley of Braddock's run and Wills' creek." The route he selected carried the road through an area known as "the Narrows," first following Wills Creek and then along Braddock's Run, passing through what is now the community of La Vale. It required the construction of two bridges, each with an approximately fifteen-foot span. "By this," Gratiot reported, "an abrupt rise of several hundred feet would be avoided." Workers completed the project in November 1834, and on the eleventh, Cumberland celebrated. Several residents paraded to Percy's Tavern, west of town, where a delegation from Frostburg joined them. Thus reinforced, they returned to Cumberland, where band music and speech making punctuated the air. Among those speaking was Lt. John Pickell, who had been in charge of the relocation.[20]

✳✳✳

Celebrations notwithstanding, not everyone was pleased with the manner in which the work was done. When Maryland's state legislature voted in 1833 to allow the change of route, the bill they passed stipulated that "substantial stone bridges" be built at stream crossings. This remained the Corps of Engineers' intent until the $300,000 appropriation that passed the following year made it necessary to scale back their efforts. One change Gratiot recommended was to build the abutments of stone with wooden superstructures. "The same ends would be attained as would result from bridges built entirely of stone," he insisted, predicting that they would last at least forty years. He conceded that the change would not comply with "the letter of the Maryland law." John Forsyth, then serving temporarily as acting secretary of war, approved Gratiot's proposal. He believed that the wooden bridges would be in "substantial compliance" with the state law.[21]

A number of Maryland politicians did not agree, including Gov. James Thomas. In a letter to Secretary Cass, he reiterated the terms of his state's law, adding his hope that there had been "some mistake or misapprehension," which could be corrected. There was no mistake, the secretary tersely replied, nor would the decision be reversed. It is not known if the governor pressed the issue further. It is clear that the work did not satisfy Meshach Frost, John Hope, and B. S. Pigman, whom the state appointed to inspect the entire road in Maryland and make a recommendation as to whether it should be accepted. As 1834 ended the trio advised against acceptance. They cited not only the wooden bridges but also reported that there were no more than three and one-half inches of "metal" on the surface for some seventeen miles west of Cumberland. The inspectors believed there should be six to eight inches.[22]

Unfortunately for Maryland, the state had little leverage in the matter. If it refused ownership of the highway, there was nothing to compel the national government to maintain repairs. Indeed, with Ohio and Pennsylvania taking control of their portions of the road, the constitutional case for federal involvement would grow even weaker. In that instance only revenues gathered by the state, likely through tolls, could fund repair projects. In April 1835 Maryland acquiesced and took possession of the National Road within its borders. By the end of the year two tollhouses were in place. Still, the Corps of Engineers did not abandon the road immediately. They continued their repair efforts during 1835 and 1836. When they finished the *Cumberland Phoenix-Civilian* congratulated them and their contractors "for the masterly manner in which the work has been executed." The traveling public, the paper continued, now had "as fine a bridge and road as were ever traveled over."[23]

The states now owned the road, and, starting with Ohio, they had asked for it. Maryland and Pennsylvania were responsible for significant portions, Virginia for a small section bisecting its northern panhandle. Ohio acquired only the portions that were completed. It would accept others as the Corps of Engineers finished their construction efforts. In 1839 the state assumed responsibility for the forty-three miles between Columbus and Springfield. In 1853 it accepted the unfinished road from Springfield to the Indiana border. All of these states would soon learn what Congress already understood—that maintaining a highway was an expensive proposition, one that tolls would not be sufficient to cover.[24]

✳✳✳

CHAPTER SEVEN

"An indefinite impression of great abuse"
State Control of the Road

ONCE CONGRESS ABANDONED its responsibilities for the National Road, the states that took control of it adopted a number of approaches to the highway. Illinois, after receiving the road in May 1856, took the simplest method and ignored it. Canals and railroads by then had gained the state's attention, and the National Road there, in the words of an Illinois historian, "lapsed into a neglected dirt tract."[1]

Congress ceded the portion of the road that crossed Indiana to the state in August 1848. It was not a welcome acquisition. The state legislature had invested heavily in canal-building projects, many of which had proven to be financially disastrous. With railroads the obvious wave of transportation's future, Indiana politicians wanted nothing to do with the road they had so eagerly coveted when Uncle Sam was footing the bill.[2]

In early 1850 the Wayne County Turnpike Company received a state charter to operate the road for the twenty-two miles in that county. The company completed construction of the road and surfaced it with gravel. They operated it as a toll road until 1893, when the townships through which it passed purchased their individual sections and made it a free road. A private company also operated the road in Henry County.[3]

The most ambitious turnpike company was the Central Plank Road Company, which received a charter from the state in 1849. It gained control of the road through Hancock, Marion, Hendricks, and Putnam Counties. Under the terms of the charter, the company was required to surface the road with timber, plank, or gravel. The directors chose plank, and in 1850 they began working east from Indianapolis. Workers first laid the stringers so they were about level with the ground. They then placed the planks, three inches thick and eight feet long, on top of them. They were laid along the north side of the grade, giving westbound wagons the right-of-way. They did not nail the planks in place, and frequently they turned up at the ends, producing a dangerous nuisance for travelers. Later the company put a gravel surface over the planks. Toll gates dotted the road, including one at the White River Bridge in Indianapolis and another at the east end of the city. Travelers considered this to be excessive, and the company eventually agreed to remove the eastern gate when the city took over maintenance of that part of the road that passed over Washington Street. The plank company operated the road until 1889, when the individual counties purchased it.[4]

✳✳✳

In Maryland the statute setting down the terms for the state's acceptance of the road authorized no more than two tollhouses within its borders. The federal government agreed to pay for both. The first, a brick building, which went up seven miles west of Cumberland, was in place by the end of 1835. A December 22 advertisement in a Cumberland newspaper informed travelers that "a GATE has been erected, according to law, upon that part of the National Road within the limits of the State of Maryland, the toll collector appointed and duly authorized to receive tolls."[5]

Early in 1838 the state legislature modified the toll regulations. Wagons carrying coal and timber and returning the same day only had to pay the toll one way. The act set the salary for the toll collector at three hundred dollars a year. It further called for the governor to appoint "some disinterested person or persons" to audit the accounts of the superintendent quarterly. The auditors were to receive two dollars a day. Three months later the state began putting the toll receipts to work. On June 2 an ad appeared in the *Cumberland Phoenix-Civilian* calling for sealed proposals for stone, preferably limestone, for effecting repairs. The work was to stretch from Frostburg to the Pennsylvania line.[6]

By late 1837 Thomas Shriver, Maryland's superintendent, was reporting, "The repairs during the past year have been heavy and expensive." Many sections, he explained, had required "an entire new covering of metal." Tolls were barely covering expenses. As of October 1, the fund had a balance of $85.39. By then

Shriver was already cutting corners. He informed the legislature, "The paved part of the road through the town of Cumberland having given way in many places, and it being ascertained that the renewal of the pavement would be attended with too much expense, a covering of McAdamised stone has been placed upon the whole, which at a comparatively moderate cost has put the streets in excellent condition."[7]

In 1842 the second Maryland tollbooth went up some twenty-five miles west of the first. By then Jonathan Huddleson was superintendent of the road in the state. His concerns were similar to Shriver's. "The difficulty and cost attending a supply of good metal on many suffering parts of the road, calls for all the means that the road can honestly claim," he asserted. Specifically, Huddleson asked for a third tollgate along the western portion of the road, although he conceded that the original law did not provide for one. He also recommended that some means be established to collect tolls on miles two through six west of Cumberland, which travelers were using free of charge.[8]

The following year Thomas Thistle, Huddleson's successor, reported that toll receipts were "entirely insufficient to keep the road, even in tolerable good repair." Toll receipts, he added, were down $1,600 from the previous year. He blamed much of this on the legislature allowing individuals hauling coal or timber to pay tolls only one way. "This law," Thistle complained, "has never been of any benefit to the citizens in general, but to a few individuals in the Frostburgh district, and those living immediately on the road between Frostburgh and Cumberland." Stagecoach companies, he went on, also traveled both ways. "If one set of men goes through for half price," he asked, "Why not all?"[9]

Maryland's General Assembly did not act upon the advice of its superintendents. Instead, in January 1843, the legislators voted to reduce tolls for "all wheel carriages" with wide wheels. Maryland's surviving records of the road end there; we do know, however, that the state kept the tolls in place until 1878.[10]

There is also a dearth of records for state operations in Pennsylvania and Virginia. The Keystone State formally accepted the road on April 1, 1835, when it was satisfied that the Corps of Engineers had adequately completed repairs. Officials erected six tollhouses along the route. They remained in operation longer than in any other state. Pennsylvania did not make travel free until June 1905.[11]

When Ohio took control of the road in 1831, its portion extended from the Ohio River to Zanesville, a distance of about eighty miles. The following summer the state legislature agreed to start acquiring sections west of Zanesville as soon as they were completed and received the requisite nine inches of stone. The law also authorized the governor to erect tollgates "about every ten miles." This made them twice as frequent as under the state's original legislation. At the same time, however, the act reduced tolls by half. Stagecoach companies could pay a flat, yearly fee, as could private citizens who lived within eight miles of the road. Individuals evading tolls were subject to a five-dollar fine. Finally, the governor could set the salaries of toll collectors not to exceed $180 annually.[12]

It did not take long for the highway to begin to deteriorate. As 1835 ended, George W. Manypenny, superintendent of the road, reported, "The masonry is in a gradual state of decay, and the tolls are insufficient to reclaim it, and keep up the pavement at the same time." During the year, he added, the state had accepted an additional ten miles of road west of Zanesville. This gained Ohio an extra tollgate, but it also added to the state's responsibilities.[13]

In 1836 the Ohio General Assembly, controlled by Jackson Democrats, reorganized the state's system of public works. The legislators created a Board of Public Works, which included the state's canal board as well as the superintendent of the National Road. The board consisted of two statewide "acting commissioners" and four "advisory commissioners," each of whom represented one of four districts established by the law. In keeping with the Jacksonian principle of "rotation in office," the commissioners served two-year terms, the legislature naming three each year.[14]

The National Road became the responsibility of William Wall, one of the acting commissioners. Manypenny retained the post of superintendent at an annual salary of $1,200. In April 1836 Wall, assisted by an engineer, inspected the road "and found [it] to be very much out of repair." In many places the covering was entirely cut through, and the culverts were in need of major repairs. The bridge across Salt Creek, nine miles east of Zanesville, had collapsed, and "several other bridges were tending rapidly to the same result." Wall believed it would take $100,000 to put the road in complete repair. Tolls received from April through November amounted to only $22,531.[15]

Wall was not alone in his view. "This spring has been unusually severe upon the road," the editor of the *St. Clairsville Gazette* reported, "and has left it in an extremely bad condition, a large amount of it between Wheeling and Zanesville being entirely cut through." The newspaperman urged the state legislature to make an appropriation sufficient to put the road in "complete repair." If they did, he predicted, future tolls would be sufficient to maintain it. If not, "The National Road in Ohio will be entirely destroyed."[16]

Despite legislative inaction, the editor's dire prediction did not come true. Manypenny had enough funds on hand in 1836 to advertise for repairs to the road, extending from the Ohio River to a point twenty-two miles west. The following spring Thomas Drake, Manypenny's successor, called for bids to work on the road from the Ohio to the seventy-fourth mile. He also advertised for proposals to rebuild the Salt Creek bridge. By then the Corps of Engineers had completed much more of the road and turned it over to the state. As a result, Drake asked for bids to build "three or four" tollhouses between Hebron and Jefferson.[17]

All three projects were completed by the end of 1837, although Drake had to advertise a second time for bids to build the tollhouses after the initial proposals submitted were too expensive. The state also repaired a serious slip at Bridgeport and installed a new culvert and drains to prevent the problem from reoccurring. The superintendent further reported that "slight repairs" had been made at various locations. Workers built four new culverts and repaired masonry seven miles west of the Ohio River. Drake made "an arrangement" with the warden of the state penitentiary, which allowed "considerable repairs" to be made in the Columbus area.[18]

Heavy rains fell during the fall of 1837, extending into the early part of the winter. They returned the following spring. An April 1838 inspection revealed that the wet weather had "produced results of the most disastrous character upon the spongy bed and attenuated covering of the road." Heavy traffic compounded the effects. Working with limited funds, Drake had laborers fill deep ruts with whatever large stones they could find. He conceded that this was not a permanent solution. "The traveling public were," he further admitted, "more indebted for the tolerable condition of the road in the summer, to the drying and settling of its bed, than to any efforts which could be made for its immediate repair." The patchwork repairs continued into 1839. A full cover of stone went down from the forty-first to the sixty-eighth mile. "The balance of the road has been patched according to its necessities and the state of funds," Drake explained. The Corps of Engineers, meanwhile, completed their work to Springfield during the summer of 1839, and two more tollgates went up.[19]

As the 1840s progressed, toll revenues tended to fluctuate. In the year ending November 15, 1840, the state realized $51,443 from tolls. This was down nearly $1,100 from the previous year. The Board of Public Works blamed a small reduction in toll rates and a decrease in emigration from eastern states for the drop. The next year toll receipts rose to $60,875. This allowed the superinten-

Note: The photographs in this gallery are presented in geographic sequence, traveling from east to west.

This painting of the "Fairview Inn or Three Mile House on Old Frederick Road," by Thomas Coke Ruckle (ca. 1829), shows typical traffic on the National Road at the time. (Courtesy of the Maryland Historical Society)

The Casselman (originally Little Youghiogheny) River Bridge in Maryland ca. 1913. It was the first major bridge project on the National Road. (National Archives)

The end of Maryland road maintenance in 1913 (National Archives)

An artist's rendering of traffic on the National Road during the 1840s (Library of Congress)

Searight's Tollhouse in Fayette County, Pennsylvania (Ohio Historical Society)

Wheeling, Virginia, in 1855, showing the suspension bridge across the Ohio River (Library of Congress)

"S" bridges were common on the road. This one was located near Hendrysburg, Ohio. (Ohio Historical Society)

The road showed the result of age and neglect in this photograph taken eleven miles west of Zanesville, Ohio, November 27, 1913 (National Archives)

A repair project at Amsterdam, in Licking County, Ohio, in 1914 (National Archives)

The road's iconic mile markers were placed at one-mile intervals. (Ohio Historical Society)

This impressive covered bridge spanned the East Fork of the Whitewater River at Richmond, Indiana. (Indiana Historical Society)

Washington Street in Indianapolis in 1825. Five years later it would become the route of the National Road through the city. (Indiana Historical Society)

Artists rendering of the White River Bridge west of Indianapolis in the 1840s or '50s (Indiana Historical Society)

The White River Bridge in the 1890s (Ohio Historical Society)

An Indianapolis tollhouse in the 1890s (Indiana Historical Society)

Vandalia, Illinois, was the western terminus of the road. (Ohio Historical Society)

dent to make enough repairs to "render its condition much better than it has been for many years previous." Receipts dropped dramatically in 1842. The state collected only $32,280, a sum far too low to address damage caused by an unusually rainy winter. Revenues remained roughly the same for the next two years. Despite the lack of funds, the board reported at the end of 1843 that the road was "in better condition than for several years preceding." The following year they asserted, "The work is now in very good repair, and the Board believe in much better condition than it has been at any period since its reception by the State, from the General Government."[20]

Throughout this time, the state attempted to find an efficient system for operating a road that now stretched some 180 miles. In 1840 the Board of Public Works divided the road into two districts, roughly equal in length, and assigned a superintendent to each. Drake was put in charge of the eastern district, Richard Stadden of the western, which started sixteen miles west of Zanesville. Each divided his district into sections for the purpose of maintenance work. Drake employed day laborers. Stadden hired supervisors at thirty dollars a month and paid the hands working under them seventy-five cents a day. The system lasted until May 1841, when the General Assembly required the board to employ just one superintendent.[21]

In 1842 the board modified the system and divided the road into four-mile sections. Under the arrangement, contractors delivered stone to points on each mile where it was most needed. Workers, paid by the day, applied it during spring and fall months.[22]

In March 1843 the General Assembly gave the board authority to appoint a resident engineer who was to be in charge of repairs and the collection of tolls. That position superseded the superintendent's. Two years later the legislature again divided the road into eastern and western divisions and called for the employment of a resident engineer, to be paid $700 annually, on each. The law also required that the engineers take an oath to "faithfully and honestly discharge the duties of their office." It called upon them to make a detailed yearly statement of all their financial transactions.[23]

✳✳✳

Despite these safeguards, the system failed to prevent the machinations of a dishonest superintendent. On September 15, 1842, the board named John Yontz superintendent of the road. He remained on the job when the title was changed to resident engineer. Yontz employed as his assistant William Mulrine, a young man reportedly in his early twenties, who was the son of one of Yontz's neighbors. In January 1845 the *Ohio State Journal,* a Columbus newspaper, began reporting rumors concerning the Board of Public Works. "An indefinite impression of great abuse in that department of the public service prevails," the Journal observed, "and this is not confined to party lines."[24]

In April 1845 the board discovered that "the claims upon the road-fund far exceeded the amount acknowledged or reported by Mr. Yontz." More investigation revealed that "the finances of the road were . . . in a ruinous condition; the road was largely in debt—its creditors impatient from frequent disappointment, and no means in hand to satisfy them or to pay current repairs." According to its annual report, the board tried repeatedly and unsuccessfully to secure from Yontz a schedule of the certificates he had issued on behalf of the road fund. They learned that Yontz had failed to deposit toll receipts into the state treasury. Instead he collected the funds "and [disbursed] the same without limit or discretion." Indeed, the board concluded, "No restraint beyond his own discretion was placed on the Engineer in his disbursements." The board did not attempt to explain how they had allowed this state of affairs to occur. The near total lack of record keeping forced them to place advertisements in newspapers asking contractors holding certificates Yontz had issued to come forward. This they did, presenting certificates totaling nearly $66,000.[25]

The General Assembly already had its suspicions. On March 6, 1845, the legislators appointed a three-member board of commissioners "to examine the books, accounts and proceedings of the Board of Public Works." They empowered the commissioners to examine all records of the board and its employees, and they received the power to compel the attendance of witnesses. The board convened in late April, naming Roswell Marsh president. Simeon Nash and Demas Adams Jr. were the other two members.[26]

The commissioners would eventually issue at least three reports. The first was laid before the Ohio House of Representatives on December 26, 1845. It addressed a wide range of the board's responsibilities, including supervision of the state's canals, and covered 566 pages. Forty of those pages dealt with Yontz, Mulrine, and the National Road. They began by studying the contracts and certificates issued for payment to the various contractors. In many cases the pair had destroyed old contracts and issued new ones. They also consolidated certificates issued to several contractors into one. These provided virtually no information identifying on what section or mile of the road any work had been done. Many did not even give the name of the contractor. "They present nothing but absolute confusion," the commissioners concluded.[27]

One thing the investigators did learn was that, "Soon after Mr. Yontz took charge of the road, a system of favoritism sprang up." Six individuals secured virtually every contract let along the road, and generally at double or triple what had been paid for similar work in the past. Further investigation suggested that these men did not carry out the projects but were fronts for Yontz and Mulrine's duplicity.[28]

One of the contractors was James Taggart of Norwich. He spoke willingly and apparently openly with the commissioners about his dealings with Yontz and Mulrine. Taggart conceded that he made an arrangement with the pair to make bids for repair work along the entire length of the road in Ohio. He sent his bids to the two men "with the expectation, if contracts were awarded to him, of having said contracts sub-let by William Mulrine, and an account of the profits rendered to him by said Mulrine." Taggart insisted that he was never aware that his actions were part of a dishonest scheme. The commissioners believed him, feeling he acted largely out of ignorance. "We find no testimony showing that he was cognizant of fraudulent practices on the part of the engineer or his assistant," they wrote. "Yet we now know . . . that contracts were announced in his name where he was not the lowest bidder, to the prejudice of the public interests."[29]

Two of Yontz's other favorite contractors, Daniel McDonald and Bernerd O'Neill, were employed as stonebreakers on the road before they suddenly became, at least on paper, major contractors. Both disappeared before the commissioners could examine them. McDonald was illiterate, unable even to write his name, and a certificate he allegedly filled out, the commissioners learned, was in Mulrine's handwriting. Receipts supposedly signed by O'Neill were also signed by Mulrine, they believed. The fact that his first name was incorrectly and repeatedly signed "Barnard" tended to support their contention.[30]

A number of contractors, real and phantom, told the commissioners that Yontz and Mulrine urged them to submit unreasonably high bids. One testified that he originally put in bids for delivering stone at rates ranging from $2.37 to $2.50 per rod. Yontz and Mulrine informed him that they would not consider bids below four dollars. Several others offered similar testimony. The board concluded that such contractors "were mere men of straw, and that Mr. Yontz and Mr. Mulrine were the real contractors."[31]

The commissioners concluded, "These facts, thus far detailed, show that there have been great frauds committed, in the management of the road by the late Resident Engineer and his assistant." The lack of reliable record keeping rendered it impossible for them to determine the amount of the state's loss "with any exactness." Based on the records they had, the commissioners concluded that at least $70,000 "must have been taken from the state unjustly."[32]

In addition to the state, the board reported that the subcontractors and their laborers were heavy losers. In lieu of direct payment, they received certificates, which, as a result of Yontz and Mulrine's frauds, depreciated dramatically as word leaked out concerning their deceptions. "Instances of great hardship and of individual suffering have pressed themselves upon the attention of the Board," they wrote. They urged the General Assembly to "indemnify all innocent sufferers from the misconduct of its own officers." They admitted that the means of accomplishing this was "a question much more difficult [than a] solution." Revenues from tolls, they went on, were not enough to pay off questionable claims and at the same time keep the road in proper repair.[33]

The board attempted to secure Yontz's voluntary testimony, but he continued to delay, citing both personal and legal concerns. Finally, on June 1, 1846, they dispatched the sheriff of Franklin County to Yontz's home in Brownsville, some forty miles east of Columbus, to bring him before the board. Once there, accompanied by his lawyer, the former resident engineer submitted to two days of questioning. His memory was less than sharp, his answers unspecific. This was one exchange:

> Question. Were not numerous certificates wholly in the handwriting of W. Mulrine, repeatedly shown to you, and by you pronounced to be all correct?
>
> Answer. No; not numerous—there may have been instances of that kind.
>
> Question. As nearly as you can recollect, how many certificates have been issued by Mulrine in your name?
>
> Answer. I cannot pretend to recollect of any, (except where I was present;) there must have been but few, I think.
>
> Question. Was he, Wm. Mulrine, in the habit of signing your name to certificates in your presence; and if so, how often was it done?
>
> Answer. He did it sometimes; but how many I cannot recollect. It occurred when I was examining calculations, and he engaged in writing certificates for those already looked over, or examined by me.[34]

The board reported that at least fifteen contractors they had examined stated that they had received certificates from Mulrine, and that he often signed Yontz's name to them. In most cases they added that they later showed the certificates to Yontz, who pronounced them proper. As for subletting contracts,

Yontz said he believed Mulrine acted as "an agent for contractors, in some instances." He claimed not to know the prices of those contracts.[35]

The board informed Yontz that they wanted him to return and to "produce certain books and papers connected with his management of the road." After consulting with his attorney, Yontz agreed to return on June 11 and to bring his records with him. This he failed to do. Shortly before Yontz was scheduled to reappear before the board, the group received a letter from one of his attorneys. His client would supply everything the commissioners desired, he wrote, "excepting it should conflict with, or prejudice his interest in the case now pending against him by the State." The commissioners considered this response to be a tacit admission of guilt. "This refusal of Mr. Yontz to submit to a full examination upon the grounds on which it is placed," they wrote, "is an admission on his part of misconduct in the management of the road."[36]

The later fate of Mulrine is not known. The State of Ohio attempted at least three times to try Yontz. On June 21 and September 20, 1847, and again on October 12, 1848, juries were seated, but the case was continued each time, reportedly because of the inability to secure the attendance of witnesses. By then it was reported that Yontz was living in Illinois. The final continuance came on January 30, 1849, at which time the name John Yontz disappears from court records. In June 1850 a Cleveland newspaper reported that he had relocated to Utah, converted to Mormonism, and was serving as treasurer of the territory.[37]

✳✳✳

In addition to disreputable engineers, weather continued to present challenges to the road. In their report for 1847, the Board of Public Works noted that repairs were conducted that year "upon a more extended scale" than in recent years. A flood that spring washed out a large stone culvert at Zanesville. The bridge that workers put up in its place cost the state $1,283. Floodwaters also claimed a culvert along the South Fork of the Licking River. A forty-four-foot bridge replaced it, at a cost of $1,234. Often during the year, they reported, two feet of water covered the road near Kirkersville, chasing the toll collector at gate 11 from his post.[38]

These challenges did not remain the state's responsibility much longer. In 1853 the Central Ohio Railroad, projected to run from Columbus to the Ohio River community of Bellaire, was completed from Columbus to Zanesville. Workers finished the rest of the line the following year. By the end of 1853, stagecoach companies had abandoned service from Zanesville to Springfield.

This led some to fear a dramatic decrease in tolls, making it impossible to maintain the road. Tolls decreased as predicted, but with the heavy mail stages gone, maintenance costs plummeted more sharply.[39]

The completion of the Central Ohio line made the National Road largely a local thoroughfare through Ohio. The state's General Assembly recognized this, and on May 1, 1854, it authorized the Board of Public Works to lease the road to the highest bidder. Joseph Cooper and Company received the lease for $6,105 per year. On June 1 the National Road in Ohio passed into their hands. It remained under private control until 1876, when the General Assembly turned it over to the counties through which it passed.[40]

※※※

During the years of state control, tolls were contentious matters between the states and those who used the road. Often politics entered into the fray. Soon after Ohio accepted its portion of the road, the *St. Clairsville Gazette,* a Democratic newspaper, complained that the gatekeeper east of that community told those who objected to the tolls that Andrew Jackson was responsible for the erection of the gates. The *Gazette* suggested that he secure a copy of the state law authorizing the structures. If he did, the paper noted, he would learn "that a majority of the legislature passing the law were friends to H. Clay."[41]

Shifting political winds changed the sources—if not the tone—of moral indignation. In 1836 a Democratic state legislature raised the rate of tolls and also gave Superintendent Manypenny a substantial pay raise. This prompted the Whig-oriented *Zanesville Republican* to ask, "Farmers, you who live along the road east and west, will you support the Van Buren candidates who justify this enormous tax on you, by doubling the tolls, to increase the salary of an office holder?"[42]

Attempts at evading the tolls were common and took a variety of forms. Riders who were familiar with the countryside could often divert around the houses. Ohio was among the states that gave exemptions to those attending church or funeral services. As one local historian observed, "Church-goers were frequently more numerous than church attendants, and there were more funerals than deaths."[43]

Drovers conducting large herds of cattle, hogs, and sheep to eastern markets sought out alternate routes wherever they could. Such detours ended when they reached the mountainous country of Pennsylvania and Maryland and had little choice but to follow the only route through the wilderness. Owners of Conestoga wagons and similar freight vehicles soon adopted wider wheels, which allowed them to pay lower tolls.[44]

The Ohio Board of Public Works complained that "a great evil prevails in some neighborhoods, which tends much to the injury of the road, without yielding any income." The evil to which they were referring was "neighborhood roads and bye-paths," which served as detours around the tollhouses. They further asserted that the gates were often located distant from thriving towns. This meant tolls frequently were not collected at "places of great business . . . where travel is immense at the very worst seasons of the year." To correct these problems, the board asked the General Assembly to approve the erection of new gates that would collect quarter or half tolls for short-distance travelers. "This," they contended, "would discourage many of the plans which are now resorted to, in order to evade and violate the law." The General Assembly failed to act on the board's recommendation.[45]

In Indiana the Wayne County Turnpike Company also fought a stiff battle against toll evaders. The opening of Twenty-Third Street in Centerville in the 1850s allowed westbound vehicles to turn south on that thoroughfare to avoid the tollgate on Twenty-Second Street. The company promptly moved its gate to Twenty-Third Street. They soon discovered that people were turning south on nearby Henley Road and entering town from the south side. This led to another move, this time to the southern end of Henley Road. Travelers responded by turning south on Garwood Road. Finally the company made one last move, back to Twenty-Third Street.[46]

Both Ohio and Pennsylvania passed laws exempting from tolls stagecoaches carrying the US mail. Stage companies soon took advantage of these measures by tossing one or two mailbags on every coach. Pennsylvania took the companies to court, and in 1845 a state court ruled that the state could collect from individuals passengers riding in those coaches. In 1843 Ohio's Board of Public Works approved a toll of ten cents on every passenger. "At least one half of the whole wear of the road, is caused by the running of stage coaches," the board explained, "and if tolls cannot be collected on them, it is a well established fact that the road cannot be kept in repair, except at an increased rate of tolls on other travel."[47]

Neil, Moore, & Co., Ohio's largest stage company, refused to pay the toll. The state went to court, claiming they owed about $4,700 in tolls. In 1846 the parties reached a compromise. The state allowed one westbound and one eastbound mail stage to travel the entire length of the road toll-free each day.

The company agreed to pay fifty cents at each tollgate for all other coaches with three seats and sixty cents for those with four seats. The legal case continued as Neil, Moore, & Co. still declined to pay the back tolls that Ohio insisted they owed. The US Supreme Court eventually ruled in the company's favor. The 1846 arrangement held until 1851, when the Post Office Department required a second daily mail stage to be carried over the road. The company did not run an extra stage but put the second mail on one of the stages it was already running and for which it had been paying a toll. The state believed it should continue to pay the toll. Neil, Moore, & Co., of course, disagreed. Within two years the completion of the Central Ohio made the question moot.[48]

Legal disputes for the most part did not trouble the passengers who rode the stagecoaches along the National Road. To them they were the most efficient forms of conveyance on the route. For residents living in communities along the road, they were sources of the latest news and bearers of visitors from far-away lands. Their drivers were celebrities leading adventurous lives that were the envy of grown men and the source of young boys' dreams. They spanned the practical and the fanciful—and they eventually became a key component of the romance and nostalgia of the National Road.

CHAPTER EIGHT

✳✳✳

"You are sure to be passed by Pete Burdine"

The Traveler's Road

TRAFFIC ON THE NATIONAL ROAD took a variety of forms. Many individuals plodded along on foot, toting knapsacks as they went. Riders on horseback were also common, as were farm wagons or covered wagons bearing emigrants westward. Heavy Conestoga wagons lumbered along, hauling all variety of freight to eager recipients. At the apex of National Road society, however, were the lavishly gilded stagecoaches and their equally colorful drivers. To boys living along the route, the drivers occupied a position of esteem that astronauts would hold more than a century later. As one man who grew up along the road later recalled, "I honestly believe that had the choice been given me, or any other small boy, between taking [the stage driver's] place and that of the President, we would not have hesitated a moment,—the driver was the greatest, the most envied man in the world."[1]

The first stage line on the National Road was started in 1818 by James Kinkead, the noted bridge builder, along with Jacob Sides and Abraham Russell. Each man owned a separate section. Russell was the proprietor from Cumberland to Little Crossings, Sides from the latter point to Somerfield, and Kinkead between Somerfield and Brownsville. The same year the *Hagerstown Advertiser* reported that an unnamed stage line had commenced operations between Washington, DC, and Baltimore and Washington, Pennsylvania. Plans were under way to extend the service to Wheeling. The *Virginia Northwestern Gazette,* a Wheeling paper, later reported that the line began operation in early September, making the run from the nation's capital to Wheeling in five days. It likely was the line owned by "Joseph Boyd & Co." On April 27, 1819, this firm announced four-day runs between Washington and Baltimore to Wheeling and Pittsburgh. Another early stage line was started in 1818 by the firm of Hill, Simms, and Pemberton, running between Brownsville and Wheeling.[2]

The most prominent proprietor of stage lines along the road was Lucius Witham Stockton. Born in New Jersey in 1799, he was a grandnephew of Richard Stockton, a member of the Continental Congress and signer of the Declaration of Independence. In 1821 Stockton and Richard Stokes began operating a line of stages between Hagerstown and Gettysburg, connecting the National Road and the Pittsburgh-Philadelphia Pike. Soon after that, Stockton relocated to Uniontown. He entered into business with Daniel Moore of Washington, Pennsylvania, who was already operating a stage company. Stokes also joined the firm, as did Moore N. Falls of Baltimore and Dr. Howard Kennedy of Hagerstown. Their National Road Stage Company quickly absorbed most of its competitors, forming, as historian Arch Butler Hulbert observed, one of America's earliest trusts.[3]

Although Moore was his senior—and later his father-in-law—Stockton ran the company. He installed agents at every community from Baltimore to Wheeling, usually a tavern owner. He made frequent inspection tours from his home in Uniontown, traveling to Wheeling in twelve hours and to Cumberland in a day. His private carriage was the *Flying Dutchman,* pulled by sorrel mares "Bet" and "Sal." It was often reported that Stockton always had a little whiskey added to their water and that they became so accustomed to it that the animals eventually refused to take their water straight. Stockton later extended his company's reach as far as Columbus. He established branch lines as well, one running from Washington, Pennsylvania, to Pittsburgh, another from Washington to Cadiz, Ohio.[4]

Although Stockton enjoyed preeminence on the road, he did not possess a monopoly. James Reeside, a native of Scotland, whose family came to Baltimore in 1789 when he was still an infant, provided him with worthy competition. Bolstered by a grub stake he built hauling freight during the War of 1812, Reeside relocated to Hagerstown and established a stage line that connected that city with McConnellstown, Pennsylvania. Sensing opportunity with the opening of the National Road, he moved to Cumberland in 1818. The entrepreneur managed a tavern for two years before turning his full attention to his stage companies. They required that full attention. Reeside eventually operated lines both east and west of the Mississippi. He owned most of the lines running out of Philadelphia and New York. Adding in extensive contracts to carry the US mail, he employed over four hundred men and over a thousand horses.[5]

In 1836 Reeside purchased from John Weaver the People's Line, which ran between Cumberland and Wheeling. He changed it from a triweekly operation to a daily, later making runs twice a day. Before long his renamed Good Intent Line and Stockton's People's Line were fierce competitors. Passengers benefited from rates that were slashed to ridiculously low levels. Finally the two parties realized that they could not continue their cutthroat competition and agreed to return to their former fares. The fact that Reeside had recently sold his interest to Alpheus Shriver, William Wurt, and William Still may have played a part in the restoration of amity.[6]

West of the Ohio, Stockton faced competition from Neil, Moore, & Co. William Neil, a Kentucky native, began the line about 1820. His brother, Robert, soon became involved in the business, buying out William in 1831. Henry Moore of Wheeling, a veteran stage line operator, joined him. Their Citizens' Line at first ran from Wheeling to Cincinnati via Dayton. They later expanded into Pennsylvania, New York, Indiana, and Michigan. Like Stockton and Reeside, Neil was not afraid to enter into a fare war. When competitors threatened in 1837, the line announced reductions. Five dollars could secure a ticket from Columbus to either Wheeling or Cincinnati.[7]

Further west, a fierce competition arose between the Great Western Stage Company and lines owned by Fink & Walker of Chicago. A coveted contract to carry the mail from Chicago to St. Louis was the source of the rivalry, but it quickly spilled over onto the National Road. The tactics were savage. Both lines drove their horses literally to death in their effort to make time. Drivers would swing their vehicles over into a passing stage, driving it off the road, or suddenly rein back their horses as a rival stage closely approached from behind. The competition ended in 1846 when Otho Hinton & Company, owners of the Great Western, failed, and one of the owners absconded with thousands of dollars in company funds.[8]

✳✳✳

The coaches themselves evolved over the years. The first, dating back to about 1815, were known as "turtle backs" or "turtle hacks" because of the shape of their roofs. They were uncomfortable for passengers, and by the late 1820s Troy and

Concord coaches, named for their places of manufacture in New York and New Hampshire, respectively, had replaced them. Square in shape, they had an iron railing on top to prevent packages and carpetbags from falling off. A protected space under the driver's seat held mail and baggage, and at the rear a projecting frame covered with heavy cloth, called a "boot," carried trunks. Metal springs had not yet been invented, but leather springs, called "thorough-braces," eased the jolting somewhat. According to one man who recalled traveling over the road, "This arrangement gave the body of the coach free play and a kind of swinging motion."[9]

The Troy and Concord coaches weighed between 1,400 and 2,250 pounds and cost between five and six hundred dollars. They seated nine passengers inside in three richly upholstered seats. The trio occupying the front seat faced to the rear, the other six faced forward. A tenth passenger could ride next to the driver, a position that was coveted in favorable weather. In a pinch, more could ride on the roof.[10]

"No boy who beheld that old coach will ever forget it," Thomas Searight waxed about one particularly opulent vehicle. He added, "The coaches were all handsomely and artistically painted and ornamented, lined inside with soft silk plush." It was a competitive business, and even in the early 1800s entrepreneurs understood the value of eye-catching designs. Stages were brightly painted, with landscapes or portraits of prominent individuals painted on them. Stagecoach names were just as colorful. Well-known people of the day and of earlier times were frequently honored. As a result passengers jolted along aboard the *Madison, Monroe, Jackson, Henry Clay, Rough and Ready, Washington, Lafayette, General Wayne, General St. Clair, Columbus, Pocahontas, Queen Victoria,* and, perhaps more strangely, the *Santa Anna.* States and cities also received namesake coaches. Others were dubbed *Ivanhoe, Loch Lomond, Beauty, Industry, Maraposa, Buena Vista,* and *Jewess.* One coach that traveled through Indiana earned the name *Prairie Flower.*[11]

The coaches rolled both day and night. Laws required stage companies to equip their vehicles with lamps, but when their supplies of oil ran dry, keeping on schedule was often a priority over stopping to refill them. Relay stations were located approximately every twelve miles. Drivers were generally responsible for just one team of horses, which they both drove and tended. Mail stage drivers would sometimes handle three or four teams. When this was the case, the teams were quickly changed at the stations. The fresh team would already be harnessed when the coach arrived. The moment it stopped the driver would throw down the reins, attendants would detach the team, attach the fresh one, and toss the reins back to the driver. Although there were almost always four horses to a team, farmers and boys would station themselves with two extra animals at the foot of steep mountains. They were detached at the summit, walking back down to await the next stage.[12]

❊❊❊

Describing a trip made in 1849, Englishman John Lewis Peyton wrote, "The drivers of the public conveyances, even those carrying the mail, were an indolent and easy going set who placed the lowest possible value upon time, consequently ours, like the rest was decidedly a slow coach." His was definitely a minority view. According to Jacob Brown, who knew many, "The stage drivers were a jolly set of men, proud of their situation, some of them of more importance in their own estimation than the Congressman or Cabinet minister riding in the coach below them." Another historian described them as "loquacious and witty," but stage drivers did not fit easily into stereotypes. They ranged from men who handled their teams carelessly to those who lashed their horses mercilessly to those who took a more "scientific approach, sparing the whip to the greatest extent possible."[13]

David Gordon, who drove for Reeside, earned "a wide reputation as a cool and skillful driver" based on an incident that occurred a few miles west of Claysville, Pennsylvania. Gordon was hauling a full load of passengers when his team began running out of control. Realizing that he could not halt them, the resourceful driver pulled the coach off the road and turned it over against a high bank. He then righted the vehicle, got it back on the road, and continued on his way. Gordon's passengers, though frightened, were uninjured, and they credited the driver for their good fortune.[14]

Archie McNeil was the son of a blacksmith who lived near Cambridge, Ohio. As a boy he would head into town and spend time at the stage stations. McNeil ran errands for the drivers, and as time wore on they let him ride on the driver's seat to the next station, returning with another driver. Over time he learned to handle the reins, and by adulthood he was ready to pursue his chosen vocation. McNeil ventured east, operating primarily between Brownsville and Wheeling. He earned a reputation as one of "the class of merry stage drivers" who "enlivened the road with his quaint tricks and humorous jokes."[15]

Redding Bunting was among the most widely known and respected of all National Road drivers. He stood six foot six and was "straight as an arrow, without any redundant flesh." Bunting drove for the Stockton line and was reportedly a favorite of the boss. He was acting as an agent for the company when President Van Buren composed a special message to Congress. Presidential messages were top priority missives in those days, with newspapers eager to get them quickly into print. Bunting went to Frederick, Maryland, then the western terminus of the Baltimore & Ohio Railroad. He sat by the drivers the entire distance back to Wheeling. They made the 222-mile trip in twenty-three hours, thirty minutes. Along the way, Homer Westover rode into National Road folklore by driving the coach from Uniontown to Brownsville, some twenty miles, in forty-five minutes. In 1846 Bunting personally drove the stage bearing President James Polk's war message from Cumberland to Wheeling. He left at two in the morning and arrived at Wheeling, 131 miles distant, twelve hours later. According to Thomas Searight, "Despondency and depression of spirits seemed to have encompassed him, when business ceased on the road, and he appeared as one longing for the return of other and better days."[16]

Peyton's observations notwithstanding, National Road stagecoach drivers were competitive men who placed speed at a premium. Peter Burdine drove for the Reeside line and was "noted for his dashing qualities." He composed a brief poem, projecting his confident attitude, which became well known along the route: "If you take a seat in Stockton's line / You are sure to be passed by Pete Burdine."[17]

Stage racing was illegal in most states, the measures likely being sponsored by legislators who had been either jolted or frightened by speeding drivers. The drivers routinely ignored these laws. On May 13, 1837, the driver of a mail stage attempted to pass a Neil, Moore, & Co. stage on Main Street in Zanesville. In making the effort, one of the passing stage's horses fell, broke a leg, and had to be shot. The outraged editor of the *Ohio Republican* wrote, "We are surprised at the Proprietors of stage lines, permitting such driving where the lives of passengers are put in so much jeopardy, and such outrageous cruel treatment exercised towards that valuable animal—the horse."[18]

Not all accidents involving racing were the fault of a stage driver. On July 9, 1839, a man driving a farm wagon some four miles east of Indianapolis decided to race a stagecoach. He succeeded in passing the vehicle and stood up and appeared to be swinging his hat above his head in celebration. In so doing the man lost his balance and fell, becoming entangled in the harness as the startled horses dragged him along the ground. When they stopped, a local newspaper reported, "he was quite dead, and his body was found to be much mutilated."[19]

Considering the volume of traffic on the road—and the competitive nature of the drivers—wrecks appear to have been rare. However, they were not unheard of, and some produced injuries or fatalities. On December 9, 1831, a westbound stage tumbled over a steep bank at the Mud Run bridge between Cambridge and Old Washington, Ohio. One passenger suffered a broken collarbone, and the driver was reported to have been even more seriously hurt. Other passengers "suffered more or less in the flesh."[20]

On October 31, 1841, a westbound stage "broke down" about two miles west of West Alexander, Pennsylvania. The driver commandeered a road wagon, loaded both the passengers and the mail he was carrying on it, and continued on his way. He had gone only a short distance when the horses took off on a run, throwing the driver and the passengers off the wagon. The driver and a local resident who had gone to help him were "somewhat injured." One of the passengers ended up with a badly broken leg.[21]

A July 1842 accident some twenty miles west of Columbus, just east of the village of Lafayette, left two people with serious injuries and a US court judge with bad bruises. According to the *Springfield Republic,* "The horses were running at the time, and threw the stage off the side of the road." The paper also observed, "As in almost every upset we ever hear about, those who jump from the stage are the ones who are injured, while those who keep their seats are the ones who are uninjured." That proved to be the case for three passengers who remained in their seats.[22]

In March 1845 a westbound Neil, Moore, & Co. coach was descending Lloyd's Hill, a few miles west of St. Clairsville, Ohio. A lever attached to the lock broke, throwing the vehicle forward onto the horses. They panicked and took off at a gallop, upsetting the stage and breaking it to pieces. According to one report, the driver suffered a broken collarbone. Another said it was a broken leg. Both agreed that he received serious injuries. The passengers' injuries ranged from deep cuts and heavy bruises to slight wounds.[23]

Winter weather added to the hazards of travel on the road. In early January 1832, the "upsetting and breaking of the mail stage" near Fairview, Ohio, forced the driver to procure a sled for himself, the mail, and his seven passengers. He set out despite the fact that the road was "completely covered with ice." The party reached the bridge at Crooked Creek, near Cambridge, where there was a sharp turn in the road. The sled was traveling too quickly to make the turn, and it skidded and was thrown against the parapet wall. Three passengers were thrown over the wall and into the stream below. Although they fell some twenty feet, none were badly hurt. Those who remained on the bridge suffered bruises but also avoided serious injuries.[24]

Icy roads were responsible for at least two wrecks along the road in early December 1845. One happened near Zanesville. The coach was reportedly "broken to pieces," although there were no serious injuries. Another accident occurred near Cambridge. Two or three representatives of the Pottowatamie tribe were injured.[25]

A rare fatal accident occurred four miles east of Springfield, Ohio, on April 22, 1839. Something frightened the horses, and the victim, apparently riding with the driver, was thrown from the coach. He was the only passenger on the stage. The driver escaped without injuries.[26]

On November 30, 1842, seven Whig members of Congress were traveling east through Ohio en route for Washington, DC, and the third session of the Twenty-Seventh Congress. About eight miles west of Zanesville, the stage skidded on ice, slid off the road, and fell twenty feet over an embankment. Representative Robert Caruthers of Tennessee and Rep. David Wallace of Indiana were seriously injured. For a time doctors feared that Caruthers might not survive, but he recovered and lived another forty years. Representatives William B. Campbell and Meredith Gentry of Tennessee and Henry S. Lane of Indiana received slight injuries. Representative Patrick Goode of Ohio and Sen. Oliver H. Smith of Indiana were unhurt. Another passenger, described simply as "a young man," suffered a broken arm.[27]

A pedestrian was killed in Cambridge on March 6, 1835, when a stagecoach struck him. Two westbound stages were entering town, the second immediately behind the first. John Dixon, a pioneer settler, saw the lead stage and stepped out of the road. He had a handkerchief tied around his ears and presumably did not hear the second team. Dixon stepped back onto the road, and one of the lead horses of the second team knocked him down. The driver jerked on the reins, but before he could bring the stage to a stop, the wheels passed over the victim's body. He died seconds later. A similar accident took place on March 24, 1847, about a mile east of New Concord, Ohio. William Foster was riding a skittish horse that was frightened by an approaching stagecoach. The animal threw him, and he landed in the path of the stage. As was the case at Cambridge, the wheels passed over Foster's body before the driver could halt the coach. He died half an hour later.[28]

In October 1839 a stagecoach from Columbus arrived at Zanesville without a driver. He had been thrown off about eight miles to the west. The passengers were unaware of the situation until the horses stopped at the Muskingum River bridge. The driver, slightly injured, walked into town several hours later. A potentially more serious incident, which could have been a scene in a Hollywood western, was reported by the *Ohio Republican,* a Zanesville newspaper, on May 28, 1842. A Neil, Moore, & Co. stagecoach was descending a hill when the lever broke, throwing the driver from his seat. The horses started off at a full gallop. A passenger, who was inside the coach, managed to climb to the roof and make his way to the driver's seat. He then jumped on one of the horses and brought the team to a halt. "There were several passengers inside," the *Republican* reported, "and all of them testified to the coolness of the gentleman who risked his own life to save his fellow-passengers." The paper failed to report whether or not the driver was injured.[29]

Not all accidents involved stagecoaches. On June 19, 1820, John Withrow, sheriff of Union County, Pennsylvania, was taking his wife and another woman out for a ride in a gig. The horse took fright, running the vehicle off the road and down over a twenty-yard bank. The horse was killed, and Withrow suffered serious injuries. The two women jumped out and were only slightly hurt. In July 1835 a family of German emigrants was descending a mountain some twenty miles east of Uniontown. Their wagon overturned, throwing a woman and her child against a tree. Both died instantly. Other family members fell down a steep embankment but escaped serious injury.[30]

✳✳✳

Travelers on the National Road could encounter a wide variety of their fellow citizens, ranging from a farmer hauling produce or herding livestock to the president of the United States. Nine US presidents made one or more trips over the road, some many years before or after their time in the White House. Four traveled it as part of their journeys to be inaugurated.

The first president to traverse the road was James Monroe, who made an extensive summer tour in 1817, just months after his first inauguration. The trip carried him north into New England, through upstate New York, and on into Ohio. From Zanesville he followed the future route of the road to Washington, Pennsylvania. (It was on this portion of the trip that he discussed the challenges of Wheeling Hill with John McClure.) After a visit to Pittsburgh, he arrived at Brownsville—and the National Road—on the evening of September 9.

The citizens were ready, and when Monroe appeared on the opposite bank of the Monongahela, they fired twenty-one blasts from a cannon. He forded the river on horseback. Upon reaching the shore, a "committee of arrangement" greeted him and escorted the distinguished guest to a local hotel, where a reception was planned. There a member of the committee delivered a lengthy welcoming address. The president responded with a few remarks that the *Brownsville American Telegraph* termed "extemporaneous but very apposite to the occasion." The paper added, with approval, "The president's dress and behaviour, as symbols of our government, were extremely plain."[31]

Following a similar ceremony in Uniontown, Monroe continued east on horseback, accompanied much of the way by David Shriver, then serving as superintendent of the road. On his way to Cumberland, one of the contractors for the project hosted an open-air reception "in a style and manner which afforded much gratification to his distinguished guest." The chief executive also inspected the Youghiogheny River bridge, then under construction. He was "very free in expressing the pleasure he received" in viewing the project. Along the way Monroe visited with the laborers at work on the road. "He complimented [them] warmly upon their orderly and peaceable deportment towards travelers—and urged them to persevere in that praiseworthy course of conduct." The president arrived at Cumberland on October 12, where a modest reception, based on the concept of "republican simplicity" took place.[32]

After losing the presidency in the House of Representatives in 1825, Andrew Jackson took the National Road as part of his return to Tennessee. Despite the loss, a reception committee at Washington, Pennsylvania, arranged for "an excellent supper, of which the general and a large party partook." Four years later Jackson reversed his route, this time as president-elect. On such occasions stage companies would build a special new coach or refit their best vehicle, decorating it even more ornately than they normally did. Jackson, however, refused to launch the tradition. According to an oft-repeated account, James Reeside had won a new Troy coach, the first one on the road, in an election year bet. He offered it to Jackson for the remainder of the trip, but Old Hickory, scrupulously alert to any appearance of impropriety, politely declined the offer. He did, however, allow family members who were accompanying him to make use of the Reeside coach.[33]

Jackson's successors were less concerned with appearances, and William Henry Harrison, James K. Polk, and Zachary Taylor all traveled the road in opulent style. Harrison, elected in 1840, was no stranger to the turnpike. One of his journeys had occurred four years earlier, as his unsuccessful campaign for the presidency was winding down. Harrison "was received in the most fantastic manner" at Zanesville. A local committee met him at the Guernsey County line in late October and escorted him to a downtown rally.[34]

When Zachary Taylor headed to the capital for his 1849 inauguration, Thomas Shriver led a delegation of Whigs from Cumberland to the Ohio River to greet the Mexican War general. They proceeded on a road that was covered with ice and sleet. Coming down Meadow Mountain, the coaches "danced and waltzed" and skidded from one side of the road to another. However, the most skillful drivers available were at the reins, and the party headed east without incident. Taylor, known for his calmness under fire, seemed more interested in the winter scenery than in the condition of the road. He made it safely to Cumberland, continuing to the capital on the B&O.[35]

In 1843 ex-president John Quincy Adams, seventy-seven years old and in poor health, made an arduous trip to Cincinnati. An avid astronomer, Adams had been invited to preside as the cornerstone was placed for the city's observatory. After touring upstate New York, the congressman traveled by lake to Cleveland then took the Ohio & Erie Canal to Hebron. Continuing west on the National Road, he met the welcoming committee dispatched by the astronomical society at Kirkersville. The group, which had arrived too late to meet him at Cleveland, escorted Adams to Columbus. After taking part in the ceremonies on November 9, he traveled to Wheeling. There he again took the National Road, this time eastbound. The former chief executive spent nights at Washington and Uniontown, participating in public receptions at both places. From Washington he departed in "a new and splendid Coach of the Good Intent Stage Company."[36]

Martin Van Buren also traveled the road after his term ended. Like his mentor Andrew Jackson, the eighth president did not generally support federally funded internal improvements. During the 1840s, as he was touring Indiana, the ex-president's coach upset when it struck a deep mud hole at Plainfield. Some believed the alleged accident had been planned, an object lesson on the importance of keeping the road in proper repair.[37]

Two future presidents spent time on the road in 1846. James Buchanan, ten years away from his election to a single term, had already served in Congress for a decade. At the time he was Polk's secretary of state. The other was Abraham Lincoln, who would become Buchanan's successor. He was far less famous when he passed over the road, on his way to the nation's capital, where he would serve a single term in the House of Representatives.[38]

Henry Clay frequently made use of the road he had supported as he traveled to or returned from numerous sessions of Congress. A number of stories arose from these trips, some of which may actually be true. At least two involved stagecoach accidents. On one occasion his stage allegedly wrecked on the iron bridge in Brownsville. Slightly injured, the politician was taken to a local physician, who was somewhat intimidated by his famous patient. The doctor poured a tumbler of brandy and launched into a lengthy story. Clay tried to listen patiently, but after some time had passed he interrupted, asking if he could drink the liquor and rub the glass over his wound. Following another upset in the Keystone State, Clay was said to have remarked, "This, gentlemen, is undoubtedly the mixing of the Clay of Kentucky with the limestone of Pennsylvania."[39]

What is beyond doubt is that Clay's arrival was generally a cause for celebration as each community tried to outdo all others in the warmth and enthusiasm of its welcome. One of his first sojourns over the road took place in 1818, when the youthful congressman was speaker of the house. The citizens of Wheeling feted Clay with a "sumptuous dinner" when he reached the city. During an 1829 trip, a delegation of Cumberland residents rode out six miles to greet the outgoing secretary of state and escort him to town. After arriving at his hotel, Clay spent over four hours greeting people. There followed, as one newspaper recorded, "a most splendid entertainment." The next day the politician went on to Frostburg, where another round of similar events took place. In the fall of 1842, Clay toured western Ohio and Indiana. After speaking at Dayton, the recently retired senator headed west. A delegation was waiting at the state line to escort him into Richmond and another rally. By then Clay was expected to be the Whig nominee for the presidency in 1844, and his speech was a summary of the party's positions. Following stops in Cambridge City, Knightstown, and Greenfield, Clay spoke at Indianapolis to between twenty and forty thousand. Despite suffering from a severe cold, he delivered a two-hour address.[40]

In August 1824 the Marquis de Lafayette came to the United States for a triumphal tour that lasted more than a year. On May 24, 1825, he arrived in Wheeling, remaining on the National Road as far as Uniontown. The Revolutionary War hero spent the night of May 25 in Washington. Brownsville welcomed him the next day, but the reception was brief because a delegation from Uniontown arrived and whisked the guest of honor off to their community.[41]

Among the many politicians who passed over the road were Lewis Cass, Thomas Hart Benton, Daniel Webster, and John C. Calhoun. Generals turned politicians included Sam Houston and Winfield Scott. The diminutive Tom Thumb toured along the route. So did Horace Greeley, the editor who would later famously advocate for relocation westward. In 1850 the showman P. T.

Barnum escorted singer Jenny Lind on her American tour. She and all others shared the road with foul-mouthed freight haulers, emigrants whose lives were packed into small wagons, and a wide array of livestock. It was a panoply rich in variety—and uniquely American.[42]

※※※

Whether president or plebian, National Road travelers could find hospitality at a variety of inns, taverns, and hotels, which were generally located at brief intervals. Garrett County, Maryland, boasted nearly twenty of these institutions, meaning there was one about every mile. In Fayette County, Pennsylvania, there were eight in Henry Clay Township and eighteen in Wharton Township. They included the Bull's Head, the Sheep's Ear, and Old Inks. Continuing through Ohio, travelers estimated that resting places could be found every five to seven miles. The small village of Old Washington was, for its size, rich in hostelries. Two decades before the road arrived, someone passing through described the community as "a settlement of twelve cabins, four of which were taverns." The building of the road only encouraged residents to put up more. The same pattern was true of the road's western reaches. Clay County, Indiana, had just over twelve miles of the road but offered travelers a choice of nine places to eat and stay. As the road continued westward, inns sprang up quickly, eventually reaching its western terminus. On June 25, 1838, Alex Ferguson announced that his Vandalia Inn was "now prepared to entertain travelers and others in a style and manner unsurpassed by any house in this place." The following May Thomas Redmond informed the public that accommodations at his new hotel, the Sign of the Tree, were "at least equal to those of any similar establishment in the State."[43]

Thomas Searight observed, "The outward appearance of an old tavern of the National Road was no index to the quality of the entertainment it afforded. Many of the least pretentious houses furnished the best meals, and paid the most agreeable attention to guests and patrons."[44]

At first most establishments were decidedly unpretentious. Many were log cabins with no more than two rooms. In the wilderness of Indiana, these cabins were first erected to accommodate men working on the road. A bedroom with one bed was set aside for any women or children staying in the abode, and the laborers would sleep on the floor of the common room. The lucky ones had quilts; the rest slept on animal pelts or bags of straw. Although these makeshift facilities were more common in the sparsely settled West, at least one Pennsylvania inn catered to men building the road. Three Cabins, located in Fayette County, did its best business during the construction period. Once the road was finished, nicer facilities put it out of business.[45]

As time went on, frame, brick, and stone structures began to replace the cabins. In Knightstown, Indiana, Waistell Carey built a log residence for his family in 1826. He later "amplified" the structure to serve travelers. Eventually a neighbor, Asa Heaton, offered his residence as an "annex" for surplus guests. Some time after that, Humphrey Dillon built the Dillon House. In addition to food and lodging, his facility also offered large stables and wagon yards.[46]

Even as roomier inns went up along the road, private homes continued to offer accommodations. Often this was not entirely a matter of choice. One traveler explained that a number of farmers put up signs to discourage guests. "The tide of emigrants sets past them," he wrote. "Hospitality would forbid them to turn from their doors people who might ask for food and shelter." The signs announced that they were running a business, discouraging individuals seeking a handout. In 1832 the Indiana legislature decided that these facilities, if they also sold liquor, required some regulations. The lawmakers required keepers to have at least one spare room with two beds or more, stabling facilities for at least four horses, and to post their rates in a public room.[47]

If the facilities were often wanting, the hospitality was almost always warm. In 1838 M. H. Jenks was traveling from Ohio to Muncie, Indiana. West of Richmond he stopped at a "squatters cabin and was kindly received." The family consisted of a father, mother, and their seven children. They put his horse in a log stable and invited the stranger to share supper with them. "Indian bread," pork, and milk made up the repast, which Jenks consumed "with a better relish than a 75 cent Steam boat or Hotel dinner."[48]

During an 1841 trip to Illinois, fellow travelers informed William Oliver that a nearby home was the only abode along a lengthy stretch of road. Although the place looked "very wretched," Oliver stayed since the alternative was sleeping in the woods. Soon "an inundation" of emigrants heading west arrived, crowding the small home. Supper was "rancid bacon, coffee burned black as charcoal, and Indian bread compounded with the dripping of bacon." Arriving first gave Oliver and his party seniority, allowing them to share the only room in the house.[49]

Traveling west through Indiana in 1855, Richard Beste and his family, English immigrants, stayed in two private farmhouses. At the first the family "laid us out a comparatively excellent dinner on a very white tablecloth." As an added touch they fanned the visitors with peacock feathers as they dined. The second home belonged to "a medical practitioner of no small repute in the district."

Like many others, he ran his home as a business "in order to avoid intrusive guests." The good doctor tended to Beste's horses and discussed the issues of the day. Inside the visitor encountered a man who had been lodging there for several days. He had shown symptoms of cholera and was battling them with sips of brandy and water. Beste felt fine, but he nevertheless joined the man "in taking the prescribed remedy."[50]

Owners of taverns and inns—the terms were largely interchangeable—were not shy about promoting their establishments. When "S. Magill" took over a tavern in Cumberland, he boasted, "Good Beds, a careful Hostler, attentive servants, the best of grain and Hay, will be provided and constantly kept." In 1816 John Conolley opened the Sign of the Black Horse in Brownsville. He announced that the business "will be supplied with the best articles which the market or the season affords" and would always have on hand "a constant supply of the best oats and hay." John Valentine, promoting his Golden Swan Tavern in Washington, Pennsylvania, promised that "LIQUORS OF ALL KINDS, and of the best quality will be constantly kept." Valentine continued, "His stables are large and commodious—and no pains shall be spared to accommodate those who may think proper to call." The owner of the Sign of the Indian Chief and Green Tree in Manhattan, Indiana, was less specific but equally hyperbolic. "No exertion on the part of the proprietor will be wanting to render guests comfortable and at home," he assured potential visitors. "The house will be second to none on the road and is expected to recommend itself."[51]

Boasting aside, most innkeepers devoted more attention to substance than they did to style. As a result, their priorities were having plenty of good food, plenty to drink, and supplying reasonably clean and comfortable beds. The sleeping rooms were generally small and sparsely furnished. The floors were sanded, and the beams in the ceilings were uncovered. Dining rooms had one large table where all white patrons dined together.[52]

In the early days of the road, guests as well as road workers frequently slept on the floors of the log cabin inns. How long this practice continued is uncertain, but on December 1, 1824, a traveler reached a Brownsville inn and wrote, "We laid down on the floor, feet to the fire, and slept till 6." Even in later years, a private bed was far from a certainty. An unwritten rule of the road was to lodge all comers, even if this meant doubling up. Two travelers, complete strangers, would often share a bed, and more than one bed would often be found in a single room.[53]

Maid service, like privacy, ranged from rare to nonexistent, especially outside the large cities, and bedding was seldom changed for every new guest.

Travelers often encountered bed vermin and flies. Stopping at an inn in Richmond, Indiana, in 1843, Sarah Henderson and her party "became very uneasy when we discovered to my utter amazement that the bed was pre-occupied by a little animal which has received various names." Another guest joked that he had caught one of the creatures trying to "carry off" a female patron. A patron at an inn in western Illinois wrote approvingly, "The Vandalia Inn, where I spent the night, was air-tight, and the bed was free of bugs." He paid a dollar for the room and three meals.[54]

If innkeepers considered clean sheets to be a nicety, the quality of the food and drink they offered was a top priority. About an hour before the arrival of an evening stagecoach, a proprietor would swing into action. He would begin the transfer of liquors from demijohns to bottles and arrange glasses at the bar. Meanwhile he directed whatever help he had to get supper prepared. At the same time locals would gather to await the stage, hoping to learn the latest news from arriving passengers and the driver.[55]

At many inns a bell summoned the guests to meals. The bill of fare was plain, wholesome, and plentiful. Venison was found along much of the route. In eastern sections mountain mutton, turkey, pheasant, and trout were common. As one continued west, farm fare such as ham, corn, and hominy were frequently on the menu. Hostelries in large communities provided a greater variety. A guest at Bunting's Inn in Terre Haute wrote that breakfast, served at six and again at seven, included a wide variety of breads, including cornbread. There were also "little seed cakes, pancakes and fritters, milk, butter buried in large lumps of ice, molasses, preserves and blackberry syrup in large soup tureens." Tea and coffee were the drink choices. Bunting always served roast beef for dinner. Other options could include chicken pie, veal pie, beefsteak, roast lamb, veal and mutton cutlets, boiled ham, pigeon, roast veal, or roast pork. Peas, beans, hominy, potatoes, and "green Indian corn" were also on the table. Turtle soup was a frequent dish. For dessert the inn offered cherry, apple, squash, blackberry, or custard pie, along with watermelons and iced cream.[56]

Matilda Houstoun, a visitor from England, was frequently prickly in her observations of America and its National Road, complaining of the jolting ride and pedestrians who "accosted" her party. The simple fare of western Pennsylvania inns, however, won her over. Her first meal in the Keystone State came in an unidentified village consisting of a dozen log cabins. "The burly mountaineer [who] came out to receive us with a cigar in his mouth" gave her pause. So did the fact that the house was "not one of the usual stopping places for the stages" and was "little more than an overgrown shanty." The rough-looking keeper, however, earned her gratitude with both "the quantity and quality of the food which was laid on the table." Cold bear meat and hot venison steaks "of excellent quality" composed the main course. Drinks were spring water and rye whiskey. At Uniontown Mrs. Houstoun's party had beefsteak and cornbread but were most pleased by the fresh eggs. At Brownsville they again ate well. "Our evening meal consisted of delicious kinds of bread, both corn and wheat, preserves of many sorts, strawberry, apricot, and peach, rich cream, and excellent tea." She was most impressed by the "Johnny cakes," which the visitor described as "a sort of pancake" made of Indian corn.[57]

The main feature of every inn, found in the front section, was the barroom. It was lit and warmed by an immense fireplace, some as much as seven feet wide and capable of holding a wagonload of fuel. In Maryland and Pennsylvania, where outcroppings were common, most innkeepers burned coal. Farther west wood was the fuel of choice. An enormous poker, often seven feet long, stirred the fire. At many establishments this chore belonged exclusively to the proprietor, and he guarded the privilege jealously.[58]

Whiskey was the drink of choice at the taverns. Often it was all that was available, although some of the better places might offer brandy or wine. Writing in the 1890s, Thomas Searight insisted, "It did not contain the elements of modern whiskey, which excites men to revolution, insurrection, violence and insanity." Three cents a glass was the usual price, although it could sell for as much as a nickel. At some towns two glasses could be had for a "fippenny bit," a monetary unit equal to six and one-fourth cents.[59]

Many inns, particularly in larger communities, had newspapers and periodicals available. In Indiana, Methodist hymnals supplemented the reading material. Some innkeepers even kept racks of clay smoking pipes with long stems. As a puffer finished, he would break off a small piece of the end. Perhaps the most unique inducement to travelers was the sulphur spring at an inn near Old Washington, Ohio, believed to possess medicinal qualities.[60]

Inns often served a variety of purposes in their communities. Among the most versatile was the State House Inn in Garrett County, Maryland. In addition to catering to National Road travelers, the facility housed a post office and a general store, was used as a polling place and a private school, and on one occasion served as the site of a civil trial. It was one of many inns that served a local clientele as well as visitors from afar. The Fayette Springs Hotel in Fayette County, Pennsylvania often played host to "merry parties of young folks from

Uniontown," who arrived for supper and evening dances. Charley Miller's Tavern, located some ten miles east of Washington, Pennsylvania, was the inn of choice for that community's youth, perhaps because of Charley's reputation for offering "sumptuous and savory" meals.

Winter weather did not discourage the local pleasure seekers. Sleighing parties from Brownsville and Uniontown would often head to Searight's Tavern, located halfway between those two communities. Youth from Wheeling, venturing out on a winter night, would often travel a few miles east to a tavern owned by a widow known to history as Mrs. Gooding. Like Charley Miller, her meals became legendary along the road.[61]

※※※

Although Maryland and Virginia were the only slave states through which the road passed, segregation was the rule along the entire route. Blacks and whites dined at separate tables, although one traveler insisted that the fare was the same—at least at the hotel in Terre Haute where he was staying. He added that he was not sure which race refused to eat with the other, "for each seemed to despise the other equally."[62]

Both slaves and free blacks worked at the inns, usually as cooks or waiters. An exception was the Franklin House in Frostburg, Maryland, owned by Thomas Johnson. The proprietor was an accomplished fiddler, and his slave, Dennis, was an equally good dancer. Night after night, Dennis performed the "double shuffle" to the "lively music" of his master.[63]

Another Frostburg tavern keeper, Samuel Cessna, owned the Highland Hall House. He employed a "negro servant," although it is unclear whether the man was slave or free. Regardless of his status, the servant allegedly "addressed some insulting remark" to Cessna's wife. Learning of the incident, "Cessna proceeded to dispatch the negro without ceremony." He was tried in Cumberland for murder, but acquitted, a verdict that reportedly met with the approval of local citizens.[64]

William Faux, an Englishman, traveled the road as part of a tour of America in the early 1820s. At Brownsville a man asked if he and a group of slaves could ride with him and his fellow stagecoach passengers. Everyone agreed, somewhat to Faux's surprise. The man explained that he had purchased them for a planter in Missouri, and he planned to transport them down the Ohio River. Things did not work out for him as planned. After the stage had gone a few miles, his human cargo bolted for freedom. The man was able to recover six of them, but four made good their getaway—at least temporarily.[65]

Another fugitive slave encounter played out as a tragedy. It happened on July 4, 1845, at the "Old McCullough Stand," a Fayette County, Pennsylvania tavern then conducted by Nicholas McCartney. Early that day some wagoners were feeding their teams when they observed a black man walking along the road. One reportedly cried out to McCartney, "There goes a runaway nigger." McCartney asked the man if he was sure. The wagoner assured him that he was, and the innkeeper dashed off and captured the fugitive. He took his prisoner inside, fed him, and informed him that he was going to return him to his master in Maryland. The escapee seemed resigned to his fate, and McCartney left him in the charge of his brother-in-law, Atwell Holland, and went to get a horse. Seeing an opportunity, the slave again fled. Several wagoners went in pursuit. So, too, did Atwell, despite his wife's entreaties not to. The fugitive outpaced everybody but Holland, a very fleet runner, who was able to overtake him.

His accomplishment proved fatal. The slave, desperate to achieve his freedom, turned and stabbed Holland three times. He died a short time later. Local lore holds that a posse formed, resumed the pursuit, and shot and killed the slave as he made his way toward Uniontown. The truth will never be known, but it is clear that the famed hospitality of the National Road was entirely dependent upon race.[66]

CHAPTER NINE

✳✳✳

"Truly worthy of a great nation"
Responses to the Traveler's Road

ALTHOUGH THE MAJORITY of travelers on the National Road ventured out for practical reasons such as herding, freighting, or attending to business interests, there were also early-day tourists in the mix. Some jotted down their observations in diaries. Others, especially those visiting the wilds of America from abroad, later published their accounts of the road and the people and communities along the way.

Travelers who met the road at its eastern terminus were generally impressed with the Maryland community. An 1820 visitor wrote, "Cumberland is a pretty little town, delightfully situated on a branch of the Potomac, and in one of those romantic spots which are often found in mountainous and secluded situations." Two years later another observed that it was "a thriving town on the Potomac." Matilda Houstoun felt that the community had "everything to attract, both in regard to eligibility and beauty." By the time she arrived in 1850, so had the Baltimore & Ohio Railroad, leading her to predict that Cumberland would "rival in rapidity of growth any of the other mushroom-like cities of the Union."[1]

Towns and villages were well spaced through Maryland and Pennsylvania, prompting many visitors to write about the remoteness of the country. "It is at considerable intervals, that even by the road side, a small spot of settled or cleared land can be seen," one noted, "while at a distance from the road, the country is perfectly 'wild.'" Writing in a similar vein, another observed, "Notwithstanding an occasional clearing and a rude hut, with a cow and a few pigs grazing around it, the country was perfectly 'wild.'" English visitor Godfrey Vigne was moved to wax eloquent. "Silence and tranquility to a degree I never before witnessed, are, I think, the prevailing characteristics of the American forests," he wrote. "They are dark but never gloomy, excepting where they are composed of pine trees: they are solitary, and are silent as the grave, without inspiring horror." Even as late as 1850, Mrs. Houstoun wrote, "We passed no extensive clearings, but occasionally we chanced upon little cultivated spots, each of which had a neat wooden house in the centre of the newly cleared, and already half cultivated ground." In other places, she added, "The process of clearing had but just begun, a tree or two only being felled, while the hardy woodman was busy at work upon another."[2]

Travelers appear to have been unanimous in their appreciation of the mountain vistas. "Some of the scenery on this route is grand, all of it diversified, romantic, and beautiful," John Lewis Peyton wrote. Scotsman William Owen recorded in his diary, "The whole of the scenery was very romantic and beautiful, especially from the tops of the heights to which we ascended." Mrs. Houstoun agreed, noting, "We looked back occasionally from our leather 'conveniency,' and gazed upon the glorious country which was lying far beneath us." After traveling at night, William Faux wrote, "Our ride for the last three hours of our journey, was fearfully romantic, amongst huge rocks which hung over on both sides and seemed ready to fall upon us, the effect of which was greatly heightened by the moon-light." One did not have to be a native of Europe to find Maryland and Pennsylvania impressive. M. H. Jenks, an Indiana resident, marveled, "This is a wonderful rough and romantic district of Country," adding, "From many Elevated positions the Eye scans with delight of Country, wild extensive and in [the] highest degree picturesque."[3]

Winter weather, which often came early to the mountains, added to the grandeur of the scenery—and to the inconvenience and danger of travel. Crossing the Alleghenies in late October, Charles Hoffman, a New Yorker, observed, "The still cold frosty mornings gave a vigour and boldness of outline to the mountain scenery, that extended its limits and heightened its effect." Following a one-inch overnight snowfall, he enthused, "How do the dead branches smile in the frosty sunbeams; how joyously does everything sparkle in the refracted light!" Scottish visitor Thomas Hamilton was far less appreciative of the mountains' winter wonderland. Ascending Savage Mountain, he recalled, "The snow lay deeper every mile of our advance, and . . . on reaching a miserable inn, the landlord informed us, that no carriage on wheels had been able to traverse the mountain for six weeks." They continued on despite the innkeeper's advice, the passengers "having fortified their courage with copious infusions of brandy." At one point their coach became "stuck fast in a snow drift, which actually buried the horses." Despite the conditions, and an allegedly drunk driver, the stage, after volunteers extricated it, proceeded on without incident.[4]

The next morning found the winter travelers climbing Laurel Mountain in Pennsylvania, the last major summit along the route. Hamilton described the view from the top "fine and extensive, though perhaps deficient in variety." William Blaine considered it "a most beautiful and extensive view." John Woods, also a visitor from England, wrote of Laurel Mountain, "Here we had the first, and a most extensive view of the west side of the mountains." He added that there was "much cleared land in sight," a change that other travelers also noted. "From the top of Laurel Hill you look down on a very fertile valley of land," John P. Cockey wrote. "The farms are very handsomely situated, and in excellent cultivation." To Matilda Houstoun, the sight represented a dramatic metamorphosis. "We looked out and what a change of prospect before us!" she wrote. "We had emerged from the dark forests, and, to our great surprise, were looking down upon the vast plains beneath us. Far and wide, and on every side, stretched the vast expanse of country: and cultivated lands, and broad shining rivers, and thriving towns, with spires glistening in the sunshine, all were spread, as in a vast panorama, before us."[5]

In addition to viewing the forests, National Road travelers could also see the trees. Most wrote of impressive oaks, pines, and cedars, but chestnut, sycamore, tulip, and hickory trees also received mention. Some remarked on such undergrowth as rhododendrons and azaleas. Others commented on the mountain laurel. Both John Peyton and William Blaine, whose visits came nearly three decades apart, observed that it was so thick as to make the woods seem "impenetrable." For John Woods one of the saddest sights he saw along the road was the "thousands of trees, that were cut for making the turnpike [that] lay rotting by the sides of it." Woods added, "I believe I have seen more timber in this wasting state, than all the growing timber I ever saw in my life in England."[6]

Visitors often wrote of panthers, bears, deer, elk, and wolves along the road, although some accounts may have been based on conversations with local residents rather than personal observation. Wild turkeys were also common. Mrs. Houstoun commented that the American partridge was "a larger bird than our own, but not nearly as well flavored." What the Americans termed a pheasant she identified as a prairie hen. John Woods, apparently a bird watcher, wrote, "We saw but few birds on our journey; woodpeckers of several sorts, a handsome yellow bird, something like a goldfinch, a few crows, and some small birds, much like tom-tits." When a hummingbird settled on some flowers his daughter was carrying, the girl at first thought it was a large insect.[7]

Blaine and Peyton wrote that rattlesnakes were so thick in the Maryland section of the road that both hunters and surveyors avoided the road in the summer and fall. (Their presence is never mentioned, however, in construction records of the road.) A man living near Negro Mountain told Blaine that he had seen one or two dozen lying together on warm summer mornings. He further informed the visitor that the snakes quickly disappeared when an area became settled. The hogs that roamed the woods, he explained, devoured the reptiles, being protected from poisonous bites by their thick hides.[8]

Blaine observed that a "large coal formation" began at Cumberland and extended all the way to Wheeling. In mountains near the Youghiogheny it appeared at the surface "so that many people dig it out and burn it, although surrounded by so much wood." Frederick Treadway, en route to Louisiana from his home in Connecticut, wrote that virtually everyone living in the mountains burned coal because "they procure [it] without very great trouble and [at] little expense." The price, he added, ranged from three and one-half to five cents a bushel. Mrs. Houstoun also commented on the abundance of coal, but she was more pleased by the result of its abundance. "It was a cheering sight," she wrote, "to look in at the cottage doors and see the large fires blazing cheerfully within, while the whole family were gathered round the abundant supper that was spread on the table."[9]

※※※

National Road travelers were eager to comment on the impressive scenery along the route and on the flora, fauna, and wildlife that helped compose it. They were a bit more reticent about the people they encountered on their way. When they did mention the mountain people, their comments were often caustic, some calling to mind long held prejudices. Englishman Adlard Welby wrote, "The Pensilvanians resemble in many points the Scots: they go barefoot [and] they both have some dirty habits." He explained, "A medical man lately told me that the itch, a disorder which proves unclenliness where it prevails, was as rife as in Scotland." Both groups, Welby continued, were fond of "drams of whiskey and bitters." He gave the Scots the edge in culinary arts, describing Pennsylvania cooking as "the most abominable messing and spoiling of provision imaginable: nothing but frying in butter till the stomach turns even at the smell." Although he was opposed to slavery, Welby wrote that when he entered Virginia, "The white people seemed far more respectable and civilized than in the free state we had just left; almost all we met accosted us pleasantly, as if to welcome a stranger without that rude stare to which we had become accustomed."[10]

Thomas Hamilton complained of a fellow stagecoach passenger, a physician who had "a inordinate addiction to the vernacular vices of dram-drinking and tobacco-chewing." Being drunk most of the time, the man "discharged volleys of saliva, utterly reckless of consequences." This was particularly true after dark. Among the victims of his carelessness was a Quaker, "into whose eye he squirted a whole mouthful of tobacco juice," resulting in great and long-lasting discomfort.[11]

Not all observations about the Appalachian natives were negative. John Woods was grateful to a generous woman who lived a few miles west of Brownsville. She was milking a cow by the side of the road, and she shared some of the milk as well as apples from the family orchard. Mrs. Houstoun, who could be prickly in her observations, was impressed by the children she saw in the mountains. Although their homes were "very far from comfortable looking," the youngsters were "rosy faced and happy looking." She further noted that, unlike in her native England, they did not pursue the visitors "with the whining accents of experienced beggars." She also observed, "The farther we advanced, and the higher the ground to which we attained, so much the more healthy was the appearance of every one we met."[12]

Travelers also remarked occasionally on the communities through which the road passed. To John Woods, Smithfield, Pennsylvania, was "placed in a very romantic situation." During his 1819 visit he found three taverns there and about twenty houses, most made of logs. Some thirty years later, Mrs. Houstoun found that it had not grown much. Still, she considered it to be a pleasant place, writing, "There are a few, a very few, houses in it besides the inn, and these lie snugly together in a valley worthy of Switzerland." The English lady also liked Uniontown, which she described as "a clean, nice-looking village."[13]

Her view of Brownsville was decidedly different. She termed it "a most dirty town, dirty with smoke, and coal, and manufactures." She was not alone in that opinion. Thomas Hamilton was even less generous, writing, "The appearance of Brownsville is black and disgusting; its streets are dirty and unpaved; and the houses present none of the externals of opulence." John Peyton dismissed the community as "a wretched village of about 1,000 listless and thriftless inhabitants." Brownsville gained a rare advocate in William Blaine. He found it to be "a small but thriving town," noting that "several manufactories have been established there, and one of glass is in a very prosperous condition."[14]

Travelers' impressions of Wheeling were varied, apparently determined largely by whether they considered manufacturing to be a blessing or a curse. New Yorker Charles Hoffman wrote, "Wheeling is one of the most flourishing places on the Ohio. The immense quantity of bituminous coal in the adjacent region . . . gives it great advantages as a manufacturing place." Adlard Welby felt that the community was "very pleasantly situated on the Ohio, and, standing upon high ground, appears to be healthy." A number of "excellent buildings" had gone up, he added, and more were being built. Others were far less generous in their descriptions. Blaine wrote of Wheeling, "I found it but a small town, and owing to its manufactures extremely dirty." Hamilton was even more blunt: "The town of Wheeling, dirty and smoke-begrimed, could boast of no attraction." New Englander Treadway concluded, "I do not like [Wheeling] at all it is A very dirty place. The city is constantly full of this coal smoke you cannot Breath indoors nor out without inhaling this horrid stuff."[15]

✳✳✳

The road itself generally made a positive impression upon those who traveled it, although this tended to depend on the year of the journey. After going from Cumberland to Wheeling in 1820, James Hall wrote, "This section of the road [has] been completed in a manner which reflects the highest credit upon those engaged in its construction. It is a permanent turnpike, built of stone, and covered with gravel, so as to unite solidity and smoothness; and noble arches of stone have been thrown, at a vast expense, over all the ravines and water-courses." Writing a year later, Welby observed, "The National Road is a work truly worthy of a great nation, both in its idea and construction." T. S. Sears, a frequent traveler, agreed. Writing in 1847, after visiting Wheeling, he informed a friend, "I have been on this road at two other points, Brownsville and Uniontown Pa. & I never saw so fine a road. I don't think that there is another such thorough fare to be found for coaches in the Union. Every stage is crowded full as it can be. The road is almost like the floor of a house."[16]

Thomas Hamilton had a decidedly different experience. His journey occurred in the early 1830s, just before the Corps of Engineers began their repair efforts east of the Ohio. "The road was most execrable," he wrote of the area just east of Washington, Pennsylvania, "and the jolting exceeded any thing I had yet experienced." As he continued west, the road did nothing to improve his disposition. He observed, "If intended by Congress to act as an instrument of punishment on their sovereign constituents, it is no doubt very happily adopted for the purpose."[17]

As time went on, bridges spanning major streams made travel on the road more convenient. A long-anticipated bridge went up over the Monongahela at Brownsville in 1833. In 1810 the Pennsylvania legislature first authorized the governor to incorporate a company to build a bridge at the site. Nothing more came of the proposal. A similar effort in 1830 found success, and the wooden covered bridge that resulted, built by private enterprise, served travelers on the road until 1913. Few made note of the structure in their writings, but Mrs. Houstoun, who made note of virtually everything, termed it "rather a handsome bridge."[18]

Sixteen years later an even more ambitious bridge project connected Wheeling with Wheeling Island, then better known as Zane's Island. Such a project had long been a dream of the residents of Wheeling and the surrounding area. In 1816, with the National Road approaching, the Wheeling & Belmont Bridge Company received a charter from the state of Virginia and permission to issue $200,000 in stock. The Ohio General Assembly added its assent the same year. However, nothing came of the project, in part because Richmond legislators were reluctant to give enthusiastic support to a project so far removed from the state's population centers and planter class.[19]

The idea remained dormant for nearly two decades. Then, in 1836, the Ohio General Assembly petitioned Congress to support the project. The Buckeye lawmakers also instructed the state's US senators to push the effort. The following year a group of Wheeling residents added their own petition, citing dangerous winter conditions for crossing and delays to the mail. They then addressed a concern that had been brought up before by opponents of the project, the potential obstruction of navigation on the river. The petitioners asserted that there was "no reasonable ground for such fears." The House Committee on Roads and Canals agreed. The Wheeling bridge, they insisted, would be an "essential link [in] the only chain of direct communication between the capital of the United States and the seats of Government of four of the States of this Union."[20]

One of the factors motivating the committee was the fact that Charles Ellet Jr. had become involved in the project. A native of Philadelphia, Ellet had become an assistant engineer on the Chesapeake & Ohio Canal before voyaging to Europe to further his education. After returning home he became involved in a number of ambitious suspension bridge projects, including a 357-foot span over the Schuylkill at Fairmount, Pennsylvania. Congress, growing weary of anything associated with the National Road, declined to act on the committee's recommendation, but in 1836 the Virginia General Assembly reorganized the Wheeling & Belmont Bridge Company. Once again, Ohio's state legislature also gave its assent.

Still, it was not until 1847 that work began on the project, an effort that would easily exceed in ambition and length anything the self-confident Ellet had ever attempted. A pair of huge stone towers would support twelve cables, each 1,380 feet in length and containing 455,400 pounds of wire. Ellet insisted that the bridge would support 593,400 pounds of live load. Workers completed the project on October 20, 1849. A local newspaper boasted, "Centuries will roll away, another and another chain will be thrown over the Ohio . . . yet this work will stand and throw a halo of glory around the names of those who executed it." The people of Wheeling had reason to be proud. With a main span of 1,010 feet, it was the world's longest clear-span bridge. It would remain so until the Brooklyn Bridge was completed in 1883. In the meantime workers had erected a covered bridge over the narrower back channel in 1838, linking Wheeling Island with the Ohio shore.[21]

Wheeling's celebration was short lived, as both natural and legal threats to the bridge soon emerged. The legal came first. It started with Pittsburgh interests still casting a wayward eye toward Wheeling as a commercial rival. They persuaded the state legislature to support their resulting lawsuit and engaged Edwin M. Stanton as their chief counsel. They claimed that the bridge obstructed river traffic, injuring Pennsylvania's commercial interests, and in an 1852 ruling, the United States Supreme Court agreed. Bridge company officials largely ignored the ruling. Declaring the span to be an obstruction was easy. Coming to Wheeling to tear it down was not. That accomplishment bad weather nearly managed. On May 17, 1854, a strong windstorm wrecked much of the span and suspension system. Pennsylvania got an injunction to stop repair work, but the company again ignored the courts. A temporary single-lane span was in place within three months. It remained in operation until 1859, when the two-lane span was restored. In the meantime, the high court had reversed its original decision. The Wheeling Suspension Bridge was legal. It continues to carry vehicular traffic.[22]

※※※

West of the Ohio, the scenery along the road gradually began to change. "On entering the state of Ohio by this route," Welby recorded, "we find little to interest; a wild uncleared hilly country." He was interested, however, in the peach and apple orchards his party encountered, which were "literally breaking down with fruit." They purchased half a peck of peaches for six cents and made daily stops "at the first orchard to take as many apples as we want for the day."[23]

As the road progressed westward across the Buckeye State, the foothills of the Alleghenies began to give way to flatter ground. Travelers' reactions to the change were mixed. "I have been travelling to-day through a dull country," Englishman Joseph Gurney wrote, "the hills and dales being now exchanged for a flat plain, half covered with woods, and tolerably cultivated." M. H. Jenks saw the region differently. "The country through which we passed is a delightful one," he wrote as he traveled east from Dayton, "being one continued natural prairie until we approached Columbus." William Faux was impressed by the farm country of eastern Ohio. In Belmont County he experienced "fine land in grain, corn, and pasture, with a beautiful clover face, white as with a shower of sleet." To the west, after passing through Zanesville, Faux entered "a fine rich landed country, full of the natural means of living well by the sweat of the brow." His only complaint was with Ohio potato farmers, who, he asserted, produced only one-fourth as many per acre as did their English counterparts and sold them at double the price.[24]

In 1840 an anonymous traveler in Indiana found the land between Richmond and Indianapolis to be "very flat and low, so that the water cannot pass off, but stands in pools, sometimes for miles on the sides of the road." Journeying from west to east, William Miller wrote of the area just east of Terre Haute, "The country here is heavily timbered, and, among other fine trees, we saw some enormous poplars." For the most part, he added, the road ran in a straight line through flat country. This, he remarked, "renders travelling exceedingly monotonous. Hemmed in by a wall of forest the traveller can sometimes see a distance of many miles before him the cleared roadway diminished to a thread-like tenuity." Reaching the vicinity of Putnamville, Oliver found the country more interesting thanks to numerous streams, "splendid" timber, and large boulders. Eastern Indiana impressed him even more. "Centreville is situated in a fine country tolerably well cleared and thickly peopled," he wrote. "The farm houses are comfortable, in many instances with fine orchards attached to them, and not the slightest symptom of poverty or want is to be seen."[25]

Like Wheeling, Zanesville produced differing reactions among visitors. Writing in 1818, a decade before the road arrived, William Cobbett, an English visitor, termed it "a place finely situated for manufactures." He explained, "It has almost every advantage for manufacturing of all sorts, both as to local situation and as to materials." Arriving in 1837, Joseph Gurney found Zanesville to be "a neat and prosperous-looking town, of about 7000 inhabitants." Jenks, who put down his observations in 1838, wrote, "There are some fine mills at this place and fine water power and it presented a stirring and business character." He added, however, "It has a dark complexion and is a manufacturing & coal burning Town."[26]

Gurney and Jenks also recorded their impressions of Columbus. The former found it to be "a baby metropolis bursting into life, and already making some show of magnificence." A "state lunatic asylum" was under construction "on a noble plan," and the capitol building was divided into "handsome and convenient rooms." Jenks agreed that Ohio's seat of government was "flourishing and growing to an astonishing degree." He continued, "Its general appearance is clean and tidy and calculated to awaken admiration."[27]

Indianapolis also garnered positive reviews. Oliver noted that the city had "some very good hotels [and] stores." The state capitol building, he further observed, "is large and well proportioned, and forms a pleasing object." An anonymous visitor, writing in 1840, concluded, "Indianapolis covers a large area, has a population of about 4000, and contains some good buildings. The capitol is a good looking edifice, in the Grecian style, built of brick and stuccoed in imitations of marble."[28]

The same writer reported that Terre Haute was "delightfully situated on the western edge of the prairie." He termed it "quite a handsome town," but implied that it was an unhealthy place. Oliver found the western Indiana community to be "a pretty place, with a number of good houses, and some respectable stores and inns." He, too, reported that it was not a healthy town. "Some of the inmates of the hotel where we stopped were lying dangerously ill in fever," he wrote.[29]

At the western terminus, Vandalia proved disappointing to Frederick Julius Gustorf, an immigrant from Westphalia, who had been living in Philadelphia. "The houses about one hundred in all, stand on a very broken soil," he wrote in October 1835, "and since most of them are log cabins, the whole scene is dark and depressing. One can see about five or six big frame buildings containing stores. The Statehouse is a common brick building. A solitary bank, a wooden church with a small tower, and two or three state offices complete the community." Edmund Flagg, an 1838 visitor, offered a similar impression. "The streets are of liberal breadth, some of them not less than eighty feet from kerb to kerb," he wrote, "enclosing an elevated public square nearly in the centre of the village, which a little expenditure of time and money might render a delightful promenade." The buildings were "very inconsiderable" in his view, although nicer structures were under construction. Oliver was more reticent about the town: "It is a scattered place, with some good buildings, and a large open place in the centre for a square."[30]

Opinions of the western section of the road also varied from one traveler to another. In 1835 Alfred Brunson, a Methodist circuit rider venturing to Wisconsin from Ohio, encountered a bumpy stretch of road west of Columbus. One jolt tossed his saddlebags out of the wagon in which he was riding. He did not discover the loss for several miles, but a fellow traveler rode back and recovered them. The next day a mud hole broke their doubletree. Brunson concluded, "The roads through Ohio & Indiana were extremely bad." Three years later, after the Corps of Engineers had time to do their work, Jenks found the route east of Springfield to be "the most elegant road in the world." It came as a relief after having a "tedious and horribly muddy time" on the Dayton Cutoff.[31]

As he ventured through Indiana in 1835, Pastor Brunson noted that recent rains had rendered the road "intolerable." He wrote, "Sometimes we were obliged to take the woods to escape the mud." Peter Hessong, an emigrant from Maryland, wrote in May 1838, "When we got within 15 miles of Indianapolis the mud was beyond all imagination and we borrowed a chain and put six horses to one wagon and drove about three miles . . . and came back for the other [wagon], after that we got along fair." An anonymous traveler, who took the road in 1839, explained that water and traffic had combined to wear the surface into "cradle holes and gulleys which frequently become impassable." He continued, "Then a few logs are thrown in, often by the travelers themselves, just sufficient for them to get over, though not without peril." Despite the state of the road, he suspected that "there is none better in Indiana." Oliver, who passed over the highway two years later, wrote of the section near the Wabash, "The track was tortuous and narrow, interrupted with stumps and huge gnarled roots, with, now and then, an apology for a bridge, consisting of two trees laid for bearers." East of Indianapolis the situation did not improve. As Oliver and most other travelers would have agreed, the National Road ranged, depending on time and location, from a smooth, wide thoroughfare, to a rough trail, to little more than a rumor. Still, it was generally the best option available.[32]

CHAPTER TEN

✳✳✳

"It kicked up a dust"

The Post Road

IN 1818, DESPITE THE FACT that the National Road was not yet completed to the Ohio River, the government instituted mail service over the route from Washington, DC, and Baltimore to Wheeling. The first stagecoach carrying the mail over the road left Cumberland on August 1. The driver, who reached Wheeling "in due time," was William Sheets. He was a genuine "pike boy" and would also work as a wagoner and a tavern keeper before dying at ninety-five, seventy-four years after that initial mail run. James Reeside took the contract, subletting sections to a variety of companies. Stockton & Stokes carried the mail from Baltimore to Hagerstown, and James Boyd brought it on to Cumberland. Once on the National Road, Abraham Russell delivered it to Little Crossings, Jacob Sides took over to Somerfield, and James Kinkead, who seemed to be involved in virtually every aspect of the road, took it on to Brownsville. Simms and Pemberton then carried it to Wheeling.[1]

The early mail coaches, designed by the US Post Office Department, carried only three passengers. The passenger compartment, termed a "monkey box" by both drivers and passengers, sat at the front end of the coach. The mail went behind in a long wooden box that rested on the axles of the wagon. There were no springs below the boxes, and they made a loud noise as they passed over the bumpy road. Their time of service was brief. It was not long before regular passenger coaches replaced them.[2]

At that time the Post Office Department was a vastly different institution from today's United States Postal Service. Newspapers, not letters, made up a large percentage of the mail carried by the coaches. In 1820 most Americans received, statistically, under one letter per year—a figure that would rise to three by 1850 and seven four years later. Rates of postage depended upon the number of sheets a letter contained and the distance it had to travel, and those rates were high. A single sheet going thirty miles or fewer cost six cents to send. At the other end of the scale, a triple-sheet letter traveling four hundred miles merited a charge of three dollars. Postage generally was paid by the recipient. Stamps did not arrive until 1847. Before that, postmasters figured the cost and wrote it on the envelope.[3]

Six cents was not an insignificant amount in the early 1800s, and three dollars was well in excess of the average daily wage for most laborers. It is not surprising, therefore, that Americans expected the mail to be delivered quickly and efficiently. When it was not—and that was often—they complained about the Post Office Department. Local editors composed harsh missives about the department's incompetence, especially when the opposing political party was in office. Some of the criticism likely was fair, but many of the delays were beyond the agency's control. Stage companies, for example, prioritized passengers ahead of parcels, and when their coaches had a full complement of riders, mail sacks had to wait for a later coach. Snowstorms, icy roads, and ice floes on the Ohio combined in 1839 to slow stages to a point that it took a presidential message, always eagerly anticipated by editors, weeks to go from Washington to Columbus. The trip had been made previously in under two days. Sometimes local postmasters created delays. In 1838, after the Zanesville post office was removed as a distribution center, the editor of the *Gazette* complained that many of the eastern newspapers he received came from the west. "For the special information of the Wheeling distributor," he sarcastically observed, "we would suggest that Zanesville is not so far west as Columbus, and as the road is much worn, and the mails heavy, it might be well to save something more than a hundred miles of transportation by putting Zanesville packages into the Zanesville bags."[4]

Often the condition of the National Road was the culprit. In the spring of 1828, the House of Representatives directed John McLean, the postmaster general, to report any information he had concerning the state of the road and to what extent its condition affected the mails. McLean replied that recent contracts called for the "Great Western Mail" to be carried from Washington to Cincinnati in six days and to Louisville in eight. To accomplish this schedule, he continued, only three days could be allowed to reach Wheeling. The condition of the road would not allow this. "In many places, this road is represented to be so much out of repair as to be impassable to the mail stages," he informed the House. "They are driven in some instances through farms, and, in others, through the woods, to avoid these obstructions." Three years later the situation was so bad that mail contractors Moore & Stockton paid for repairs themselves at various points between Cumberland and Washington, Pennsylvania. Still, as late as 1847 conditions were such that at least one Ohio stage company was forced to employ oxen to get the coaches up certain hills.[5]

The Corps of Engineers' repair efforts in the 1830s removed many of the obstacles to getting the mail through, at least for a time. Their process, however, created a new obstacle. In the course of their work, the Engineers piled broken stone on the roadbed to be spread at a future time, forming a new impediment to travel. In reporting the problem, the *Examiner,* a Washington, Pennsylvania, newspaper, called on "the enlightened head" of the Post Office Department to pay forfeiture penalties for slow delivery.[6]

That "enlightened head" was Amos Kendall, a member of Andrew Jackson's "kitchen cabinet" as well as Old Hickory's postmaster general. A complicated personality, Kendall combined cynical and shrewd political instincts with altruism and a strong sense of duty. An example of the latter was Kendall's idea for an "express mail," which he instituted in 1836. Some historians would later dub it the "pony express," and indeed it did resemble in many ways the service that later operated between St. Joseph, Missouri, and Sacramento. In both cases wiry young riders galloped at a breakneck speed, carrying the mail between closely spaced relay stations. Both cut delivery times dramatically, and both proved to be financial losers, lasting under two years in each case.

At the time, virtually all US mail was carried by private contractors. It was delivered only to post offices, where individuals went to pick up their items. Under the system a letter could travel along a lengthy chain composed of numerous links. As a result, the incompetence of a single contractor or postmaster could slow deliveries. So, too, could problems with roads or equipment.[7]

Kendall foresaw a variety of lines radiating out from Washington, DC. One went north to New York, another southwest to New Orleans via Columbia, Milledgeville, Montgomery, and Mobile, and on to New Orleans by boat. The National Road would make up most of both the Washington to Cincinnati route and the Dayton to St. Louis route. Washington to Cincinnati service began on July 1, 1837. (Martin Van Buren had retained Kendall in his job.) The Dayton to

St. Louis operation began three months later. Postmasters had already received strict instructions concerning the service. Letters could not contain money, nor could they exceed half an ounce in weight. Neither pamphlets nor newspapers could be sent by express mail. "Newspaper slips," small single sheets, containing summaries of news items and market prices, were permitted. Finally, all items sent by express mail required triple the usual rate of postage.[8]

As the service got under way, the editor of the *Zanesville Gazette* was skeptical of Kendall's innovation. "The much talked of 'Express mail,' or rather the express saddlebags (for we doubt there being much mail) commenced running between Baltimore and Cincinnati," he wrote. Within a few weeks he had changed his mind about the service. A presidential message had reached the city in twenty-seven hours, the scribe enthused. Regular service had also improved, likely because of the roadwork of the Corps of Engineers. "Our New York papers were formerly so old when received as to be worthless, they are now and have been for some time received in a very reasonable time."[9]

The Vandalia editor of the *Illinois State Register* was also impressed with the express mail. He noted in December that the local contractor had "encountered many difficulties, and has overcome them without losing his time with any mail in a single instance." He had done so at a time when western streams were flowing at twenty-year highs and the Wabash had swollen to a mile and a half in width. "The performances of the riders, under all these adverse circumstances, are truly wonderful, and too much praise cannot be awarded to the activity and zeal which has set this vast machine in motion with such regularity," he concluded.[10]

The intrepid riders were as young as fifteen years of age. Fresh horses were waiting every five to seven miles, and the riders generally rode three daily circuits each way. There was virtually no delay at the relays. A fresh horse would be saddled, bridled, and waiting, and the youthful postilion would quickly slide over from one mount to the next. Those who rode from Cumberland to Uniontown received six dollars a month in silver for their wage. That group of riders worked for A. L. Littell, who received the contract for $5,000 a year. He later recalled:

It required a relay of nine horses on the road at once, and three boy riders. One boy left Cumberland at two o'clock in the morning, winter and summer, who rode three successive horses seven miles each, and so with the other two boys, performing the sixty-three miles in six hours and eighteen minutes. Going east they left Uniontown daily at one o'clock P.M., and rode the same horses back, and there was no office on this route where the mail was opened. At that time this express was the fastest overland mail in America, and it excited as much public interest as the arrival of a railroad train does now [ca. 1881] in a new town.[11]

The schedule called for the mail to go from Washington to Indianapolis in sixty-five and one-half hours, while the mail coaches took nearly seven days. In ideal conditions it could meet that schedule. It was not long, however, before inept contractors, who submitted unreasonably low bids, slowed the process. Bad roads and inclement weather also conspired against Kendall's project. Soon, despite the triple rate of postage, the express mail was losing money. In May 1838, less than a year after it was begun, the postmaster general discontinued the service. Thomas Searight penned a fitting eulogy: "'The Pony Express' did not remain long on the road, but when it was on, old pike boys say 'it kicked up a dust.'"[12]

※※※

Mail stages made tempting targets for robbers along the route, and while attempts were relatively rare, there were a few daring thieves willing to make the try. Among them was a pair of less than competent highwaymen who undertook to rob a Wheeling to Baltimore mail stage on the night of August 6, 1834. The two had cut some brush and thrown it across the road near the top of Savage Mountain, close to a gloomy pine grove known as the "Shades of Death." As the stage slowly ascended the mountain, one of the robbers sprung out from the brush and seized the bridle of the lead horse. After stopping the stage he ordered the driver to dismount. The man misjudged his intended victim, Samuel Luman, described as "a young man of splendid physique and perfectly fearless." Not only did he refuse to come down but he also aggressively applied the whip to his horses. The first robber cried to his accomplice, "Shoot the driver you damned coward, why don't you fire at him?" The reason was simple. The second man had taken a look at the baggage rack. Spotting a large number of trunks, he determined that the stage was also carrying a full load of passengers, one of whom might be armed. He therefore chose to avoid the doors of the coach, remaining safely behind the vehicle. At this point, the first man attempted to unhitch the traces, but Luman lashed his face with his whip, forcing him to lose his grip. The robber then leveled his pistol, a flintlock, at the driver, but it misfired, due perhaps to the evening fog. Luman then drove his team relentlessly until they reached the safety of Frostburg. The passengers gave their courageous driver a reward, one that a Cumberland editor considered inadequate. It led him to posit, "Query. Wonder if the safety of the mail and lives of the passengers were valued at only five dollars?"[13]

Even a successful robbery attempt did not guarantee a large haul. On the night of June 17, 1836, a stealthy thief stole a large mailbag from the boot of an eastbound stage about a mile east of Old Washington, Ohio. He cut the bag open and scattered its contents "in all directions." Unless he was seeking information, his effort was for naught. "The robber or robbers," the *Guernsey Times* reported, "made but a water-hawl, as fortunately the bag in question contained only newspapers."[14]

Equally unlucky was the miscreant who attempted to rob an express mail rider on the night of August 8, 1837. The robber concealed himself near a bridge that crossed Alum Creek, some three miles east of Columbus. As the rider approached, he rushed forward and seized the bridle reins in an attempt to stop the horse. The rider applied his whip, broke the man's hold, and continued on his way. The robber not only failed at his task, but he also received a lecture from the *Ohio State Journal*: "Highway gentlemen should remember that no money is ever sent by the Express Mail, and that therefore they are doing a bad business to risk detection for an act which cannot benefit them if successful."[15]

A pair of robberies took place between Columbus and Springfield in September 1837. The first happened on the night of the twenty-first and was apparently accomplished by stealth. Every letter on the stage was taken. The perpetrator was arrested two months later in Detroit. The man entered a bank and attempted to cash a $1,000 note drawn on a New Jersey canal company. The transaction aroused the suspicion of the bank's cashier. It turned out that the note had been mailed by a St. Louis merchant on September 14. The second robbery occurred west of Lafayette on the morning of the twenty-seventh. The theft was not detected until the stage reached Columbus. Local newspapers provided few details of the incident. Two robbers stopped a mail coach bound for Columbus about three miles east of Springfield on the night of March 9, 1840. They leveled their pistols at the driver and demanded the Cincinnati mailbag. After rifling through its contents, they left the bag along the road.[16]

In late February 1839, a sleepy wagon driver left Terre Haute heading west. He drove to the Wabash River ferry crossing and blew his horn to summon the boat. By the time it arrived he was, by his own admission, "fast asleep." His nap provided the robber with an opportunity to make off with the mailbag. A group of boys discovered the theft when they found some of the letters scattered along the banks of the river.[17]

Accounts of individual travelers being robbed on the road are virtually nonexistent. One of the few was reported on July 20, 1819. Two men were traveling together when a band of six or seven robbers confronted them on Laurel Mountain and ordered them off the road and into the woods. They tied the pair and relieved one of them of $150. The gang then returned their victims to the highway, one of them explaining that they did not wish to harm them but hoped some travelers would soon be along to release them.[18]

Certain sections of the road developed reputations for nefarious activities, although the evidence may have been more anecdotal than actual. William Oliver learned of one when he attempted to cross the Wabash into Terre Haute during a dark night in 1841. The ferry operator was tired and irritable following a busy day, vowing that he would not conduct any more passengers until morning. He added that the bottomland along the river was a dangerous place to be after dark. "You wont give over coming through that ere dark bottom till you get murdered," he warned. "It was only the other night that one got himself skivered between here and Paris. I wouldn't pass through that bottom after sundown for fifty dollars." After Oliver explained that he and his party were strangers to the country, the reluctant ferryman relented and carried them across. Oliver and his group continued safely on their way.[19]

In Effingham County, Illinois, one "Kit" Radly kept what he termed a hotel along the road. According to one local historian, the facility was in reality "a gambling den, which was for years the rendezvous of a gang of blacklegs and cutthroats as rough and worthless as himself." Rumor held that a number of travelers who stopped there were never again seen or heard from. "The general supposition seems to be that a systematic plan of robbery and murder was pursued for years on the unsuspecting passersby, but, as Radly was universally feared, no efforts toward an investigation were . . . made." After Radly died, his son, Nick, inherited the property. Nick appears also to have inherited his father's penchant for mischief. On several occasions he was arrested for "complicity in some very bold thieving scrapes." Once he reportedly threw a hatchet at a man who had been deputized for the purpose of arresting him. He left the county for parts unknown after savagely stabbing a man with whom he had gotten into an altercation.[20]

Perhaps the most accomplished robber along the National Road, at least in terms of the amount of his haul, was Dr. John F. Braddee, described as "the most notorious individual that ever lived in Uniontown." His background is murky, but Braddee was a native of Kentucky, where he was a servant to a prominent physician. His employer often sent horses east, and sometime in the 1820s he went along as an assistant on one of the drives. Along the way he fell ill. After recovering, Braddee, who was penniless, showed up in Uniontown. He immediately announced that he was a physician, and despite his lack of education, he soon enjoyed a thriving practice. As many as fifty horses could be seen hitched around his office as patients sought treatment and purchased such remedies as Braddee's Cordial Balm of Health and Cancer Salve. When not treating the masses, the doctor acquired racehorses and spent much of his time at the local track. He rose quickly in Uniontown society, despite a few brushes with the law and rumors of unsavory activities.[21]

Braddee's success allowed him to purchase the Old National House, one of Uniontown's most prominent properties. At the time he bought the place, it consisted of a three-story brick house. Braddee added a wing to the structure, which served as his office. It stood adjacent to Lucius Stockton's stage yard, a busy place that saw numerous arrivals every day. Many of the coaches delivered large mail sacks, a sight that was not lost on the good doctor.

Braddee recruited William Corman, a young and apparently gullible stagecoach driver. The doctor persuaded him that robberies of mail stages were common occurrences, they were never detected, and the participants always shared large hauls of money. They began the operation in 1839, but it was their activities beginning in late 1840 that attracted the attention of postal officials. Corman was driving between Smithfield and Uniontown at the time. At first Braddee sent Peter Mills Strayer, another accomplice, to meet the driver. Often riding in a sleigh, Strayer would take one of the bags from the coach while Corman was watering his horses at a remote point east of Laurel Mountain. Later, at intervals of one to two weeks, the driver would leave one mailbag in his coach when stages were changed at Uniontown. Braddee would then have an associate surreptitiously remove it. The doctor gave Corman three to five dollars from time to time, often telling him there had been nothing of value in the bags they stole.[22]

On about November 14, 1840, postal authorities noticed that the New York City mailbag had disappeared somewhere between Wheeling and Frederick, the first of seven such occurrences. The pouches included all the mail destined for New York from such points as Cincinnati, Louisville, Nashville, and St. Louis. According to Dr. Howard Kennedy, a special agent of the Post Office Department, they would have contained, on average, $20,000 to $30,000 apiece.

After investigating the matter, postal authorities determined that the sacks were going missing at or near Uniontown. They had already assumed that a driver had to be involved as an accomplice, and soon their suspicions centered on Corman. They secured an arrest warrant, and on the evening of January 7, 1841, Agent Kennedy arrived in Uniontown. He did not want to arrest Corman there for fear of alerting his cohorts. Instead Kennedy rode on the box with the unsuspecting driver on his run to Washington. Once he was apprehended, Corman "betrayed great alarm" and gave the local justice of the peace a detailed account of his activities. He not only implicated Braddee and Strayer, but also William Purnell, a clerk in the doctor's office. To the surprise of postal officials, Corman further confessed that their crimes dated back to November 1839, one year earlier than they had suspected.[23]

Braddee, Strayer, and Purnell were soon arrested, and Corman was returned to Uniontown, where he joined them in the county jail. The driver remained there, but a US marshal conducted the other three to a federal facility in Pittsburgh. According to the *Washington Reporter*, Braddee's arrest did not come as a surprise. "His life is dissolute and depraved," the paper observed, "and no doubt has existed for a long time, in the minds of the public, that his career is one of secret crime and perfidy." Meanwhile the *Washington Examiner*, a Democratic paper, was content to note that the men in custody had been active in Whig politics and "during the last canvass shouted lustily for 'Tippecanoe and Tyler too.'"[24]

Corman told investigators that Braddee had disposed of the mailbags, after he rifled through them, by throwing them into a privy on his property. They went there and located five sacks. A search of his barn uncovered treasury drafts, bank bills, and other paper valued at $30,000, all wrapped in a silk handkerchief. A few days later, a work crew making an excavation for a new street in the vicinity of the privy found another bag. Inside it they discovered letters dating back to 1839, which appeared to confirm more of Corman's story.[25]

Braddee and Strayer appeared before a judge on January 8, 1841, and both denied knowing anything about theft of the mail. Braddee was nevertheless convicted on June 4 and sentenced to ten years at hard labor. He took his own life in the Western Penitentiary in 1846. As soon as Braddee's conviction was announced, Strayer pleaded guilty. Corman and Purnell received presidential pardons, although it is not known to what extent their alleged Whig proclivities entered into John Tyler's decision. Purnell did not lack for nerve. He attempted to continue Braddee's medical practice, asserting that his close association with the convicted physician qualified him. The people of Uniontown did not seem to have agreed.[26]

A subsequent mail robbery revived memories of the Braddee episode. In March 1842 the Great Western Mail was robbed between Frostburg and Keyser's Ridge. Included in the plunder was nearly $40,000 in bank notes and drafts. Suspicion soon fell upon a number of persons who suddenly came into significant amounts of money, but definite evidence was lacking. Then, some five months later, authorities arrested Paden Sides, who had been a mail stage driver at the time of the robbery. A newspaper account of the arrest included the cryptic statement, "He is supposed to be connected with a gang of depredators of the Braddee School." It is not clear if this implied a direct connection with Braddee or a similar method of operation.[27]

Crime was rare along the road, at least in terms of reported incidents. How many solitary travelers became anonymous victims at places like the Shades of Death, the Wabash bottom, or Radly's hotel will never be known. The same is true of small-time mail robberies by one-time thieves who saw an opportunity and fought the temptation to try again. One thing is beyond doubt. Men like Braddee, who chose not to fight the temptation, as Thomas Searight would have agreed, certainly "kicked up a dust."

CHAPTER ELEVEN

"A peculiar class of men"
The Working Road

IF STAGECOACHES and their drivers captured the romantic imaginations of those living along the National Road, it was the Conestoga wagons and their profane "wagoners" that helped fulfill Washington and Jefferson's more practical dreams for the road. These vehicles linked the East Coast and the western frontier commercially. Both regions benefited from the trade they facilitated. And if plodding wagons did not offer the dash of the stagecoaches, they still managed to carve out their own niche in the folklore of the road.

The wagons took their name from a Native American tribe living in Maryland and eastern Pennsylvania when the first permanent English settlers reached Jamestown in 1607. Later attacked by the Iroquois, the tribe ceased to exist. Their memory survived through place names in Lancaster County, Pennsylvania. It was there that the earliest known reference to the vehicles is found. In 1750 the *Pennsylvania Gazette* made mention of a tavern named the "Conestoga Wagon." The wagons soon became a common sight on the road that ran between Lancaster and Philadelphia. Skilled labor for their construction was common in the region. By 1770 Lancaster itself boasted thirteen blacksmiths, five wheelwrights, twenty joiners, and seven turners.[1]

The wagon makers had to be skilled because, except for a saw and a turning lathe, they used only hand tools to create these 3,500-pound vehicles. They generally used white oak for the frame of the beds and poplar for the boards.

Wagon beds were about sixteen feet in length and four feet wide. They curved upward in the front and the rear, which transferred the weight of the load off the end gates if the cargo shifted while traversing the mountains. A series of wooden hoops, anywhere from six to thirteen in number, arched over the bed, and white canvas stretched over them.[2]

According to one historian of the vehicles, "The test of a good wagon was in its axles and hubs, and in their construction the wheelwright was most exacting." Axles were made from hickory wood, hubs from black gum, which is resistant to splitting. Iron rims covered the wooden wheels of the wagons, and attaching them taxed a blacksmith's skill. In the early days of the road the wheels were generally narrow, but over time they widened, four inches being the most common. This was for two reasons. First, the wider wheels were easier to extricate from muddy sections of the road. Second, after states took control of the road, the tolls they imposed were less for vehicles with wider wheels. The front wheels were generally about three and one-half feet high. The rear wheels ranged from four to four and one-half feet high. With a blue body, red running gear, and a white canvas top, the typical Conestoga wagon would have been right at home in an Independence Day parade. A new one cost about $250.[3]

The wagons were almost always pulled by six-horse teams, although occasionally eight equines bore the burden. The harness was as impressive as the wagons themselves. Back bands could be as wide as fifteen inches, hip straps as much as ten inches in width. Heavy black housing reaching the bottom of the hames protected the horses' shoulders. The traces were heavy hand-forged chains.[4]

According to one local historian, "Many experiments in different types of wagons were tried, but the standard conestoga was the one that best stood the test." Among those "experiments" was a wagon designed and built by a resident of Wheeling. Its tires were eight inches wide, the goal being to avoid tolls. Nine horses, three abreast, pulled it. The vehicle impressed the editor of the *Examiner*, a newspaper published in Washington, Pennsylvania. In May 1843 he wrote that local residents had seen the passing wagon "loaded with 96 hundred pounds; and the horses, several of which were of an inferior stock, moved with apparent ease." Despite this endorsement, the Wheeling wagon did not enjoy a long career on the road.[5]

※※※

The men who piloted the Conestoga wagons were invariably termed wagoners, not teamsters. They were, recalled one individual who grew up in eastern

Ohio, "a peculiar class of men, rough, hearty, whiskered and sunburned, fond of grog, voluble in their stories of adventure, and shockingly profane." Occasionally the wagoners worked in pairs, but the overwhelming majority traveled alone except for the bulldog that many tied to the rear of their wagons. While stagecoach drivers worked for one of the stage lines that sprang up along the road, wagoners were almost always independent operators. Among the rare exceptions were those who conducted "line teams," controlled by companies that changed horses every fifteen miles in an attempt to move shipments more quickly. Others made their own arrangements. Among them were wagoners Samuel and William Scarborough, who lived on a farm owned by William Hogg, a Brownsville merchant. To pay their rent, the brothers made a yearly trip to Baltimore, returning with a load of goods for Hogg's store.[6]

There were two classes of wagoners on the road. "Regulars" were the men who drove the large Conestoga wagons, making a career of the work. "Sharpshooters" were individuals, usually farmers living along the route, who hauled goods in their farm wagons when demand for shipping spiked or work on the farm slackened. The farm wagons they pressed into service tended to be smaller than the Conestoga wagons, with flat beds and narrow wheels. The regulars disdained the sharpshooters, whom they regarded as interlopers. This often resulted in heated arguments when two stubborn drivers refused to give way when meeting.[7]

The sharpshooters generally made shorter runs. For example, those who lived in Guernsey County, Ohio, seldom ventured farther east than Wheeling, some fifty miles away. Isaac Hurst, a sharpshooter from Fayette County, Pennsylvania, limited his activities to hauling flour from his father's mill to Cumberland. Another Fayette County resident, Robert Hogsett, sold corn from his own farm throughout the mountains as he ventured to Cumberland. He returned with loads of merchandise for Brownsville store owners.[8]

Two items became indelibly associated with the wagoners. One was the "hunting shirt," a woolen garment that many wore, covered by a cape trimmed in red. The second is the "stogie." The wagoners were inveterate tobacco users, and most shunned pipes for cigars. They also preferred their smokes to be cheap. To meet this demand, George Black, a Washington, Pennsylvania tobacconist, developed a slim cigar that he sold at a rate of four for a penny. Soon after Mifflin M. Marsh of Wheeling began turning out his own cheap cigars, founding a business that survived until 2001. At first dubbed "conestogas," the name was soon shortened to "stogies."[9]

※※※

Conestoga wagons were pulled by Conestoga horses, a breed whose lineage is unclear. They weighed about 1,800 pounds and were described as "docile and steady." Historians have placed their cost at anywhere from two hundred to twelve hundred dollars for a team of six. The wagoners did not make use of mules, which they considered too light in addition to being helpless in mud.[10]

The rear pair of horses, the "wheel horses," were attached to the wagon tongue. The wagoner put his best and heaviest horses in that position because they were responsible for turning and backing. The middle pair, known as "middle leaders," were hitched to doubletrees hung at the tongue. The "leaders" were hitched to a long chain fastened to the end of the tongue. The left side of the teams was the "near" side, and the right was the "off" side. The driver's saddle was on the near wheel horse, but he seldom used it. Typically the wagoners walked beside their teams, guiding them with a single line. A bar connected the bridle bits of the two leaders, meaning when one turned, so did the other. Both verbal and physical signals guided the teams. A steady pull on the line and the command "haw" called for a left turn. Two or three short jerks and the command "gee" were the signal for a right turn.[11]

If those signals were not enough, the wagoners also wielded five-foot-long whips. Battley White of Washington County, Pennsylvania, made the ones most favored, a rawhide instrument. The "Loudon whip," produced in Loudon, Pennsylvania, featured "an elastic wooden stock." It was rarely used by National Road wagoners but preferred by drivers along the Glade Road, a highway that ran from Pittsburgh to Philadelphia.[12]

A minority of wagoners attached bells to their teams. They were cone-shaped with an open end and were connected to a thin iron arch sprung over the tops of the hames, three to five composing a set. The bells remained in memory long after the road's freighting days were over, becoming an important element of the "romance of the pike." One legend, often repeated, held that a wagoner who pulled another out the mud or some other difficulty could claim his beneficiary's bells.[13]

The regular drivers averaged about fifteen miles a day. Sharpshooters, with their lighter wagons, could cover twenty miles. The average load ranged from six thousand to eight thousand pounds. Occasionally the wagoners boasted of hauling "a hundred hundred," a cargo of ten thousand pounds, shipments they got over the mountains with difficulty. The freight rates ranged from $1.75

to $6.00 per hundred pounds. Distance played a role in how much the men received. In 1846 a pair of wagoners arrived in Terre Haute after a two-month journey from Hagerstown, Maryland. They received six dollars a hundred.[14]

The men earned their pay, especially in mountainous country. "They had no trouble getting up," former wagoner John Deets recalled of his colleagues, "but the trouble was getting down." Locking the wheels tightly would soon wear them out. Instead many wagoners cut a small pole about ten feet long and tied it to the bed with a lock chain, bent it against a rear wheel, and tied it to the rear of the bed. According to Deets, the men would wear out fifteen to twenty poles between Baltimore and Wheeling.[15]

Icy mountain roads complicated the process. Often the wagoners would utilize a rough lock, which was a short chain with large, rough links, and an ice cutter, which resembled a small sled and was secured to the rear wheels. Despite these precautions, Deets conceded, "The wagon would sometimes be straight across the road, if not the hind end foremost." Snow could be so deep that it forced the wagoners to go through fields, shoveling drifts as they went. If conditions were bad enough, they engaged sleds to get their cargos over Negro Mountain. At the Monongahela and Ohio Rivers, where the drivers had to ferry across, winter often meant waiting several days until ice floes passed or the channel froze over.[16]

Whether it was warm or cold, the wagons had to be greased. Drivers carried their own tar pots, which they hung from a hook on the rear axle. They stopped and heated them about every fifty miles, applying the tar to friction points after jacking up the wagon and removing the wheels. One wagoner was said to have remarked, "A good driver is known by the amount of tar he gits on Wheels and not on hisself."[17]

On June 6, 1832, Rep. T. M. T. McKennan of Pennsylvania, a future secretary of the interior, rose to speak in the United States House chamber. Before the National Road was completed, he intoned, it had cost between $120 and $200 a ton to haul goods from Baltimore to the Ohio River, and it had taken from four to six weeks. After the road was built it took half the time and cost half as much. In Illinois, according to a local historian, the realities of freight transportation were more informal. "People could go to Terre Haute, and even to St. Louis, and thus reach markets and sell the little portable stuff they had, and buy such things as their necessities demanded and haul them home."[18]

The bulk of the freight traffic flowed between Wheeling and Cumberland, thence on to Baltimore and back. The "down loads," as those moving eastward were termed, consisted largely of farm products. Bacon made up a large portion of these cargoes. Charles and James Brownlee of Washington County, Pennsylvania, drove exclusively for a local pork packer. A school teacher, traveling in the vicinity of Wheeling, recorded in her diary that she had seen 105 wagons, all laden with flour, headed for Baltimore. In 1842 John Snider hauled a load of butter from Wheeling to Washington, DC. He sold some along the way but delivered the bulk of his shipment safely to the capital.[19]

In 1825 tobacco was added to the list of farm products shipped from eastern Ohio. Some 120,000 pounds were raised in the vicinity of Zanesville that year. Soon a daily line of wagons, each transporting over two tons of the crop, was on the roll, making the journey from Wheeling to Baltimore in eight days. A Wheeling newspaper reported that the National Road was "literally covered" with wagons bound for Baltimore. The tobacco was shipped in hogsheads, which were about four feet high and three and one-half feet in diameter at the bulge. They weighed from nine to eleven hundred pounds. In 1835 a wagoner was en route to Wheeling with eleven hogsheads. Some locals at St. Clairsville persuaded him to pause and weigh his laden wagon on the hayscales. It weighed in at 13,280 pounds. The six-horse team later ascended a hill of eight degrees from the river into Wheeling "with ease." This prompted the editor of the *St. Clairsville Gazette* to remark, "The Buckeyes of Belmont [County] may challenge competition in this line."[20]

As wagoners returned westward, they brought with them a variety of goods, many intended for merchants along the route. These included firearms, clocks, medicines, spices, books, linens, window glass, furniture, soap, pottery, and glassware. Heavier loads included such items as lead, nails, millstones, and iron. The wagoners almost always knew the destination of the goods they were bringing, having made previous arrangements. An exception was Robert Bell, who often bought the goods he carried, selling them to individuals along the road from his rolling store. Despite a reputation for honesty, he was known to people along the route as "Stingy Robert."[21]

In the early 1830s Col. Henry Orndorff, owner of a Zanesville hotel, arranged to have fresh oysters shipped from the coast, retailing them locally and selling them as far away as Columbus and Chillicothe. Fifteen years later George W. Cass established a line of daily express wagons, traveling at the speed of a stagecoach, solely to deliver oysters from Cumberland to the Ohio River. Described as a "box upon four wheels," the wagons were twelve feet long, six to seven feet high, and five feet wide. They were further described as "dangerous and very liable to topple."[22]

Before the Baltimore & Ohio Railroad (B&O) reached Wheeling, wagon traffic on the road was immense. As one historian of the road observed, "Warehouses in Cumberland, during spring and autumn, were congested with towering piles of goods waiting to be moved." This was particularly true after the B&O was completed to the western Maryland city in 1842. Over fifty wagons would depart from the loading platforms in one day. They clogged the road to a point that stagecoach drivers became annoyed as they waited at bridges and ferry crossings.[23]

According to a story related by former wagoner Jesse J. Peirsol, a break in the Pennsylvania Canal in the mid-1840s created a sudden and tremendous demand for wagons. By sunrise the next morning, Peirsol was at a warehouse in Brownsville, where he secured a load of tobacco, bacon, and wool, "and whipped off for Cumberland." Once there he discovered warehouses and freight cars filled with goods. Armed guards stood vigil on the platforms, keeping watch over large boxes of merchandise. The wagoner secured a load, which he returned to Brownville at a rate of $1.25 a hundred.

Peirsol loaded up again, went back to Cumberland, and returned with a shipment for a Wheeling merchant, this time earning $2.25 a hundred. "In coming back," he recalled, "it looked as if the whole earth was on the road; wagons, stages, horses, cattle, hogs, sheep, and turkeys without number." Cumberland's merchants, seeing all the wagons, tried to reduce the rates. This led to a meeting of the wagoners, who decided to make "a vigorous kick against the proposed reduction." The strike held until a pair of sharpshooters drove their wagons to one of the warehouses, prepared to haul at the lower rate. When the regulars found out, they descended on the two men, pelting them with buckets, oyster cans, and whatever else they could grab. Police ended the melee, and the sharpshooters loaded. They drove sixteen miles out of town only to discover the next morning that their harness had been cut and their axles sawed off.[24]

⚹⚹⚹

During the summer months, wagoners generally camped out with their teams. In colder weather they sought the shelter of a "wagon house." These facilities were more numerous than the inns that catered to stage drivers and their passengers. They were most often located in the country or on the edges of towns because they required ample space to accommodate Conestoga wagons and their teams. The wagon houses tended to be smaller than inns, and they offered far fewer amenities. The greater number of them were log or frame structures.[25]

Upon reaching a wagon house, the driver first saw to his team. He removed feeding troughs from the rear of his wagon and attached them to the wagon tongue, filled them with grain, and tied the horses to feed. Spring water was always available close by. Wagoners did not shelter their equines except in extremely inclement winter weather. Instead they covered them with blankets to protect the animals from the elements.[26]

Only after they had tended to their horses did the wagoners see to their own needs. All had their own bedding, which they carried into the main room of the wagon house and tossed on the floor. Generally it was little more than just a straw tick bed and a blanket. A pump in the yard provided a place to wash off the road dust, and a single towel hanging on the porch served all the guests. The drivers then enjoyed a meal of ham and eggs, beef steak, or trout. Also generally available were hot cakes, fried potatoes, cheese, pie, and cake. Meals usually cost twelve and one-half cents. At the inns, whiskey was three cents a glass or two for a nickel. For $1.15 a wagoner could procure two meals, feed for his horses, all the drinks he desired, and a place to sleep. Both black and white wagoners gathered together at the wagon houses, but they dined at segregated tables.[27]

After supper the men drank, sang, engaged in practical jokes that could border on the cruel, and swapped stories about life on the road. Wagon stands whose proprietors were adept with a fiddle were especially popular because the men particularly enjoyed a "hoe down," with as many as forty boisterous wagoners dancing to their host's music.[28]

The frolicking generally ended around midnight, when the men spread their bedding for their night's rest. They lay on the floor side by side, sleeping, as one later recalled, "with their feet near the fire, as soundly as under the paternal roof." As was the case at taverns, the fireplaces that kept them warm throughout the night were enormous. Some were open hearths capable of holding six-foot logs. Others were deep iron grates, where a wagonload of wood or a ton of soft coal was burned. The keeper presided over the fire with a poker, a possession many of them prized. Indeed, this was so important a duty that one wagon stand owner was said to keep his poker under lock and key.[29]

As the B&O stretched to the west, the Conestoga wagon became less and less significant. When the railroad reached Wheeling, the wagoners composed a poem concerning their plight that they often repeated. If not on a par with Keats, it offered an accurate assessment:

Now all ye jolly wagoners, who have got good wives,

Go home to your farms, and there spend your lives,

When your corn is all cribbed, and your small grain is good,

You'll have nothing to do but curse the railroad.[30]

CHAPTER TWELVE

"A continual stream"

The Moving Road

In late 1824 William Owen and his father, both natives of Scotland, came to America to inspect land in Indiana for possible purchase. On November 30 they reached Cumberland. Even before then, "We met continually droves of hogs, often 600 together, being driven, usually from Ohio and even Indiana." Three years earlier Englishman William Blaine wrote that he had "met vast droves of hogs, four or five thousand in a drove, going from the State of Ohio across the mountains to the Eastern States." His fellow countryman John Lewis Peyton, who traversed the highway in 1849, recalled, "It was soon obvious we were approaching a land of abundance, for we met daily droves, and large ones, of kindly, well-fed, and handsomely-shaped bullocks, weighing on an average, nine hundred pounds."[1]

Hog droving from Ohio predated statehood, going back to the late 1700s. In the early days the hogs were feral beasts, "long of limb and tremendous of snout," according to the recollections of someone who grew up along the road. They roamed the woods, subsisting on the mast of beech, oak, and hickory trees. When young, their owners marked them for identification. It was a cruel process that involved cutting notches or holes in their ears or slicing off portions of one or both ears, creating what were termed "full-crops," "half-crops," or "swallow-forks." The owners recorded these marks at the county courthouse, and they became as indisputable as cattle brands.[2]

Between one and one-half and three years of age the animals were considered ready for sale. Some farmers ventured eastward themselves, but many engaged professional drovers. Shrewd businessmen, they purchased as cheaply as possible and had no qualms about doing anything to maximize their profits. For example, many would give the hogs salt as they approached Baltimore then load them up with water, increasing their weight and, of course, their selling price.

Most droving was done in autumn, winter, and early spring, when lower temperatures made for more comfortable travel and less weight loss. After a drover had put a neighborhood under contract, he would show up on an appointed day, accompanied by a crew of men, boys, and dogs. They would scour the woods and drive the hogs into a field surrounded by a strong, tall fence. Riders on horseback, abetted by the dogs, then chased them around the field until they were tired enough to be handled and weighed. Many of the animals were reluctant to leave their native woods, often leading drovers to resort to cruel measures. Some would sew down their eyelids so they could not see to return, while others filled their eyes with sand, accomplishing the same purpose.[3]

While the exact number of hogs driven eastward is uncertain, there is no doubt that it was significant. In 1856 a Cincinnati newspaper put the number for that year at nearly half a million. An innkeeper near Somerfield, Pennsylvania, recalled that droves of four or five hundred were not uncommon and insisted that one included 1,323 "by actual count." Another reported that nearly one hundred droves passed his stand during the course of one year. In late 1848 a Cumberland newspaper reported that there were about twenty thousand hogs at that city awaiting railroad transport to Baltimore. "It is also stated," the paper added, "that the National Road is literally lined with hogs, and that corn is becoming scarce, west of Cumberland." The size of the droves occasionally grew when drovers purchased hogs en route from farmers headed to market who had grown weary of the road and were eager to return home.[4]

It did not take long for wild hogs to disappear from the scene. Farmers bred them with animals imported from Europe, creating domesticated breeds that were easier for their owners to lead to market. Still, it was not unusual to see a man at the head of the drove scattering shelled corn to bait them along. The journey over the mountains was especially arduous. Frozen roads would often halt the drovers for two or three days because they cut the hogs' feet and made them lame. Many avoided the mountains altogether. Indiana and Illinois drovers would often divert to Cincinnati, whose many packinghouses earned the Queen City the less romantic nickname "Porkopolis." Ohio hogs often headed westward toward the same destination—and the same fate.[5]

As time went on, cattle replaced hogs as the primary livestock driven on the National Road. Transmontaine cattle drives began in the late 1700s, when Kentucky farmers began taking their stock to eastern markets over the Wilderness Road, which passed through the Cumberland Gap. To the north, cattle were also driven from the Ohio River town of Point Pleasant, (West) Virginia through the Kanawha River Valley on what was known as the Old State Road.[6]

The first known cattle drive eastward from Ohio occurred in the spring of 1805, when George Renick drove sixty-eight head over the mountains from the Scioto Valley. Renick had settled along the river near Chillicothe in 1802. At the time the area was beginning to emerge as a major cattle-raising region. Farmers at first had to import grain from Pittsburgh, but by 1803 their neighbors were producing surpluses of corn, catching up with the demand. Stock raisers were well aware of the possibilities offered by eastern markets. At the same time, they were equally cognizant of the risks, worrying that their stock would be of little or no value after making the difficult journey. Renick's drive, which terminated in Philadelphia, proved to be a profitable success, and others quickly followed.[7]

The Scioto Valley's feedlots soon proved to be a magnet for western cattlemen. As America's farm population spread westward, herds from Illinois were driven east into Ohio to be fed and fattened before moving on to eastern cities. By 1820 at least five thousand were arriving there annually. They remained outdoors during their time in Ohio, pasturing in the summer and being fed corn and grass in open lots in the winter.[8]

As with hogs, farmers sometimes drove their own cattle to the markets and sometimes engaged professional drovers. In the summer of 1846, a Columbus newspaper reported that "one of the finest lots of steers and heifers" ever seen had passed through the city. A speculator from New York state had come to nearby Madison County to purchase them and was driving them himself. The drovers conducted two grades of cattle over the mountains. Three-year-old "stock cattle" were destined for eastern Pennsylvania, where farmers purchased them to fatten for future sales. Four-year-old bullocks, already well fattened, went straight to the stockyards of eastern cities.[9]

William Oliver, an Englishman who spent much of 1841 in Illinois, described the start of a drive. "The drovers come into the country in the beginning of a summer, or as soon as there is a sufficiency of grass to afford a supply to their droves on their passage through the woods," he wrote. After a drover had purchased as many head as he wanted in a certain neighborhood, he would announce a rendezvous day for all to be assembled at a crossroads or near a village. According to Oliver, "On the evening previous to the appointed day, herds are seen approaching in all directions across the prairie, attended by men on horseback." The drover and his assistants were waiting. They drove the animals they intended to take east into a strongly fenced enclosure as those rejected bolted across the prairies to return home.[10]

One of the terms of the bargain was that farmers selling to the drovers had to supply someone to assist in getting the drive started. These individuals generally remained with it for about a mile. If Oliver's assessment of the start of a drive is accurate, they were needed. The horsemen positioned themselves to stay between the cattle and the woods, the potential route of escape. "The barriers were pulled down, and out rushed the cattle pellmell amidst a torrent of shouts and yells." It was with difficulty that the men kept the herd together, and while a few would bolt away, the well-trained horses helped keep most in line.[11]

Once the drive was under way, the drover was known simply as "the boss," and he had absolute control of the operation. Depending on the size of the herd, his crew ranged from three to seven members. A man or boy, leading an ox with a rope attached to its horn, walked in front. The boss rode behind the first forty head much of the time, occasionally riding ahead to seek the best river crossing, to find a place to rest the herd at midday, or to make arrangements at a "drove stand" for spending the night. One or more riders remained on the flank to keep the stock in place while passing beside a forest. Another member of the crew, generally on foot, remained at the rear of the herd.[12]

The boss, the flank riders, and the man bringing up the rear all wielded "black snake" whips. According to an individual who conducted three droves east, a harness maker in Centerville, a village in Belmont County, Ohio, turned out the best whips and did so at reasonable prices. "These whips had linen or silken crackers and when used by a man who knew how, would make a report like the firing of a rifle," the drover recalled.[13]

Although the National Road was well south of the cattle regions of Illinois, herders utilized the highway because there were no passable east-west roads in the northern part of the state. The same was true in Indiana, where good roads ran south from the state's stock-raising regions to Indianapolis. Once in Ohio, cattle destined for the feedlots of the Scioto Valley often turned south onto other routes at Springfield. They were replaced by Licking County herds that met the road at Jacksontown, or Fairfield County stock that reached it at Zanesville. Cambridge was a dividing point. Herds bound for New York and, to an extent, Philadelphia headed northeast on the road to Steubenville. Those going to Baltimore remained on the highway. Some destined for Philadelphia also stayed on the National Road, turning northeast at Cumberland or Frederick.[14]

Stock cattle covered about nine miles a day, fat steers seven. When the drovers put stock hogs behind the cattle, the drive slowed. Many chose to do so, however, due to economic considerations. The hogs would consume the corn that the cattle wasted, so bringing them along cost virtually nothing.[15]

The drovers faced a variety of problems along the way. The stones that garnished the macadamized sections of the road cut the cattle's feet to the point that the bovines could be rendered lame. Blacksmiths along the route were able to address this threat by shoeing the animals with the aid of stalls and machinery that lifted the steers. A few members of the herd would usually drown when large streams had to be forded, and ferrymen were always ready to gouge drovers wishing to avoid this hazard. To minimize the expense, drovers would put the ox and ten to twelve steers on a single boat. They became the leaders of the herd, the rest following behind by swimming the river. East of the Ohio more dangers lurked in the form of poisonous mountain laurel and wolves eager for a meal of beef.[16]

Contemporary newspapers do not contain accounts of stampedes along the National Road. One historian of the beef cattle industry in Ohio, however, observed that getting the herds through villages was difficult. "The cattle were likely to fright," he observed, "at children playing, horses being trotted along the street, or the pounding of a village blacksmith." A resident of Granville, Ohio, located about eight miles north of the road, recalled of the highway passing through his hometown, "Sometimes it happened [the drovers] would be passing through town on Sunday morning when the bells were ringing for church, and occasionally it would cause a stampede." The droving crews, the man added, would make great exertions to set the animals in the right direction. If they did not succeed, "The whole herd would be galloping back in an irresistible tide."[17]

The drovers also faced economic concerns. Often, when they were some three or four days from their destination, speculators would ride out to greet them. These men, who were well posted on the current market reports, would try every trick to persuade the drovers to sell at bargain prices. They offered tales of depressed and glutted markets, and occasionally they would fool a rookie drover. The veterans, however, were usually immune to their inducements.[18]

On July 1, 1841, Benjamin Franklin Harris started from Illinois to Pennsylvania on what would be his seventh, and last, drive. At 430 head, it was also his largest herd. Along the way, "Frank" Harris left his wife with her father in Circleville, Ohio. The year had been extremely dry in the East. The grass had dried up, and Pennsylvania farmers were less than eager to buy cattle. As he headed eastward, Harris met a number of drovers returning from Lancaster who advised him to turn back. Many had been forced to sell at a loss, sacrificing three or four years' profits in the process. Harris decided to press on, feeling he could not afford to return with his herd. He would hold on to his cattle until cold weather set in, and he would return to Circleville to fetch his wife, concluding, "If wife was with me I could hold out longer." In the meantime fortuitous rains fell, the grass grew, and the demand for cattle grew with it. Because his expenses were high, Harris's profits were slim, but he at least turned a profit, avoiding financial disaster.[19]

Drove stands provided overnight accommodations for drovers, their crews, and their herds. Like ferry operators, proprietors of these facilities would often take advantage of any opportunity to overcharge for their services. To avoid this, many drovers sought out farmhouses, whose owners tended to offer more reasonable rates. According to one drover, Ezekiel Bundy, whose farm was located just east of Barnesville, Ohio, enjoyed a sterling reputation as a host. "He set the best table and furnished the best beds to sleep in, of any of them, and his bills were not higher than those whose accommodations were much inferior." Grazing for the night was usually five cents a head, although drovers who were adept at negotiating could sometimes reduce the cost to just a dollar for a herd of a hundred head. Lodging for the human members of the party ranged from thirty-seven to eighty-seven cents per person. The crew might instead pay a group rate of three to nine dollars, which included meals. Sometimes the boss would trade calves born along the way or sick animals for accommodations.[20]

✳✳✳

According to one historian of the road, "No more stupid creatures ever thronged the road than thousands of sheep with their witless antics and mournful baa-baa." He supported his assertion by writing of a traveler shocked as he witnessed "the dumb beasts follow one another to their death over a Pennsylvania cliff." A tavern keeper located near Uniontown agreed, observing that while he would willingly host herds of cattle or hogs, he did not want either sheep or shepherds at his establishment. He had three reasons: "1. Sheep were damned fools. 2. So were shepherds. 3. Both smelled."[21]

Those views notwithstanding, merino sheep, introduced to Ohio during the first decade of the nineteenth century, held out the promise of extraordinary profits. At a time when ordinary wool was bringing about forty cents a pound, the merinos' long fleece was fetching $2.75. So prized were the Spanish animals that Paul Fearing of Marietta reportedly traded 1,600 acres of land for a full-blooded ram in 1811. Heavy importation soon brought prices down to a more reasonable level, but they remained a sound investment. By the early 1820s, a Pennsylvania storekeeper estimated that 50,000 sheep had passed his establishment during a twelve-month period. More definite figures came from Ohio's superintendent of the road. During the year ending November 30, 1835, he reported that 69,105 sheep, 54,207 hogs, and 105,912 head of cattle had passed through the state's eleven tollgates. Many, of course, had passed through more than one gate. Gate 3 had the greatest number of sheep at 8,586. Gate 5 saw the most hogs with 8,397, and Gate 7 passed the highest number of cattle, 14,540.[22]

While hogs, cattle, and sheep generally headed eastward, horses, usually driven in groups of about twenty, went both ways. Virginia breeders drove their animals to Wheeling, often taking them all the way to Vandalia. They were tied by halters, in pairs, to a rope running from the axle of a buggy in front, back to another buggy at the rear. They averaged about twenty-two miles a day. Mules also passed over the road, most coming east from Missouri.[23]

Great flocks of fatted geese and turkeys could be seen along the road as holidays approached. In most cases they were herded into pens as night fell. Others, especially on the western section of the road, were crammed by the dozens into coops placed on wagons covered with ducking. The men who drove these wagons were known as "marketers." Many drove their loads west to St. Louis.[24]

※※※

Sadly, droving along the National Road was not limited to livestock. Both Maryland and Virginia were slave states, and the highway through Pennsylvania was a convenient route connecting the two. "Some of the old citizens of Uniontown," Thomas Searight wrote in the 1890s, "well remember the time, when scores of poor slaves were driven through that place, handcuffed and tied two and two to a rope that was extended some 40 or 50 feet, one on each side." An Ohio traveler left a graphic account of one such drive:

> In the winter of 1828–29, I put up for a night at [Frostburg], on the national road. Soon after there came a slaver with a drove of slaves. I then left the room and shortly afterwards heard a scream, and when the landlady inquired the cause, the slaver

cooly told her not to trouble herself, he was only chastising one of his women. . . . It appeared that three days previously her child had died on the road and been thrown into a crevice in the mountain, and the mother weeping for her child was chastened by her master, and told by him, she "should have something to cry for."[25]

Few people living along the road in the allegedly free state of Pennsylvania seem to have objected to their state's role in the interstate slave trade. Among those who did was the editor of the *Washington Examiner*. On November 15, 1825, he wrote that three droves had passed through his community in the previous three months. "The men in two of the droves were all chained together by the necks and hands," he reported, "and such was the cruel brutality and mock cry of suffering on the part of the drivers, that they were compelled to sing and shout as they passed through our town, that we might see and be convinced how happy they were." Describing one of those drives of human beings, he wrote, "A number of negroes, chained and hand cuffed, were driven through our town towards Wheeling. The poor creatures were not only thus manacled, but there was also an iron collar round the neck of each, and a large chain bound them together two and two like a team of horses."[26]

✳✳✳

As William Owen and his father ventured west in 1824, they overtook "several parties of emigrants, all bound for Ohio." Traveling over the road in Pennsylvania in 1849, Englishman John Lewis Peyton observed of the pioneers heading west, "We were seldom out of sight of them." To the editor of the *Indiana Democrat,* writing during the fall of 1834, they were "one moving mass." He added, "Never have we seen such a number of travelers and movers, and it is with pleasure that we behold this general influx of wealth and population to our borders." The editor of the *St. Clairsville Gazette* was also pleased to welcome the emigrants. Of those passing through the Ohio community in the spring of 1839 he wrote, "Such are the emigrants we want to open the forest or prairie, to cultivate the boundless plains, to make improvements, to rear villages and towns, to open roads, canals, &c., to build schools and public edifices, and to diffuse the blessings of civilization."[27]

Despite the enthusiasm of the *Gazette* editor, historians have tended to downplay the importance of the National Road as a conduit for western expansion. It started with Archer Butler Hulbert, whose pioneering book on the highway was published in 1904. "The Cumberland Road was not to Indiana and Illinois what it was to Ohio," he wrote, "for somewhat similar reasons that it was less to Ohio than to Pennsylvania, for the further west it was built the older the century grew, and the newer the means of transportation which were coming rapidly to the front." Since then others have pointed out that Ohio had been a state for twenty-two years by the time construction began there. Indiana joined the Union in 1816, and Illinois entered two years later. Work on the road through the Hoosier State began eleven years after statehood, and a dozen years later in Illinois.[28]

Clearly the road arrived too late to be a factor in creating the states through which it passed, nor in the population explosions that immediately followed statehood in Ohio, Indiana, and Illinois. However, anecdotal evidence, while indefinite by its very nature, strongly suggests that subsequent waves of settlers made extensive use of the road. Owen, Peyton, and the editors of the Indianapolis and St. Clairsville newspapers are among numerous observers who testified to heavy emigrant traffic passing over it. Historians who point to the fact that many pioneers left the road at Wheeling to continue down the Ohio are correct. Their argument, however, ignores an important point. By the time they reached Wheeling, the National Road had made the most difficult portion of the journey, the arduous passage over the Appalachians, much easier than it would have otherwise been.[29]

A man who grew up along the road in Indiana described the emigrant traffic between June and November: "From morning till night there was a continual rumble of wheels, and, when the rush was greatest, there was never a minute that wagons were not in sight, and, as a rule, one company of wagons was closely followed by another." Others were more specific. M. H. Jenks, in his journey from Ohio to Indiana in 1838, wrote that the Dayton Cutoff "was lined with immigrants." He counted fifty families in just one day, even though Jenks was traveling in the same direction. The *St. Clairsville Gazette,* which hailed the arrival of emigrant parties, reported that twenty wagons had rolled through the community on May 18, 1825, although the road was not yet begun in Ohio. Forty more passed through during the next three days. The emigrants were, the paper added, "cheerful and contented . . . and many had every appearance of being wealthy."[30]

In 1834 a resident of Richmond, Indiana, took it upon himself to take a census of immigration. In October he informed the *Palladium* that 427 wagons, bearing 2,005 individuals, had passed through the town on the National Road. In May 1836 the same paper reported that forty wagons had been counted in one day. Finally, in October 1840, the *Palladium* reported that 544 wagons went through Richmond during a five-week period. Most were from Ohio and were destined for either Illinois or Missouri.[31]

In recalling the National Road's salad days, an Illinois resident placed the emigrants in two categories. "First," he insisted, "there was the poverty-stricken class who plainly had reason to be looking for a better country." He described their wagons as "rickety," their horses as "sway-backed," the women as "slatterny," and the children as "dirty-faced [and] frowsy-headed." The other class, he asserted, was of a "vastly more attractive type." Their horses were "fat and sleek," their wagons "staunch," their women and children "clean and neat in their apparel and modest and well-mannered."[32]

His observations were vastly oversimplified. At the same time, all emigrants were not equal in their socioeconomic circumstances, and they headed west in a variety of conveyances that reflected those circumstances. Some were able to travel in expensive Conestoga wagons, pulled by teams of four or six horses. The bulk of families, composing a "middle-class" of travelers, went in two-horse wagons. A few had two of these vehicles. Inside were bedding, household goods, and farming utensils. Some brought packhorses, which carried extra clothing and other supplies. Sometimes cattle, sheep, or hogs trailed the wagons. Often the family dog, tied to the wagon, brought up the rear.[33]

Less affluent families started west with small one-horse wagons. Some did so to avoid the higher tolls that larger vehicles were charged, knowing horses could be purchased at comparatively cheap prices in the western country. To avoid taxing the solitary animals' strength, the older family members seldom rode in the wagon unless the weather was inclement. The father could generally be seen leading the horse. His wife and the older children walked a short distance behind. The older boys generally saw to the livestock.

Individual travelers often rode packhorses, and both individuals and families could be seen walking, carrying with them all their possessions or pushing them along in hand wagons. In the fall of 1833 a Cambridge, Ohio, newspaper described a passing party of emigrants: "It consisted of a wagon filled with such articles of furniture, &c. as usually belong to a emigrating establishment bound for the 'far west'—drawn by two men and a boy, all duly harnessed, acting in the capacity and doing the work of a team of horses!" The paper added that the group, composed of German immigrants, "appeared cheerful and patient in the exercise of their laborious employment."[34]

Families covered eighteen to twenty miles a day. Most traveled individually, but sometimes five or ten families would compose a wagon train, a sight that one witness described as "quite lengthy and imposing." In the spring of 1834, a Richmond, Indiana, newspaper reported that a caravan of some two hundred Mormons "with a long train of wagons" passed through the town. Seven years later a traveler in western Indiana encountered another group of Latter Day Saints, "bound to some place in Missouri, where there is a settlement consisting entirely of that sect of religionists."[35]

Most emigrant wagons were covered with a white cotton sheet or blanket, furnishing cover for sleeping. If a family was too large to fit in the wagon, and with eight or more children many were, a sheet thrown over four saplings provided an improvised tent. If camping kept expenses low, it was not without its drawbacks—at least one emigrant complaining of stagecoaches running all night and keeping her family awake.

West of the Ohio, the emigrants found hotels bearing signs proclaiming, "Rooms for Movers." Some appear to have been operated by earlier emigrants, offering bargain prices to those who followed. After staying at one in Etna, Ohio, just east of Columbus, one grateful traveler wrote, "We staid all night . . . at a house kept to acomodate movers we took a room and got our breakfast there it went very good to sit and eat instead of standing." A native of Richmond, Indiana, later recalled that these establishments were located at five- to six-mile intervals and were "well patronized."[36]

✳✳✳

As the road worked its way west, a number of towns and villages grew up. Among those founded in Pennsylvania were Centreville, a Washington County community so named because it was roughly equidistant between Uniontown and Washington. Three miles to the west, Jonathan Knight surveyed the site of Beallsville. In September 1819 the public was informed that they could purchase lots at a public auction that month. Two months earlier an auction had been held a few miles west at the new village of Hillsborough. A post office opened that October. The town's name was later changed to Scenery Hill. Some two miles east of Washington, Pancake was established, named in honor of George Pancake, a local tavern keeper. Over the years residents changed its name to Martinsburg and later Laboratory. (Lots were sold on December 17, 1819, for another town named Martinsburg, this one located midway between Washington and Claysville.)

When tavern keeper John Purviance learned that the National Road would pass by his establishment, he surveyed and laid out lots for the town of Claysville, naming his town in honor of one of the road's most prominent congressional supporters. He auctioned off the lots on May 18, 1817. The first major community west of Washington, Claysville grew quickly. The same year Purviance established his town, Charles De Hass added a number of lots to the village of West Alexander, located on the Virginia border.[37]

On July 29, 1829, the Commonwealth of Virginia granted a charter for the village of Triadelphia. Josias Thompson, the National Road surveyor, owned most of the property on which the town was located and became the first mayor. Thompson, John D. Foster, and Aurasa Brown received the charter, thus the word "Triad" gave the town its name.[38]

Although southeastern Ohio was well settled by the time the road arrived, the project led to the establishment of a few new settlements. In February 1830 Charles Hendry announced that he was offering for sale "a number of lots in a town he has recently laid out and called Hendrysburg." Located in western Belmont County, the community was twenty-five miles west of Wheeling. "Its distance from Wheeling," he assured potential buyers, "will prevent from having its business injured by that place." Hendry added that he planned to erect a steam mill, a rolling mill, a carding machine, and "an extensive Distillery."[39]

In March 1828 Judge Davis Findley, who had lived in the area since 1806, laid out the town of Concord on the eastern edge of Muskingum County. Soon businesses from nearby Zane's Trace relocated to the new village, which adopted the post office name of New Concord. The town prospered as taverns and other businesses sprang up to accommodate travelers. Its future became assured in 1837, when the Ohio General Assembly passed a law incorporating Muskingum College.[40]

Meanwhile, a few miles west, Norwich was founded in January 1827. The village was named for a town in England that had been home to one of its early settlers. Within six years Norwich boasted over four hundred residents. Its extensive business community included three taverns and six stores. Norwich also had "2 regular physicians [and] 4 Indian root doctors." Keeping with its location along a major thoroughfare, it was also home to three blacksmiths, five saddlers, and four wagon makers.[41]

The road led to the founding of a number of towns as it continued west into Licking County. The easternmost is Gratiot, laid out by Adam Smith and named in honor of the chief general of the Army Corps of Engineers. Continuing west, Brownsville, Linnville, and Amsterdam owed their existence to the road. Thomas

Harris, described as "a zealous Jacksonian" in his politics, named Jacksontown in honor of his hero. Wagoners and other denizens of the road often referred to the community as "Jacktown." In 1832 Dr. William Kirker laid out the village of Kirkersville and opened a tavern there. The town thrived during the years that the road did, declined during the railroad years, and revived somewhat as a part of US Route 40.[42]

In Clark County at least three villages were established east of Springfield as the road came through. The easternmost is Brighton, platted by David Ripley and Marvin Gager in 1833. Two years earlier John H. Dynes had laid out Vienna, a short distance to the west. Just west of Vienna and six miles east of Springfield, Laybourn Newlove established Harmony in 1832. Despite the allure of the Dayton Cutoff, "Capt. Abram Smith" established Donnelsville, a community located seven miles west of Springfield, in 1832.[43]

As the road continued into Indiana, it passed a short distance south of the Wayne County community of Vandalia. In 1836 the village of Cambridge City, name after the English city, was founded. Its prosperity led to Vandalia's demise. Within five years all of the community's businesses—and most of its population— had relocated to the more favorably situated town. A short distance to the east, Germantown had been founded in 1827. The road aided its growth, and in 1835 the village acquired a post office. Because Indiana already had a Germantown, residents changed its name to East Germantown. West of Cambridge City Harman Davis, a Quaker who emigrated from Bridgeport, Ohio, platted the village of Dublin in 1830.[44]

Lewis Freeman and James Harris laid out the Henry County village of Lewisville in December 1829. It soon wrested the post office away from Garnet, located a short distance to the south. To the west, Hiram Crum laid out Middletown the same month. Nine years later the Indiana legislature changed the community's name to Ogden in honor of the Corps of Engineers officer in charge of pushing the road through Indiana and Illinois. The now defunct villages of Fairfield and Raysville also owed their existence to the road.[45]

Another National Road official was honored when, in 1827, Waitsell M. Cary established the community of Knightstown. Its namesake had completed his survey through Indiana the previous year. Growth was slow at first. Into the 1830s bears could be seen wandering along Knightstown's streets. The Quaker surveyor would likely have been less than impressed with the morals of the some of the residents in the community named in his honor. According to one local historian, "A judge, the 'squire' and all the constables were seen drunk on one or more occasions in the early days, and pugilistic encounters were among the cherished amusements."[46]

In Hancock County the community of Greenfield was founded in 1828. In anticipation of the National Road's arrival, it was named county seat the same year. Greenfield would later gain fame as the birthplace of poet James Whitcomb Riley.[47]

At least three communities in Marion County, now a part of the Indianapolis metropolitan area, came into existence as the National Road passed through. Cumberland, located on the eastern edge of the county, was surveyed in 1831 by Henry Brady. Historians disagree as to whether it was named for the Maryland terminus or for the road itself. West of downtown Indianapolis, Bridgeport was founded in 1831, Stringtown in 1833. The latter reportedly earned its name because "a string of homes sprang up along the road" there.[48]

Hendricks County residents founded three more communities, Plainfield, Belleville, and Stylesville. Like so many other National Road towns, Stylesville was laid out in 1828. One local historian observed, "It was a station at which all emigrants to the great West aimed to take a dinner or a night's lodging." Belleville was laid out a year later. It prospered along the road until 1850, when the Indianapolis & Terre Haute Railroad bypassed it just over a mile to the north.[49]

The road also spawned three communities in Putnam County. Manhattan was founded in 1829, Mt. Meridian in 1833. In 1830 James Townsend laid out the community of Putnamville. He also kept the first store there. The following year Townsend placed an advertisement in the *Indiana Democrat,* an Indianapolis newspaper, hoping to attract more settlers. "It is believed to be as healthy as any town in the west," he boasted. He further predicted, "Judging from the . . . acts of Congress we may anticipate an appropriation at the next session [of Congress] that will complete the grading and bridging to this place next season."[50]

John Graves platted the Clay County village of Harmony in 1839. However, his insolvency led to the plat being vacated, although it later became a railroad town. Cloverland, located in the western portion of the county, near the Vigo County line, fared better. Charles Modesitt established the community in 1834. It gained a post office sixteen years later. In 1844 Owen Thorpe founded a town site along the road and named it Brazil. Growth was slow, the 1850 census listing only eighty-four residents. The arrival of the Terre Haute & Richmond Railroad and the development of the coal industry later in the decade spurred a population boom in the late 1850s. In 1876 Brazil became the seat of Clay County.[51]

Entering Illinois, the National Road first passed through Clark County. There, on September 22, 1835, Col. W. B. Archer issued a circular announcing that he was laying out the town of Marshall. "It is decidedly the handsomest site for a town between Terre Haute and Vandalia," he boasted. Twenty years later Marshall became the county seat. To the west a settlement grew up consisting mainly of boardinghouses for the accommodation of those working on the road. In 1832 John Chancellor established the town of Martinsville at the site. Further west the community of Casey also grew up along the road.[52]

On July 10, 1834, former National Road superintendent William Greenup and Joseph Barbour announced that they would offer for sale lots in Cumberland County for a new town. It was to be named Greenup. "The Lots are laid off on each side of the National Road, with spacious streets and alleys," the two men announced. They promised to donate adjacent land "for public, charitable, and beneficial purposes."[53]

The Effingham County community of Teutopolis was laid out in 1837. It became a haven for Germans from Cincinnati, who purchased ten thousand acres of land at $1.25 an acre, except for the eighty-acre town site, for which they paid four hundred dollars. To the west William Hankins surveyed and platted Ewington in September 1835. It later became the county seat until Effingham, which was founded in 1855, wrested away that honor in 1859. Further west Freemanton was established in June 1834. It became a gathering place for workers on the road, earning a reputation as "a great place for drinking and fighting." As one local historian observed, "The building of the National Road gave it birth; the building of the Vandalia Railroad sounded its death-knell."[54]

Afterword

Decline, Rise, and Nostalgia

THE B&O AND ITS connecting lines did not kill the National Road, not entirely. They did, however, render its moniker largely obsolete. By the end of the Civil War the road was almost exclusively used for local travel. A few vestiges of its days of glamour and importance remained. Stagecoaches continued to run between Wheeling and St. Clairsville at least through the Civil War. In Pennsylvania the stages carried both passengers and mail into the early twentieth century, but the romance was largely gone. The once proud coaches were by then referred to as hacks. They were purely local concerns, connecting Washington, Brownsville, and Uniontown. Meanwhile Ohio landowners encroached upon the original right-of-way, extending their fences several feet. This posed a problem when interurban railroads sprang up along the route. Agreements had been made on the fly many years previous, and the state was hard pressed to assert its legal claims.[1]

The formerly bustling highway quickly became the object of a piteous nostalgia, the word "old" invariably coming up in written accounts of the road. Writing for *Harper's Magazine* in 1879, William Rideing referred to it as "a glory departed." Subsequent writers were more blunt. In a 1905 history of Muskingum County, Ohio, J. Hope Sutor observed, "This great highway is now only a neglected county road." One year later, writing about the road in Pennsylvania, William H. Koontz agreed, "Today it is simply a country road, kept in repair just as other roads are." He added, "That such should be the fate of this once great highway, with all its bustle and business, was foreseen only by few, the many believing that its great tide of traffic must continue to flow on indefinitely."[2]

Time would, to an extent, vindicate "the many." In a sense, William Neil, of Ohio's Neil, Moore, & Company stage line had offered a glimpse into the road's

future as early as the 1830s. At the time he was simply viewed as an individual
who was "scaring the horses." Neil proposed running a line of "steam carriages"
over the road, and in 1833 he petitioned the state legislature for permission to
do so. The proposal met with the vehement disapproval of the editor of the
Guernsey Times, a Cambridge newspaper. "The project, to say the most of it, is
one of very doubtful expediency," he wrote on February 22. "The consequence
would be that the road would be entirely abandoned, so far as relates to the use
of horse power, and an odious monopoly be secured to the company holding
the charter."[3]

The Ohio General Assembly was no more enthusiastic than the Cambridge
scribe, and for six more decades horses enjoyed the monopoly of travel and
transport along the road. That began to change with the development of the
safety bicycle in the early 1890s. The invention led to a cycling craze, along
with calls from such organizations as the League of American Wheelmen for
improved roads. As the century ended, the Post Office Department began
experimenting with a system of rural free delivery of the mail, adding to the
need for better highways.[4]

Of course, it was the automobile that supplied the main impetus to what would
become the Good Roads Movement. At first a novelty, Henry Ford's assembly
line and the 1908 introduction of the Model T made the "horseless carriage" a
practicality and soon, in the minds of many people, a necessity. Unfortunately,
this twentieth-century innovation faced roads mostly mired in the nineteenth,
and the National Road was no exception. At one point west of Zanesville, where
it intersected with a county road, travelers were greeted by a sign warning, "Any
Persons Traveling This Road, Do So At Their Own Risk."[5]

In most places the situation was not so dire. Maryland worked on the road
between Cumberland and Frostburg in 1902, and Pennsylvania repaired lengthy
stretches over the next decade. Beginning in 1914 the infamous section west
of Zanesville received sixteen miles of concrete pavement. An experimental
project, it secured partial funding from the national government, which represented the first federal monies allocated for the highway in nearly eighty years.
After passing over the road in 1910, one traveler wrote that it had "met with
varying fortunes" under county and township control. "At the present time
the old Cumberland Road is in pretty fair shape, in parts." He then added, "A
good deal of it is in rather bad disrepair."[6]

In 1909, after a special session of the 61st Congress, Rep. Albert Douglas of
Ohio and his wife decided to forsake the railroad and return home in the Ford

they had christened "Betsy." The twentieth century had dawned, but they found a road "thronged with teams" in sections. Although the road was "very good" at some points in Maryland, the portion that ascended Big Savage Mountain was one of the worst they encountered. Loose stones combined with sand and dust, forcing Betsy "to fairly plow her way." The situation improved in Pennsylvania, where much of the road had received recent repairs with crushed and rolled limestone, "and we flew over it." Leaving the Keystone State, the road was "fine" the short distance to Wheeling. The Douglases left the highway at Zanesville, turning southwest for their Chillicothe home. The highway, the congressman concluded, was "good, bad, and indifferent," depending on locale. "In spots it is excellent, and in spots it is execrable." He closed presciently: "Our children may see its glories revive, its way repaved with modern metal." Someday, he continued, "Its sides [will be] lined with colossal advertising signs, 'darkening the view,' and its old taverns renovated, rebuilt, re-established,—but with 'soft drinks' perhaps substituted for the 'fifteen-cent-a-gallon' of other days."[7]

By the time Betsy embarked on her journey, a nascent good roads movement was beginning to stir. At first the American Automobile Association, founded in 1902, spearheaded it, abetted by numerous local and regional clubs. Soon the American Association of State Highway Officials became involved in the effort. Quickly joining them were those with commercial interests, including automobile makers, tire manufacturers, the oil industry, and companies that produced paving materials. The American Road Builders Association held its first annual convention in 1903.[8]

There was general agreement on the need for improved roads. There was far less unanimity as to the priorities. State and local officials tended to support improvement of farm-to-market roads, which would benefit their constituents. Automobile clubs preferred the construction or improvement of trunk roads, traversing several states and opening wide stretches of highway to a growing number of motorists.[9]

The federal government was not yet on board, so advocates of interstate roads took matters into their own hands. One of the first was Carl G. Fisher, founder of the Indianapolis Motor Speedway and a prominent Hoosier businessman. In 1912 he made the audacious proposal to construct a hard surfaced road from coast to coast. Henry Joy, president of Packard Motor Car Company, suggested that the highway serve as a tribute to America's sixteenth president. On July 1, 1913, the Lincoln Highway Association was organized. Road maps were virtually nonexistent, so the association used railroad maps and timetables to sketch out a route from New York to San Francisco. The need for such highways was rapidly becoming obvious. The same year the association formed, automobile registrations in the United States reached 1,258,062.[10]

Other ideas for highway projects soon followed. The Dixie Highway would stretch from Mackinaw to Miami, the Meridian Highway from Laredo to Winnipeg, Manitoba, the Jefferson Highway from New Orleans to Winnipeg. By 1920 boosters had also proposed a Pikes Peak Ocean-to-Ocean Highway, a Yellowstone Trail, and a Midland Trail, among others.[11]

The National Road—at least on paper—became a part of what was termed the National Old Trails Road. The brainchild of Charles Henry Davis, president of the National Highways Association, the route would utilize historic trails to form a highway from New York to the West Coast. Included were Braddock's Road from Alexandria to Cumberland, the National Road from Cumberland to Vandalia, and a variety of western trails, most notably the Santa Fe Trail. (During the 1920s Harry Truman served as president of the association, a fitting role for the avid motorist and history buff from Independence.) In calling for federal involvement in the improvement of these trails, Davis wrote, "Our people are demanding of Congress the construction of not only the National Old Trails Road, but likewise national highways in the length and breadth of these United States of America."[12]

Congress finally got involved in 1916, passing the Federal Highway Aid Act. The bill was a victory for advocates of local projects as opposed to federally funded interstate routes. It allotted a paltry $75 million to be distributed as matching funds to states with functioning highway departments. The secretary of agriculture assumed the responsibility for making allotments representing 50 percent of the cost of state highway projects, with post routes being the priority. States had to agree to maintain the roads once they were improved, but they were not allowed to charge tolls.[13]

For the first two decades of the twentieth century, property taxes, bond issues, and automobile registration fees were the states' main sources of revenue for highway projects. After 1916, federal aid was also included. Then, in 1919, Oregon became the first state to enact a gasoline tax. New Mexico and Colorado quickly followed. By 1925 forty-four states had approved such a tax. Four years later New York became the forty-eighth. Congress added a national tax in 1925. In most states the measures sailed through the legislatures with little opposition. At least three passed the bills unanimously. In Tennessee the chief tax collector exclaimed, "Who ever heard, before, of a popular tax?" Even the oil industry voiced few objections at first, although their attitude changed as the rates rose over the years.[14]

World War I demonstrated to the national government the need for a "system of national highways under federal control." One publication described the sending of a convoy of military trucks from Detroit to Baltimore in December 1917 as a "daring adventure." Not only was it a challenge for the vehicles, it was a threat to the roads over which this and other caravans passed. They damaged the roadbeds terribly. After the war huge tractor-trailers began to emerge, leading to similar destruction.[15]

After the war the military decided to find out just how capable America's highways were of "moving an army across the continent." They did so by organizing the First Transcontinental Motor Train. Thirty-nine officers and 258 men shepherded eighty-one vehicles, ranging from motorcycles to heavy trucks, over three thousand miles of roads from Washington, DC, to San Francisco. They largely followed the Lincoln Highway. Among the officers was Lt. Col. Dwight D. Eisenhower, who would later admit that he went along "partly for a lark and partly to learn." (Mainly, Ike had fun at the expense of gullible junior officers. In western Wyoming, abetted by fellow officers and local civilian residents, he convinced an eastern lieutenant that an Indian attack was imminent. They armed him with a shotgun, the shot surreptitiously removed, and put him on guard duty. After the victim had marched his post for awhile, the pranksters slipped into the darkness and let loose with "war yelps," drawing fire from both barrels.) East of the Mississippi, road conditions varied from quality pavement to mud. West of the river, they were almost uniformly bad. The convoy's commander described the route through Nebraska as "graded sand and gumbo badly rotted and four to ten inches deep in dust." In Utah the train encountered a gooey silt beneath a thin crust of sand. Practically every vehicle became mired in it. In Nevada tanker trucks sank to a depth of five feet in "wet quicksand." All along the route crews had to strengthen or rebuild bridges too weak to handle the heavy trucks. The convoy had expected to cover about seventy-five miles a day. It made closer to fifty.[16]

To the US Army the moral was clear. Brig. Gen. Charles Drake, head of the Motor Transport Corps, wrote, "The necessity for a comprehensive system of highways . . . is real and urgent." Business lobbyists and automobile associations continued to press the case for good roads. Congress listened. In 1921, the year that Warren G. Harding became the first president to ride to his inauguration in an automobile, the legislators passed the Federal Highway Act.[17]

The law was the brainchild of Senator Charles E. Townsend of Michigan. It attempted to balance the concerns of advocates of local projects and those who favored interstate roads, but it clearly emphasized the latter. The bulk of federal funds were to go to "such projects as will expedite the completion of an adequate and connected system of highways, interstate in character." Unlike the original National Road bill, the act did not call for the national government to build the highways. This the states would do. The law required each state to submit a list of roads within their borders, not exceeding 7 percent of their total highway mileage, which would contribute to an interstate system. This meant about 200,000 miles of roads. The states complied, and by 1923 Thomas MacDonald, who headed the Bureau of Public Roads, had put together a tentative map of a national highway system.[18]

By then the National Road had become a beneficiary of the measure. A paving project began in 1922, and by the following year, the route was surfaced with concrete from Cumberland to Indianapolis and most of the way to Terre Haute. Before long the hard surface extended to St. Louis. Much of the pavement covered the original roadbed, and it seldom strayed far.[19]

As it gained a hard surface, the National Road lost its identity. The national government did not want its highways to have names; it preferred numbers. In 1925 the Joint Board on Interstate Highways developed a system. East-west roads would have even numbers, often ending in zero, that grew larger as they continued southward. North-south highways received odd numbers, growing as the system moved to the west. The Lincoln Highway, at least in the eastern part of the country, became US 30. In 1926 the National Road was rechristened US 40. The board also adopted a system of standard signage, including the shield-shaped signs that identified US highways. Route 40 would eventually stretch from Atlantic City to San Francisco. Ironically, after being stripped of its name, the National Road became a truly national highway. Today it terminates a few miles east of Salt Lake City, its traffic diverted onto Interstate 80.[20]

Just as inns and wagon stands had sprung up along the National Road, accommodations soon appeared on US 40. Most larger communities, in which the highway was already Main Street, had existing hotels. On the edges of those communities, in smaller towns, and at points between, campgrounds opened. Some were privately operated, others part of county fairgrounds or courthouse lawns. Generally travelers packed their own tents, but they were often available for rent. It did not take long for entrepreneurs to erect cabins for those not desiring to rough it. These eventually gave way to structures with multiple sleeping units under a common roof, called "motor courts" at first and later shortened to "motels." Filling stations dotted the road, as did truck stops, catering to both the mechanical and culinary needs of those who succeeded the Conestoga wagon drivers. Restaurants ranged from the elegant to the "drive-ins" and fast food eateries that popped up after World War II. All served an ever-growing number of motorists. Writing in the early postwar years, Philip Jordan, a historian of the road, observed, "U.S. 40 never sleeps," adding, "at no time in the National Road's long life of 140 years has it been busier."[21]

This activity was not destined to last. Like its first incarnation as a major artery, the National Road would again be superseded. In 1952 Dwight Eisenhower was elected president of the United States. He arrived with memories of the mud and dust that had plagued the First Transcontinental Motor Train. He also had more recent memories of Germany's efficient autobahns, and he yearned for a similar system of dependable, high-speed highways for the United States. In 1956, at his State of the Union address, Ike called for an appropriation of $25 billion for the construction of 41,000 miles of limited-access highways. On June 29 Congress passed the National Interstate and Defense Highways Act. (The inclusion of the word "Defense" was enough to persuade a few skeptical but hawkish congressmen.) Madison, Monroe, and Jackson had harbored their constitutional qualms, but now the federal government had virtually no misgivings. The national share of construction costs was to be 90 percent.[22]

Although individual projects would continue, by the end of the 1970s, Ike's autobahns were largely in place. For some fabled highways, including the iconic Route 66, this sounded their death knell. For US 40 it represented an end to its days of prominence. The Eisenhower Interstate Highway System became America's primary network of roads, the fastest, most efficient way to get from point A to point B. For some travelers, it also represents the end of an era when the travel itself was part of the pleasure.[23]

✖✖✖

From Cumberland to Keyser's Ridge, Maryland, the National Road parallels I-68, a relative newcomer to the interstate grid. It exists as Alternate Route 40. At the latter point the road again becomes US 40, separates from the interstate system, and heads northwest into Pennsylvania. Some sixty-two miles later it reaches Washington, Pennsylvania. From there to Vandalia, it runs close to I-70, joining it in places.

Along the way travelers can still encounter vestiges of the old National Road and of Route 40's salad days. Many of the original ubiquitous mileposts still stand, as do more recent replacements. There is an original "S" bridge a few miles east of Claysville, Pennsylvania, and two more in the vicinity of New Concord, Ohio. The Little Youghiogheny Bridge, completed in 1814, proudly stands at Casselman River Bridge State Park, just east of Grantsville, Maryland. Although not technically part of the National Road, the Wheeling Suspension Bridge, which carried much of its traffic across the Ohio River, still delivers cars and trucks to Wheeling Island. A few original inns remain in business, many under different names, particularly in that portion of western Pennsylvania where the road escapes the interstate grid. A number of businesses that served US 40 travelers in its heyday survive, especially in communities along the route and at locations fortuitously close to I-70 exits. Elsewhere they are either vacant or serve as offices or local businesses. In the case of old motels, many have a new life as efficiency apartments. Along the way there are National Road societies at the state and local levels. A number of community libraries and historical societies work to preserve the heritage of the road. Those wishing to learn more about that heritage can visit the National Road & Zane Grey Museum in Norwich, Ohio, or the National Road Interpretive Center in Vandalia.[24]

It is likely that today's National Road traveler trends older, more local, and in less of a hurry. The interstate system's speed and efficiency are both highly prized in the twenty-first century. US 40 instead offers charm, nostalgia, and a slower pace. To those of a certain age or attitude, these are also prized.

After his 1909 journey over the road in "Betsy," Congressman Douglas ventured his assessment. For those who still find pleasure in escaping the antiseptic bustle of the interstates to venture over the National Road, it is a fitting conclusion: "To fond students of the past, to men who love to revive in imagination the days of the pioneers and to dwell in thought among the days that are no more, the romance of this old pathway of the nation will live forever."[25]

Notes

ABBREVIATIONS

H.	House
IHS	Indiana Historical Society, Indianapolis
ISL	Indiana State Library, Indianapolis
MHS	Maryland Historical Society, Baltimore
NA	National Archives and Records Administration, Washington, DC
OHS	Ohio Historical Society, Columbus
PSA	Pennsylvania State Archives, Harrisburg
RG	Record Group
S.	Senate
WRHS	Western Reserve Historical Society, Cleveland

INTRODUCTION

1. Cumberland Road, S. Doc. No. 195, 9th Cong., 1st Sess. (Dec. 19, 1805).

2. Philip D. Jordan, *The National Road* (Indianapolis: Bobbs-Merrill, 1948), 73–74; Theodore Sky, *The National Road and the Difficult Path to Sustainable National Investment* (Newark: Univ. of Delaware Press, 2011), 15–16.

3. Jeremiah Simeon Young, *A Political and Constitutional Study of the Cumberland Road* (Chicago: Univ. of Chicago Press, 1902), 5.

1. "THE TOUCH OF A FEATHER"

1. Ron Chernow, *Washington: A Life* (New York: Penguin Press, 2010), 16–19.

2. Chernow, *Washington*, 20–21, 31–32.

3. Chernow, *Washington*, 32; Charles H. Ambler, *George Washington and the West* (New York: Russell and Russell, 1936), 39; Philip D. Jordan, *The National Road* (Indianapolis: Bobbs-Merrill, 1948), 21–22.

4. Chernow, *Washington*, 33–37; Ambler, *Washington and the West*, 44–46; Jordan, *National Road*, 22–24.

5. Chernow, *Washington*, 40–45; Jordan, *National Road*, 34–36.

6. Chernow, *Washington*, 45–50; Jordan, *National Road*, 36–38.

7. Ambler, *Washington and the West*, 95–99; Chernow, *Washington*, 52–55; John Kennedy Lacock, "Braddock Road," *Pennsylvania Magazine of History and Biography* 38 (Apr. 1914): 3–4; Jordan, *National Road*, 41.

8. Lacock, "Braddock Road," 6–7; Jordan, *National Road*, 42–45; Ambler, *Washington and the West*, 104; Chernow, *Washington*, 56–57.

9. Chernow, *Washington*, 57–60; Ambler, *Washington and the West*, 105–6; Lacock, "Braddock Road," 33–36; Jordan, *National Road*, 53.

10. John W. Wayland, "Washington West of the Blue Ridge," *Virginia Magazine of History and Biography* 48, no. 3 (July 1940): 197; Chernow, *Washington*, 149–50.

11. Ambler, *Washington and the West*, 174–78; Chernow, *Washington*, 463–66, 479–81; Wayland, "Washington West of the Blue Ridge," 198.

12. Ambler, "Washington and the West," 177–84; Chernow, *Washington*, 481; entries for Sept. 11–12, 1784, George Washington Diary, in *The Diaries of George Washington*, ed. Donald Jackson and Dorothy Twohig, 6 vols. (Charlottesville: Univ. Press of Virginia, 1976–79), 4:17–18.

13. Entries for Sept. 12–14, 1784, in Jackson and Twohig, *Diaries of Washington*, 4:19–21; Nicholas Dungan, *Gallatin: America's Swiss Founding Father* (New York: New York Univ. Press, 2010), 36; Richard Beale Davis, ed., *Jeffersonian America: Notes on the United States of America Collected in the Years 1805–6–7 and 11–12 by Sir Augustus John Foster* (Westport, CT: Greenwood Press, 1954).

14. Entries for Sept. 13–14, 1784, in Jackson and Twohig, *Diaries of Washington*, 4:19, 21; Ambler, *Washington and the West*, 178, 182.

15. Washington to Benjamin Harrison, Oct. 10, 1784, in *The Writings of George Washington from the Original Manuscript Sources, 1745–1799*, ed. John C. Fitzpatrick, 47 vols. (Washington, DC: US Government Printing Office, 1931–44), 27:475.

16. Washington to Harrison, Oct. 10, 1784, in Fitzpatrick, *Writings of George Washington*, 476–79.

17. For an analysis of these questions, see John Lauritz Larson, "'Bind the Republic Together': The National Union and the Struggle for a System of Internal Improvements," *Journal of American History* 74, no. 2 (Sept. 1987): esp. 365–71.

18. Chernow, *Washington*, 718–20; Dungan, *Gallatin*, 45.

19. Gary S. Williams, *Spies, Scoundrels and Rogues of the Ohio Frontier* (Baltimore: Gateway Press, 2005), 127–32.

20. Williams, *Spies, Scoundrels and Rogues*, 132–41.

21. Clement L. Martzolff, "Zane's Trace," *Ohio Archaeological and Historical Publications* 13 (1904): 299–300; Thomas W. Lewis, *Zanesville and Muskingum County Ohio [. . .]*, 3 vols. (Chicago: S. J. Clarke, 1927), 1:57.

22. Williams, *Spies, Scoundrels and Rogues*, 30–31, 64; Martzolff, "Zane's Trace," 303–5.

23. Petition to Congress by Ebenezer Zane, Mar. 25, 1796, in *The Territorial Papers of the United States*, ed. Clarence Edwin Carter, 28 vols. (Washington, DC: US Government Printing Office, 1934–62), 2:550–52.

24. Martzolff, "Zane's Trace," 306–7; *History of Muskingum County, Ohio, with Illustrations and Biographical Sketches of Prominent Men and Pioneers* (N.p.: J. F. Everhart, 1882), 67; Lewis, *Zanesville and Muskingum County*, 59–60.

25. Jordan, *National Road*, 59–60; Martzolff, "Zane's Trace," 312–15; *History of Muskingum County*, 67.

26. Martzolff, "Zane's Trace," 315–19.

27. Rufus Putnam to Oliver Wolcott, Feb. 5, 1800, in Carter, *Territorial Papers*, 3:75; *History of Muskingum County*, 67–68.

28. Martzolff, "Zane's Trace," 320–23; Jordan, *National Road*, 66.

2. "THE MOST EFFECTUAL CEMENT OF UNION"

1. Dungan, *Gallatin*, 49–50, 60, 67; James Holley, "The Constitution, Parties and the Cumberland Road, 1801–1822" (master's thesis, Univ. of Iowa, 1965), 5.

2. Beverly W. Bond Jr., *The Foundations of Ohio*, vol. 1 of *The History of the State of Ohio*, 5 vols., ed. Carl Wittke (Columbus: Ohio State Archaeological and Historical Society, 1941), 446–63; George W. Knepper, *Ohio and Its People* (Kent, OH: Kent State Univ. Press, 1997), 89–93.

3. Albert Gallatin to William B. Giles, Feb. 13, 1802, in *The Writings of Albert Gallatin*, ed. Henry Adams, 3 vols. (1879; repr., New York: Antiquarian Press, 1960), 1:78.

4. Annals of Congress, 7th Cong., 1st Sess. (Apr. 3, 1802), 1124–25.

5. Jordan, *National Road*, 72; Holley, "Constitution, Parties," 6–7; Dumas Malone, *Jefferson the President Second Term 1805–1809*, vol. 5 of *Jefferson and His Time*, 6 vols. (Boston: Little, Brown, 1974), 555.

6. Cumberland Road, S. Doc. No. 195, 9th Cong., 2d Sess. (Dec. 19, 1805).

7. Cumberland Road, S. Doc. No. 195, 9th Cong., 2nd Sess. (Dec. 19, 1805).

8. Annals of Congress, 9th Cong., 1st Sess. (Mar. 21, 1806), 835–38. Emphasis added for the Jackson quote.

9. Annals of Congress, 9th Cong., 1st Sess. (Mar. 24, 1806), 839–40; Holley, "Constitution, Parties," 36.

10. Annals of Congress, 9th Cong., 1st Sess. (Mar. 29, 1806), 1236–38.

11. Annals of Congress, 9th Cong., 1st Sess. (Mar. 29, 1806), 1236–38.

12. Jordan, *National Road*, 75, 80.

13. Entry for Sept. 4, 1806, Journal kept by Elie Williams during examination of route for Cumberland Road by the Commissioners in 1806, RG 77, NA (hereafter cited as Williams Journal); Cumberland Road, Exec. Doc. No. 220, 9th Cong., 2nd Sess. (Jan. 31, 1807).

14. Entries for Sept. 4–13, 1806, Williams Journal, RG 77, NA; Cumberland Road, Exec. Doc. No. 220, 9th Cong., 2nd Sess. (Jan. 31, 1807).

15. Entries for Sept. 16–21, 1806, Williams Journal, RG 77, NA.

16. Entries for Sept. 23–Oct. 1, 1806, Williams Journal, RG 77, NA.

17. Entries for Oct. 2–11, 1806, Williams Journal, RG 77, NA.

18. Entries for Oct. 13–22, 1806, Williams Journal, RG 77, NA.

19. Entries for Oct. 23–25, 1806, Williams Journal, RG 77, NA.

20. Entries for Oct. 27–Nov. 26, 1806, Williams Journal, RG 77, NA.

21. Entries for Nov. 27–Dec. 6, 1806, Williams Journal, RG 77, NA; Cumberland Road, Exec. Doc. No. 220, 9th Cong., 2nd Sess. (Jan. 31, 1807).

22. Cumberland Road, Exec. Doc. No. 243, 10th Cong., 1st Sess. (Feb. 19, 1808); Cumberland Road, Exec. Doc. No. 258, 10th Cong., 2nd Sess. (Dec. 13, 1808).

23. Gallatin to Jefferson, Apr. 13, 1807, in Adams, *Writings of Gallatin*, 2:334–35; Thomas Jefferson to Joseph Kerr, Thomas Moore, and Elie Williams, Aug. 6, 1808, Jefferson to Gallatin, Aug. 6, 1808, in *The Writings of Thomas Jefferson*, ed. Albert Ellery Bergh, 17 vols. (Washington, DC: Jefferson Memorial Association, 1907), 12:117–18.

24. Cumberland Road, H. Doc. No. 263, 10th Cong., 2nd Sess. (Feb. 16, 1809).

25. Holley, "Constitution, Parties," 26–27; Annals of Cong., 11th Cong., 2nd Sess. (June 10, 1809), 465–66.

3. "ENTIRELY IN THE WOODS"

1. United States Western Road, Nov. 6, 1810, Correspondence and Other Records Pertaining to the Cumberland Road, 1810–24, RG 77, Records of the Chief of Engineers, 1789–1999, RG 77, NA (hereafter cited as Cumberland Road Records).

2. Henry McKinley to Albert Gallatin, Feb. 13, 19, 1811, James Cochran to Gallatin, Feb. 1, 4, 1811, Cumberland Road Records, RG 77, NA.

3. Gallatin to David Shriver, Feb. 28, 1811, Cumberland Road Records, RG 77, NA; Cumberland Road, Misc. Doc. No. 311, 12th Cong., 1st Sess. (Feb. 3, 1812).

4. Gallatin to Shriver, Mar. 28, 1811, National Road Reference File, 1806–1935, Hunter Collection, RG 12, Department of Highways, PSA (hereafter cited as Hunter Collection).

5. Shriver to Gallatin, Apr. 29, 1811, Cumberland Road Records, RG 77, NA; Shriver to Gallatin, Apr. 22, 1811, Henry McKinley to Gallatin, Apr. 23, 1811, Hunter Collection, RG 12, PSA.

6. Shriver to Gallatin, Apr. 22, 1811, Hunter Collection, RG 12, PSA; C. Randle to Gallatin, Apr. 30, 1811, Cumberland Road Records, RG 77, NA.

7. Jordan, *National Road*, 84–85.

8. Jordan, *National Road,* 84–85; Shriver to McKinley, June 12, 1812, Hunter Collection, RG 12, PSA; Shriver to Gallatin, Oct. 21, 1811, Cumberland Road Records, NA.

9. Shriver to Gallatin, Oct. 21, Nov. 24, 1811; Shriver to W. Jones, July 9, 1813, Hunter Collection, RG 12, PSA.

10. Shriver to Alexander J. Dallas, June 30, July 8, 21, 1815, Cumberland Road Records, RG 77, NA; Dallas to Shriver, July 11, 1815; David Shriver Jr. Papers, 1811–52, Mss. 3245, WRHS.

11. Shriver to William Jones, June 21, July 9, 1813, Hunter Collection, RG 12, PSA; Richard Delafield to "Lt. Vance," May 29, 1834, Correspondence of engineers in charge of repairs of the Cumberland Road, East of the Ohio, 1832–1833, RG 77, NA.

12. Shriver to Gallatin, May 13, 1811, Cumberland Road Records, RG 77, NA; Cumberland Road, Misc. Doc. No. 311, 12th Cong., 1st Sess. (Feb. 3, 1812); Cumberland Road, Misc. Doc. No. 339, 12th Cong., 2nd Sess. (Mar. 2, 1813); Shriver to Gallatin, June 15, 1812, Hunter Collection, RG 12, PSA.

13. Cumberland Road, Misc. Doc. No. 379, 13th Cong., 3rd Sess. (Jan. 2, 1815).

14. *Allegany Freeman* (Cumberland, MD), Dec. 18, 1813, Jan. 8, Dec. 10, 1814; Shriver to Dallas, Apr. 15, 1815, Cumberland Road Records, RG 77, NA.

15. Shriver to Dallas, Apr. 15, 1815, Cumberland Road Records, RG 77, NA.

16. Shriver to Gallatin, June 7, 1812, James Cochran to Gallatin, July 6, 1812, Cumberland Road Records, RG 77, NA; Shriver to Gallatin, Apr. 3, 1813, Hunter Collection, RG 12, PSA.

17. Cumberland Road, Misc. Doc. No. 311, 12th Cong., 1st Sess. (Feb. 3, 1812); Cumberland Road, Misc. Doc. No. 356, 13th Cong., 2nd Sess. (Jan. 19, 1814); Shriver to George W. Campbell, May 28, 1814, Hunter Collection, RG 12, PSA; Shriver to Dallas, Mar. 25, 1815, June 12, 1816, Cumberland Road Records, RG 77, NA; Cumberland Road, Misc. Doc. No. 403, 14th Cong., 1st Sess. (Mar. 13, 1816); Shriver to Dallas, June 12, 1816, Cumberland Road Records, RG 77, NA.

18. Cumberland Road, Misc. Doc. No. 403, 14th Cong., 1st Sess. (Mar. 13, 1816).

19. Cumberland Road, Misc. Doc. No. 403, 14th Cong., 1st Sess. (Mar. 13, 1816); Progress Made in Making Roads by Authority of the United States, Misc. Doc. No. 443, 15th Cong., 1st Sess. (Jan. 23, 1818).

20. Shriver to Gallatin, May 13, 1811, Jan. 6, June 12, 1812, Cumberland Road Records, RG 77, NA.

21. Abraham Kerns and John Bryson to Shriver, Nov. 17, 1814, Hunter Collection, RG 12, PSA; Stephen Schlosnagle, *Garrett County: A History of Maryland's Tableland* (Parsons, WV: McClain Publishing, 1978), 135.

22. Shriver to Dallas, May 20, June 30, 1815, Cumberland Road Records, RG 77, NA.

23. Cumberland Road, Misc. Doc. No. 317, 12th Cong., 1st Sess. (Apr. 14, 1812); Cumberland Road, Misc. Doc. No. 379, 13th Cong., 2nd Sess. (Jan. 2, 1815); Shriver to Dallas, Apr. 15, 1815, Cumberland Road Records, RG 77, NA.

24. Shriver to Dallas, July 21, 1815, Shriver to Crawford, Dec. 31, 1817, Cumberland Road Records, RG 77, NA; Dallas to Shriver, July 11, 1815, David Shriver Jr. Papers, 1811–1852, Mss. 3245, WRHS; James Shriver to Mother, July 21, 1815, Shriver Family Papers, MHS.

25. Shriver to Gallatin, June 7, 1812, Shriver to Dallas, July 21, 1815, Cumberland Road Records, RG 77, NA; James Shriver to Mother, July 21, 1815, Shriver Family Papers, MHS.

26. Thomas B. Searight, *The Old Pike: A History of the National Road with Incidents, Accidents, and Anecdotes Thereon* (1894; repr., Bowie, MD: Heritage Books, 1990), 101; Dallas to James Madison, May 19, 1816, Cumberland Road Records, RG 77, NA.

27. Elie Williams to Shriver, July 17, 1816; Shriver to Williams, Aug. 1, 1816; Dallas to Shriver, Sept. 6, 1816; Dallas to Williams, Sept. 6, Oct. 28, 1816; Williams to Dallas, Sept. 19, 1816; Crawford to Shriver, Nov. 1, 1816; Thomas Wilson to Daniel Shriver, Apr. 1817; Wilson to Crawford, Apr. 13, 1817, Cumberland Road Records, RG 77, NA.

28. Searight, *Old Pike*, 320; John Cox, letter to potential witnesses, Aug. 7, 1818, Daniel Moore to Cox, Aug. 10, 1818; A. Caldwell to Cox, Aug. 10, 1818; Richard Hardesty to Cox, Aug. 11, 1818; William Chapline to Cox, Aug. 12, 1818; James Douglas to Cox, Aug. 12, 1818; Samuel Loomis to Cox, Aug. 18; Joseph Caldwell to Cox, Aug. 13, 1818; Moses Shepherd to Cox, Aug. 14, 1818; Richard McClure to Cox, Aug. 18, 1818, Cumberland Road Records, RG 77, NA.

29. Cumberland Road, H. Misc. Doc. No, 486, 16th Cong., 1st Sess. (Mar. 10, 1820); Shriver to Crawford, Oct. 2, 1819, Cumberland Road Records, RG 77, NA.

30. Cumberland Road, H. Misc. Doc. No. 220, 9th Cong., 2nd Sess. (Jan. 31, 1807).

31. John Connell to Dallas, Feb. 19, 1816; James Marshall to Dallas, July 1, 1816; John Danagh et al. to Thomas Wilson, Feb. 9, 1816; James Blaine et al. to the president, ND, Cumberland Road Records, RG 77, NA.

32. Robert Mitchell and 19 other members of Congress to the president, July 17, 1816, Cumberland Road Records, RG 77, NA; L. Diane Barnes, "Urban Rivalry in the Upper Ohio Valley: Wheeling and Pittsburgh in the Nineteenth Century," *Pennsylvania Magazine of History and Biography* 123, no. 3 (July 1997): 207, 210–13.

33. Archibald Woods et al. to Henry Clay, Benjamin Ruggles, and James Caldwell, Feb. 6, 1816, Cumberland Road Records, RG 77, NA; Dallas to Elie Williams, Thomas Moore, and Joseph Kerr, June 2, 1816, Hunter Collection, RG 12, PSA; Jordan, *National Road*, 75.

34. *Washington (PA) Reporter*, Nov. 16, 1816; *Brownsville American Telegraph*, Nov. 20, 1816.

35. Franklin Ellis, *History of Fayette County, Pennsylvania [...]* (Philadelphia: L. H. Everts, 1882), 255; Boyd Crumrine, *History of Washington County, Pennsylvania [...]* (Philadelphia: L. H. Everts, 1882), 377; Charles A. Winegerter, *History of Greater Wheeling and Vicinity* (Chicago: Lewis Publishing, 1912), 137; Searight, *Old Pike*, 319–20.

36. Shriver to Crawford, Feb. 8, 1817, Cumberland Road Records, RG 77, NA; John Kennedy and James Kinkead to Shriver, July 15, 1819, Shriver to Crawford, July 17, Aug. 5, 1819, Shriver Family Papers, MHS.

37. Josias Thompson to Crawford, Jan. 22, 1818, Cumberland Road Records, RG 77, NA.

38. Ellis, *Fayette County*, 255, 430.

39. Entries for June 19, 23, 1816, "Uria Brown's Journal," *Maryland Historical Magazine* 10, no. 3 (Mar. 1915): 275, 278–79.

40. Thompson to Crawford, Dec. 15, 1817; Feb. 8, 1818; June 7, 1819, Cumberland Road Records, RG 77, NA.

41. *Washington (PA) Examiner,* May 31, Sept. 6, Nov. 28, 1819; *Hagerstown Advertiser,* July 27, 1819; Crumrine, *Washington County,* 378.

42. Shriver to Crawford, Apr. 28, 1817, Cumberland Road Records, RG 77, NA.

43. Shriver to Crawford, Dec. 31, 1817; June 1, 1818; Dec. 27, 1819; Mar. 31, 1820; Shriver to Crawford, June 30, 1818, Hunter Collection, RG 12, PSA; Shriver to Crawford, Mar. 19, 1819, Shriver Family Papers, MHS.

44. Shriver to Crawford, Aug. 5, Dec. 24, 1819, Shriver Family Papers, MHS.

45. Crawford to Shriver, Mar. 7, 1823, David Shriver Jr. Papers, 1811–1852, Mss. 3245, WRHS; Shriver to Crawford, July 12, Sept. 29, 1823, Sept. 8, 1824, Cumberland Road Records, RG 77, NA.

46. Shriver to Crawford, Oct. 27, 1823, Cumberland Road Records, RG 77, NA.

4. "A SCENE OF ZEAL AND INDUSTRY"

1. James D. Richardson, ed., *A Compilation of the Messages and Papers of the Presidents,* 11 vols. (Washington, DC: Bureau of National Literature, 1913), 1:562; Robert V. Remini, *Henry Clay: Statesman for the Union* (New York: W. W. Norton, 1991), 142–43.

2. Charles M. Wiltse, *John C. Calhoun: Nationalist, 1782–1828* (Indianapolis: Bobbs-Merrill, 1944), 132–35; John Niven, *John C. Calhoun and the Price of Union: A Biography* (Baton Rouge: Louisiana State Univ. Press, 1988), 55–56; Remini, *Henry Clay,* 143; David S. Heidler and Jeanne T. Heidler, *Henry Clay: The Essential American* (New York: Random House, 2010), 132–33; Daniel Walker Howe, *What Hath God Wrought: The Transformation of America, 1815–1848* (New York: Oxford Univ. Press, 2007), 87; Richardson, *Messages and Papers,* 1:569–70.

3. Remini, *Henry Clay,* 143; Richardson, *Messages and Papers,* 1:586–87.

4. Holley, "Constitution, Parties," 104; Noble E. Cunningham Jr., *The Presidency of James Monroe* (Lawrence: Univ. Press of Kansas, 1996), 166.

5. Cunningham, *Presidency of Monroe;* Annals of Congress, 17th Cong., 1st Sess., 1690–91, 1734, 1875; Harlow Giles Unger, *The Last Founding Father: James Monroe and a Nation's Call to Greatness* (Philadelphia: Da Capo Press, 2009), 318; Richardson, *Messages and Papers,* 1:711–12; Harry Ammon, *James Monroe: The Quest for National Identity* (New York: McGraw-Hill, 1971), 390–91.

6. Jordan, *National Road,* 90.

7. Letter from the Secretary of the Treasury, Transmitting a Report of the Commissioners, Appointed to View and Inspect the Cumberland Road, H. Doc. No. 27, 17th Cong., 1st Sess. (Jan. 15, 1822).

8. Norris F. Schneider, *The National Road: Main Street of America* (Columbus: Ohio Historical Society, 1975), 10.

9. Billy Joe Peyton, "Surveying and Building the Road," in Karl Raitz, ed., *The National Road* (Baltimore: Johns Hopkins Univ. Press, 1996), 134; Jordan, *National Road,* 91; Cunningham,

Presidency of Monroe, 167; T. J. C. Williams and Folger McKinsey, *History of Frederick County Maryland,* 2 vols. (Frederick, MD: L. R. Titsworth, 1910), 1:149.

10. *Washington (PA) Examiner,* Apr. 30, July 16, 30, 1825.

11. Letter from the Secretary of War, Transmitting a Report of the Chief Engineer in Relation to the Road through Ohio, Indiana, and Illinois, H. Doc. No. 18, 19th Cong., 2nd Sess. (Dec. 20, 1826).

12. James Barbour to Benjamin Ruggles, Mar. 28, 1825, Letters Sent by the Office of the Chief of Engineers Relating to Internal Improvements, 1824–30, RG 77, M-65, NA (hereafter Chief of Engineers Letters); Peyton, "Surveying and Building the Road," in Raitz, *National Road,* 140–42.

13. Alexander Macomb to Jonathan Knight, ND (ca. May 1, 1825), June 30, 1825, Chief of Engineers Letters, RG 77, NA.

14. *St. Clairsville Gazette,* quoted in *Cumberland Maryland Advocate,* Sept. 5, 1825.

15. *St. Clairsville Gazette,* quoted in *Cumberland Maryland Advocate,* Sept. 5, 1825.

16. Schneider, *National Road,* 11; Macomb to James Barbour, Nov. 21, 1825, in *American State Papers: Documents, Legislative and Executive, of the Congress of the United States . . . Class V, Military Affairs,* 7 vols. (Washington, DC: Gales and Seaton, 1860), 3:139. Unless otherwise indicated, all subsequent entries will come from Class V.

17. *St. Clairsville Gazette,* Sept. 17, Oct. 29, 1825.

18. Letter from the Secretary of War, Transmitting a Report [. . .] Ohio, Indiana, and Illinois, H. Doc. No. 18, 19th Cong., 2nd Sess. (Dec. 20, 1826); *St. Clairsville Gazette,* June 21, 1826.

19. *St. Clairsville Gazette,* July 1, 1826; Morris Schaff, *A Sketch of Etna and Kirkersville* (Buffalo: Houghton, Mifflin, 1905), 72; Donald J. Ratcliffe, *The Politics of Long Division: The Birth of the Second Party System in Ohio, 1818–1828* (Columbus: Ohio State Univ. Press, 2000), 262.

20. Macomb to Knight, Apr. 27, 1826, Chief of Engineers Letters, RG 77, NA; Letter from the Secretary of War, Transmitting a Report [. . .] Ohio, Indiana, and Illinois, H. Doc. No. 18, 19th Cong., 2nd Sess. (Dec. 20, 1826); *Guernsey Times* (Cambridge, OH), May 25, 1826; *St. Clairsville Gazette,* July 29, 1826.

21. *Guernsey Times,* June 1, Dec. 28, 1827; Letter from the Secretary of War, Transmitting a Report [. . .] Ohio, Indiana, and Illinois, H. Doc. No. 18, 19th Cong., 2nd Sess. (Dec. 20, 1826); Letter from the Secretary of War, Transmitting a Copy [. . .] Cumberland Road, H. Doc. No. 14, 20th Cong., 2nd Sess. (Dec. 11, 1828).

22. Letter from the Secretary of War, Transmitting a Copy [. . .] Cumberland Road, H. Doc. No. 14, 20th Cong., 2nd Sess. (Dec. 11, 1828); Report from the Secretary of War, in Compliance with a Resolution of the Senate, Transmitting Reports from the Superintendent of the Cumberland Road, for 1829 and 1830, S. Doc. No. 17, 21st Cong., 2nd Sess. (Dec. 31, 1830); *Zanesville Messenger,* in *St. Clairsville Gazette,* Aug. 15, 1829.

23. Peyton, "Surveying and Building the Road," in Raitz, *National Road,* 136; Schneider, *National Road,* 12.

24. Ratcliffe, *Politics of Long Division*, 285, 286; Williams and McKinsey, *Frederick County,* 1:192; John F. Stover, *History of the Baltimore and Ohio Railroad* (West Lafayette, IN: Purdue Univ. Press, 1987), 21.

25. Charles Gratiot to James Hampson, Dec. 3, 1829, Chief of Engineers Letters, RG 77, NA; Capt. A. Talcott to Gratiot, Apr. 22, 1831, Letters Received by the Engineer Department Relating to the Cumberland Road (hereafter Engineer Department Letters), RG 77, NA.

26. Hampson to Gratiot, Mar. 19, 1832, Engineer Department Letters, RG 77, NA.

27. Hampson to Gratiot, Mar. 19, 1832, James R. Mulvany to David Scott, Oct. 19, 1831; Henry Flood et al. to "all whom it may concern," Oct. [?], 1831; Hampson to Scott, Mar. 31, 1832, Engineer Department Letters, RG 77, NA.

28. Macomb to Knight, May 6, 1828; unknown to Joseph Shriver, May 12, 1828; Gratiot to Hampson, Apr. 17, 1829, Chief of Engineers Letters, RG 77, NA; Report from the Secretary of War, in Compliance with a Resolution of the Senate, Transmitting Reports from the Superintendent of the Cumberland Road, for 1829 and 1830, S. Doc. No. 17, 21st Cong., 2nd Sess. (Dec. 30, 1830); *Ohio Monitor* (Columbus, OH), June 3, 1829.

29. Letter from the Secretary of the Treasury, Transmitting a Report of the Commissioners, Appointed to View and Inspect the Cumberland Road, H. Doc. No. 27, 17th Cong., 1st Sess. (Jan. 15, 1822); Report from the Secretary of War, in Compliance with a Resolution of the Senate, Transmitting Reports from the Superintendent of the Cumberland Road, for 1829 and 1830, S. Doc. No. 17, 21st Cong., 2nd Sess. (Dec. 31, 1830).

30. *Ohio Monitor* (Columbus, OH), June 3, 1829; Inspection Report on That Part of the National Road under the Supervision of James Hampson, Esq. Situated between Zanesville and the Portsmouth Canal in Ohio Made on Aug. 27, 28, 29, 1830, Engineer Department Letters, RG 77, NA; *American State Papers,* 5:188, 417.

31. Charles E. Rosenberg, *The Cholera Years: The United States in 1832, 1849, and 1866* (Chicago: Univ. of Chicago Press, 1962), 13–14, 21–39; Jordan, *National Road,* 302–3.

32. Letter from the Secretary of War, Transmitting Reports and Drawings Relative to the National Road, H. Doc. No. 74, 19th Cong., 2nd Sess. (Feb. 3, 1827); *Ohio State Journal* (Columbus), Jan. 25, 1827, June 4, 1829.

33. Letter from the Secretary of War, Transmitting Reports and Drawings Relative to the National Road, H. Doc. No. 74, 19th Cong., 2nd Sess. (Feb. 3, 1827).

34. Cumberland Road, H. Doc. No. 410, 21st Cong., 1st Sess. (May 24, 1830).

35. National Road—Springfield, Ohio, to Richmond, Indiana, H. Doc. No. 62, 24th Cong., 1st Sess. (Jan. 13, 1836).

36. Report: Change Cumberland Road, H. Doc. No. 367, 24th Cong., 1st Sess. (Feb. 19, 1836).

37. Report: Change Cumberland Road, H. Doc. No. 367, 24th Cong., 1st Sess. (Feb. 19, 1836).

38. Searight, *Old Pike,* 103–6.

39. Delafield to Gratiot, ca. Sept. 1, 1830, Engineer Department Letters, RG 77, NA; *American State Papers,* 5:416.

40. *American State Papers,* Class 4:732; Class 5:48, 188.

41. Report of the Secretary of War, in Compliance with a Resolution of the Senate, Relative to the Progress Made in the Construction and Repair of the Cumberland Road, &c., S. Doc. No. 43, 22nd Cong., 2nd Sess. (Jan. 17, 1833); *American State Papers,* 5:416; Searight, *Old Pike,* 311–12; Cyndie L. Gerken, *Marking the Miles along the National Road through Ohio: A Survey of Old Stone Mile Markers on Ohio's National Road* (Zanesville: Muskingum Valley Archaeological Survey, 2015), 8.

42. *American State Papers,* Class 6:416, 897; National Road West of the Ohio, H. Doc. No. 230, 24th Cong., 1st Sess. (Apr. 20, 1836); Schneider, *National Road,* 12–13; Capt. A. Talcott to Gratiot, Apr. [?], 1837, Administrative and Scientific Reports of Superintendents and Lesser Officials of the Cumberland Road, 1825–1840 (hereafter "Administrative and Scientific Reports"), RG 77, NA.

43. *Ohio Monitor* (Columbus, OH), July 21, 1830; *Ohio State Journal* (Columbus, OH), July 8, 1830; *American State Papers,* Class 4:732.

44. Report from the Secretary of War, in Compliance with a Resolution of the Senate, Transmitting Reports from the Superintendent of the Cumberland Road, for 1829 and 1830, S. Doc. No. 40, 21st Cong., 2nd Sess. (Dec. 31, 1830); Report from the Secretary of War, in Compliance with a Resolution of the Senate, Relative to the Progress Made in the Construction and Repairs of the Cumberland Road, &c., S. Doc. No. 43, 22nd Cong., 2nd Sess. (Jan. 17, 1833).

45. *American State Papers,* Class 5:415–17; Class 6:896–88; Class 7:699.

46. Jordan, *National Road,* 93; [?] Scott to George Dutton, July 5, 1837; D. P. Woodbury to Dutton, Oct. 3, 13, 1838, Administrative and Scientific Reports, RG 77, NA.

47. *American State Papers,* Class 5:416–17; Class 6:897; Class 7:699–700; Report of the Commissioner on Roads and Canals, S. Doc. No. 160, 26th Cong., 1st Sess. (Feb. 10, 1840); D. P. Woodbury to Dutton, Oct. 3, 1838, Administrative and Scientific Reports, RG 77, NA.

48. Report of the Committee on Roads and Canals, 26th Cong., 1st Sess. (Feb. 10, 1840).

49. Suspended Operations—Public Works, H. Doc. No. 41, 26th Cong., 2nd Sess. (Jan. 4, 1840); Message from the President of the United States to the Two Houses of Congress, at the Commencement of the Second Session of the Twenty-Seventh Congress, S. Doc. No. 1, 27th Cong., 2nd Sess. (Dec. 7, 1841).

50. Entries for May 24–28, 1841, Jane Voorhees Lewis Diary, in "The Journal of Jane Voorhees Lewis," *Proceedings of the New Jersey Historical Society* 65 (1947): 88–89.

51. Gerken, *Marking the Miles,* 273, 274, 278; Annals of Congress, 32nd Cong., 2nd Sess. (Jan. 20, 1853), 152; emphasis added.

5. "EMBARRASSMENTS AND DIFFICULTIES FROM THE BEGINNING"

1. Report of the Secretary of War, in Compliance with a Resolution of the Senate, of the Eighth Instant, Transmitting a Report of the Commissioner for Locating the Continuation of the Cumberland Road, under Act of Mar. 3, 1825, S. Doc. No. 99, 20th Cong., 1st

Sess. (Feb. 12, 1828) (hereafter cited as S. Doc. No. 99); Lee Burns, "The National Road in Indiana," *Indiana Historical Society Publications* 7, No. 4 (1919): 215–17.

2. S. Doc. No. 99, Feb. 12, 1828.

3. S. Doc. No. 99, Feb. 12, 1828; Burns, "National Road in Indiana," 217–18.

4. S. Doc. No. 99, Feb. 12, 1828.

5. Road from Zanesville, Ohio, to St. Louis, Missouri, H. Doc. No. 113, 20th Cong., 2nd Sess. (Feb. 6, 1829); Joseph Shriver, Notebook of Survey of the Cumberland Road between Terre Haute, Indiana and St. Louis, Missouri, Historic National Road Interpretive Center, Vandalia, IL.

6. Cumberland Road and Ohio River, H. Doc. No. 52, 24th Cong., 2nd Sess. (Dec. 30, 1836).

7. Homer Johnson and John Milroy to "The Honorable Speaker of the House of the State of Indiana," Dec. 14, 1829, in *Indiana State Gazette* (Indianapolis, IN), Dec. 24, 1829.

8. Charles Gratiot to John Milroy, June 15, 1830, Chief of Engineers Letters, RG 77, NA.

9. *Indiana Journal* (Indianapolis, IN), July 21, Sept. 1, 1830; *Indiana Democrat* (Indianapolis, IN), Aug. 28, 1830.

10. Cumberland Road, H. Doc. No. 12, 21st Cong., 2nd Sess. (Dec. 21, 1830); *Indiana Journal,* June 18, 1831; *Indiana Democrat,* June 11, 25, 1831.

11. *Indiana Democrat,* July 30, 1831; *Indiana Journal,* July 2, Aug. 6, 1831; Burns, "National Road in Indiana," 220–21; Logan Esarey, *History of Indiana from Its Exploration to 1922,* 4 vols. (Dayton, OH: Dayton Historical Publishing, 1924), 1:291.

12. *Indiana Democrat,* Jan. 16, Sept. 28, Dec. 11, 1833; Report from the Secretary of War, in Compliance with a Resolution of the Senate of the 14th Instant, Transmitting a Report of the Agent Appointed to Inspect the Cumberland Road, S. Doc. No. 44, 23rd Cong., 1st Sess. (Jan. 17, 1834).

13. Thomas L. Hardin, "The National Road in Illinois," *Journal of the Illinois State Historical Society* 60, no. 1 (Spring 1967): 11–13; Message from the President of the United States, Transmitting a Report from the War Department on the Condition of the Cumberland Road in Indiana and Illinois, H. Doc. No. 26, 24th Cong., 1st Sess. (Dec. 24, 1835); Message from the President of the United States, with Report on the Condition of the Cumberland Road in Illinois and Indiana, S. Doc. No. 19, 24th Cong., 1st Sess. (Dec. 22, 1835).

14. National Road West of the Ohio, H. Doc. No. 230, 24th Cong., 1st Sess. (Apr. 20, 1836).

15. Homer Johnson to Cornelius Ogden, Sept. 6, Nov. 7, Dec. 3, 1834; May 2, July 7, 1835, Administrative and Scientific Reports, RG 77, NA.

16. Cumberland Road and Ohio River, H. Doc. No. 52, 24th Cong., 2nd Sess. (Dec. 30, 1836); *Indiana Journal,* Aug. 13, 1836.

17. Cumberland Road and Ohio River, H. Doc. No. 52, 24th Cong., 2nd Sess. (Dec. 30, 1836); *Indiana Journal,* Aug. 13, 1836.

18. Cumberland Road and Ohio River, H. Doc. No. 52, 24th Cong., 2nd Sess. (Dec. 30, 1836); *American State Papers,* Class 7:701.

19. *Indiana Journal,* Aug. 13, 1836; *Indiana Democrat,* Aug. 10, 1836; Cumberland Road and Ohio River, H. Doc. No. 52, 24th Cong., 2nd Sess. (Dec. 30, 1836).

20. *American State Papers,* Class 7:702, 704.

21. *Indiana Democrat,* July 12, 1837.

22. Emory M. Thomas, *Robert E. Lee: A Biography* (New York: W. W. Norton, 1995), 95.

23. Report from the Secretary of War Relative to the Construction of a Bridge over the Wabash River at the Crossing of the Cumberland Road, S. Doc. No. 10, 24th Cong., 1st Sess. (Dec. 10, 1835).

24. *American State Papers,* Class 7:702, 704.

25. *American State Papers,* Class 7:702, 704; H. C. Bradsby, *History of Vigo County, Indiana, with Biographical Selections* (Chicago: S. B. Nelson, 1891), 461–62.

26. Report of the Committee on Roads and Canals, S. Doc. No. 160, 26th Cong., 1st Sess. (Feb. 10, 1840); Carolyn Lafever and Beth Treaster, eds., *Through the Archway of Time: Centerville, Indiana Celebrates 200 Years* (Greensburg, IN: Winters Publishing, 2014), 15.

27. William C. Greenup to T. S. Brown, June 20, 1833, Historic National Road Interpretive Center, Vandalia, IL.

28. Hardin, "National Road in Illinois," 8–9.

29. Report from the Secretary of War, in Compliance with a Resolution of the Senate, Relative to the Progress Made in the Construction and Repair of the Cumberland Road &c., S. Doc. No. 31, 22nd Cong., 2nd Sess. (Jan. 17, 1833); William Henry Perrin, ed., *History of Effingham County, Illinois* (Chicago: O. L. Baskin, Historical Publishers, 1883), 56.

30. Hardin, "National Road in Illinois," 10; Greenup to Brown, June 20, 1833, Historic National Road Interpretive Center, Vandalia, IL.

31. R. Carlyle Buley, *The Old Northwest Pioneer Period, 1815–1840,* 2 vols. (Bloomington: Indiana Univ. Press, 1951), 1:448; *Illinois Advocate and State Register* (Vandalia, IL), June 8, 1833; Inspection Cumberland Road and Its Concerns in 1833, H. Doc. No. 417, 23rd Cong., 1st Sess. (May 14, 1834).

32. Inspection Cumberland Road and Its Concerns in 1833, H. Doc. No. 417, 23rd Cong., 1st Sess. (May 14, 1834).

33. Message from the President of the United States, with Report on the Condition of the Cumberland Road in Illinois and Indiana, S. Doc. No. 19, 24th Cong., 1st Sess. (Dec. 22, 1835).

34. Unknown to C. A. Ogden, Sept. 30, 1837, Administrative and Scientific Reports, RG 77, NA; Message from the President of the United States, with Report on the Condition of the Cumberland Road in Illinois and Indiana, S. Doc. No. 19, 24th Cong., 1st Sess. (Dec. 22, 1835).

35. Unknown to Ogden, Sept. 30, 1837, Administrative and Scientific Reports, RG 77, NA.

36. *American State Papers,* Class 7:707.

37. Report of the Committee on Roads and Canals, S. Doc. No. 160, 26th Cong., 1st Sess. (Feb. 10, 1840); Hardin, "National Road in Illinois," 7.

38. *Greencastle Visitor,* in *Indiana Journal,* Apr. 6, 1839.

39. *Illinois State Register & People's Advocate* (Vandalia, IL), Apr. 26, 1839; *Indiana Journal,* May 18, June 7, 28, 1839.

40. *Indiana Journal,* July 20, 1839.

41. *Indiana Journal,* July 20, 1839; *Wabash Enquirer* (Terre Haute, IN), July 12, 1839.

42. *Wabash Courier* (Terre Haute, IN), Dec. 4, 1839.

43. Suspend Operations—Public Works, H. Doc. No. 41, 26th Cong., 2nd Sess. (Jan. 4, 1840).

44. Message of the President of the United States to the Two Houses of Congress, at the Commencement of the Second Session of the 27th Congress, S. Doc. No. 1, 27th Cong., 2nd Sess. (Dec. 7, 1841); Message from the President of the United States to the Two Houses of Congress, at the Commencement of the Third Session of the Twenty-Seventh Congress, H. Doc. No. 2, 27th Cong., 3rd Sess. (Dec. 7, 1842).

45. William Oliver, *Eight Months in Illinois with Information to Immigrants* (1843; repr., Chicago: Walter M. Hill, 1924), 187, 206–7.

6. "AN INSTRUCTIVE ADMONITION"

1. Richardson, *Messages and Papers of the Presidents,* 2:864, 873.

2. Michael F. Holt, *The Rise and Fall of the American Whig Party: Jacksonian Politics and the Onset of the Civil War* (New York: Oxford Univ. Press, 1999), 7–9; Remini, *Henry Clay,* 269–70, 273–74, 290–93; James Traub, *John Quincy Adams Militant Spirit* (New York: Basic Books, 2016), 322–26.

3. Register of Debates in Congress, 20th Cong., 2nd Sess. (Jan. 22, 1828), 102, 105, 117.

4. Register of Debates in Congress, 20th Cong., 2nd Sess. (Jan. 22, 1828), 103, 119–20.

5. Register of Debates in Congress, 20th Cong., 2nd Sess. (Jan. 22, 1828), 125; Jordan, *National Road,* 164.

6. Richardson, *Messages and Papers,* 2:1014–15, 1050, 1054–55.

7. Jordan, *National Road,* 169; Robert Remini, *Andrew Jackson and the Course of American Freedom, 1822–1832* (New York: Harper and Row, 1981), 256.

8. Remini, *Andrew Jackson,* 256; *Columbus Gazette,* Apr. 7, 1831.

9. *Journal of the House of Representatives of the State of Ohio Being the First Session of the Twenty-Ninth General Assembly [. . .]* (Columbus: Olmstead and Ballhache, 1831), 340.

10. Register of Debates in Congress, 21st Cong., 2nd Sess. (Mar. 1, 1831), 209, 828–29; Jordan, *National Road,* 170.

11. *Digest of the Laws of Pennsylvania from the Year One Thousand Seven Hundred to the Sixteenth Day of June, One Thousand and Eight Hundred and Thirty-Six* (Philadelphia: McCarry and Davis, 1837), 898–901.

12. Jordan, *National Road,* 170; Searight, *Old Pike,* 104.

13. Cumberland Road East of Ohio, H. Doc. No. 56, 23rd Cong., 2nd Sess. (Jan. 5, 1835). This document covers two years of correspondence and reports from the Corps of Engineers.

14. Joseph K. F. Mansfield to Charles Gratiot, Aug. 1, Sept. 29, 1832; Mansfield to Valentine Giesy, Aug. 13, 1832, Correspondence of Engineers in Charge of Repairs of the Cumberland Road, East of Ohio, 1832–1833, RG 77, NA (hereafter cited as Correspondence of Engineers, 1832–1833).

15. Mansfield to William McMahon, Oct. 3, 1832; Richard Delafield to Gratiot, Delafield to Andrew Stewart, Sept. 2, 1833; H. Bliss to I. F. Kennedy, Apr. 13, 1833, Correspondence of Engineers, 1832–1833, RG 77, NA.

16. Delafield to J. C. Vance, Mar. 30, 1833; Delafield to Gratiot, May 11, 1833, Correspondence of Engineers, 1832–1833, RG 77, NA; *Wheeling Gazette,* May 11, 1833, in *Washington (PA) Examiner,* May 18, 1833.

17. Cumberland Road East of Ohio, H. Doc. No. 56, 23rd Cong., 2nd Sess. (Jan. 5, 1835).

18. Delafield to Gratiot, May 14, 1834, Engineer Department Letters, RG 77, NA; Cumberland Road East of the Ohio, H. Doc. No. 350, 23rd Cong., 1st Sess. (Apr. 18, 1834); Repairs of Cumberland Road East of the Ohio, H. Doc. No. 15, 23rd Cong., 2nd Sess. (Dec. 10, 1834).

19. Cumberland Road East of Ohio, H. Doc. No. 56, 23rd Cong., 2nd Sess. (Jan. 5, 1835); *American State Papers,* Class 6:899–900; Class 7:698–99; William H. Shank, *Historic Bridges of Pennsylvania* (York, PA: American Canal and Transportation Center, 1974), 37; William H. Shank, *Three Hundred Years with the Pennsylvania Traveler* (York, PA: American Canal and Transportation Center, 1976), 51; Report of the Committee on Roads and Canals, S. Doc. No. 160, 26th Cong., 1st Sess. (Feb. 10, 1840).

20. Cumberland Road East of Ohio, H. Doc. No. 56, 23rd Cong., 2nd Sess. (Jan. 5, 1835); Repairs of the Cumberland Road East of Ohio, H. Doc. No. 15, 23rd Cong., 2nd Sess. (Dec. 10, 1834); Stegmair et al., *Allegany County,* 105; James W. Thomas and T. J. C. Williams, *History of Allegany County Maryland* (1923; repr., Baltimore: Regional Publishing, 1969), 193–94.

21. Cumberland Road East of Ohio, H. Doc. No. 56, 23rd Cong., 2nd Sess. (Jan. 5, 1835).

22. Cumberland Road East of Ohio, H. Doc. No. 56, 23rd Cong., 2nd Sess. (Jan. 5, 1835); Mr. Pigman's Report on the National Road, MSS, MHS.

23. Craig Colten, "Adapting the Road to New Transport Technology," in Raitz, *National Road,* 198; *Cumberland Phoenix-Civilian,* Apr. 21, June 16, July 14; Dec. 22, 1835, Dec. 31, 1836.

24. Report of the Committee on Roads and Canals, S. Doc. 160, 26th Cong., 1st Sess. (Feb. 10, 1840); Annals of Congress, 32nd Cong., 2nd Sess. (Feb. 24, 1853), 152.

7. "AN INDEFINITE IMPRESSION OF GREAT ABUSE"

1. Hardin, "National Road in Illinois," 22.

2. Thomas J. Schlereth, *A Roadscape of the American Experience* (Indianapolis: Indiana Historical Society, 1985), 75–76; Burns, "National Road in Indiana," 234.

3. *History of Wayne County, Indiana, Together with Sketches of Its Cities, Villages, and Towns [. . .],* 2 vols. (Chicago: Interstate Publishing, 1884), 1:454; M. C. Oakey, *Greater Terre and Vigo County [. . .],* 2 vols. (Chicago: Lewis Publishing, 1908), 1:184; Schlereth, *Roadscape,* 76.

4. Schlereth, *Roadscape,* 76; George J. Richman, *History of Hancock County Indiana, Its People, Industries and Institutions* (Indianapolis: Federal Publishing Company, 1916), 109–10; Oakey, *Terre Haute and Vigo County,* 184.

5. Jacob Brown, *Brown's Miscellaneous Writings [. . .]* (Cumberland, MD: J. J. Miller, 1896), 107; *Report of the Superintendent of the National Road in the State of Maryland* (Annapolis: William McNeir, 1837), 3–4; *Cumberland Phoenix-Civilian,* Dec. 22, 1835.

6. *Cumberland Phoenix-Civilian,* Mar. 3, June 2, 1838.

7. Report of the Superintendent of the National Road, with Abstracts of Tolls, Received from 12th Oct. 1836 to 1st Oct. 1837, Maryland State Archives, Annapolis.

8. First Semi-Annual Report of Jonathan Huddleson, Superintendent of National Road within the Limits of Maryland, Maryland State Archives, Annapolis.

9. Seventh and Eighth Semi-Annual Reports of T. Thistle, Superintendent of the National Road within the Limits of the State of Maryland, Maryland State Archives, Annapolis.

10. General Assembly of Maryland, Resolution in Relation to Tolls on the National Road, Jan. 20, 1843, Maryland State Archives, Annapolis; J. Thomas Scharf, *History of Western Maryland [. . .]*, 2 vols. (1882; repr., Baltimore: Regional Publishing Company, 1968), 1:1336.

11. Joseph F. McFarland, *20th Century History of the City of Washington and Washington County Pennsylvania and Representative Citizens* (Chicago: Richmond-Arnold Publishing, 1910), 217; James Hadden, *A History of Uniontown the County Seat of Fayette County Pennsylvania* (Akron, OH: New Werner, 1913), 426.

12. *St. Clairsville Gazette,* July 14, 1832.

13. Report of the Superintendent of the National Road, to the General Assembly of Ohio, Dec. 9, 1835, Rare Ohio Documents, OHS.

14. Harry N. Scheiber, *Ohio Canal Era: A Case Study of Government and the Economy, 1820–1861* (Athens: Ohio Univ. Press, 1969), 166–67.

15. Special Report of the Board of Public Works to the Ohio House of Representatives, Dec. 1, 1836, Rare Ohio Documents, OHS; *First Annual Report of the Board of Public Works, to the Thirty-Fifth General Assembly of the State of Ohio* (Columbus: James B. Gardiner, 1837), 12–13.

16. *St. Clairsville Gazette,* Apr. 16, 1836.

17. *St. Clairsville Gazette,* Apr. 30, 1836, May 6, 1837; *Columbus Western Hemisphere,* June 7, 1837.

18. Special Report of the Board of Public Works, Relative to the National Road, Document No. 21, Ohio General Assembly, Jan. 29, 1838; Second Annual Report of the [Ohio] Board of Public Works, Jan. 16, 1838, Rare Ohio Documents, OHS.

19. Fifteenth Annual Report of the Board of Canal Commissioners of the State of Ohio, Jan. 1839, Rare Ohio Documents, OHS; *Third Annual Report of Board of Public Works of the State of Ohio, Made to the Thirty-Eighth General Assembly* (Columbus: Samuel Medary, 1839), 22; Special Report of the Board of Public Works, Transmitting the Report of the Superintendent of the National Road, Document No. 42, Ohio General Assembly, Dec. 30, 1839; Report of the Committee on Roads and Canals, S. Doc. No. 160, 26th Cong., 1st Sess. (Feb. 10, 1840).

20. *Fourth Annual Report of the Board of Public Works of the State of Ohio, Made to the Thirty-Ninth General Assembly* (Columbus: Samuel Medary, 1841), 17–18; *Fifth Annual Report of*

the Board of Public Works of the State of Ohio, Made to the Fortieth General Assembly (Columbus: S. Medary, 1842), 18; Sixth Annual Report of the Board of Public Works of the State of Ohio, to the Forty-First General Assembly (Columbus: Samuel Medary, 1843), 21, 23; Seventh Annual Report of the Board of Public Works of the State of Ohio, the Forty-Second General Assembly (Columbus: Samuel Medary, 1844), 34, 36; Eighth Annual Report of the Board of Public Works of the State of Ohio, to the Forty-Third General Assembly (Columbus: Samuel Medary, 1844), 27, 31.

21. Fourth Annual Report, Board of Public Works, 17; Fifth Annual Report, Board of Public Works, 18; Special Report of the Board of Public Works Relating to the Management of the National Road, in Answer to a Resolution of the [Ohio] House, Feb. 3, 1841, Rare Ohio Documents, OHS.

22. Sixth Annual Report, Board of Public Works, 21–22.

23. Acts of a General Nature Passed by the Forty-First General Assembly of the State of Ohio [. . .] (Columbus: Samuel Medary, 1843), 82; Acts of a General Nature Passed by the Forty-Third General Assembly of the State of Ohio [. . .] (Columbus: Samuel Medary, 1845), 89.

24. Ninth Annual Report of the Board of Public Works of the State of Ohio, to the Forty-Fourth General Assembly (Columbus: C. Scott and Co., 1845), 25; Report of the Commissioners Appointed under the Act of Mar. 6, 1845 [. . .] to the General Assembly of the State of Ohio, Dec. 26, 1845 (hereafter cited as "Commissioners' Report"), State Library of Ohio; Ohio State Journal (Columbus, OH), Jan. 21, 1845.

25. Ninth Annual Report of the Board of Public Works, 24–27.

26. Commissioners' Report; Ohio State Journal, May 6, 1845.

27. Commissioners' Report, 40.

28. Commissioners' Report, 41.

29. Commissioners' Report; Special Report of the Auditors of State, in Reply to a Resolution of the [Ohio] House Passed Dec. 18, 1846, Ohio H. Doc. No. 24, Jan. 2, 1847.

30. Commissioners' Report, 41–42; Special Report of the Auditors of State, in Reply to a Resolution of the [Ohio] House Passed Dec. 18, 1846, Ohio H. Doc. No. 24, Jan. 2, 1847; Report of the Board of Commissioners Appointed under the Act of Mar. 6, 1845, [Ohio] H. Doc. No. 1, Jan. 20, 1847.

31. Commissioners' Report, 49–50, 52.

32. Commissioners' Report, 61–62.

33. Commissioners' Report, 71.

34. Report of the Board of Commissioners, Appointed under the Act of Mar. 6, 1845, [Ohio] H. Doc. No. 1 (Jan. 20, 1847).

35. Report of the Board of Commissioners, Appointed under the Act of Mar. 6, 1845, [Ohio] H. Doc. No. 1 (Jan. 20, 1847).

36. Report of the Board of Commissioners, Appointed under the Act of Mar. 6, 1845, [Ohio] H. Doc. No. 1 (Jan. 20, 1847).

37. Ohio Statesman (Columbus, OH), Sept. 27, 1847; Licking County Common Pleas Court Journal, 1847, 1848, 1849, Licking County Courthouse Annex, Newark, OH; Cleveland True Democrat, in Ohio State Journal, June 13, 1850.

38. *Eleventh Annual Report of the Board of Public Works of the State of Ohio, to the Forty-Sixth General Assembly* (Columbus: Chas. Scott's Steam Press, 1848), 32, 66.

39. Stover, *History of the Baltimore and Ohio*, 82–84; *Seventeenth Annual Report of the Board of Public Works, to the Fifty-First General Assembly of the State of Ohio* (Columbus: Osgood, Blake, and Knapp, 1854), 20.

40. *First Biennial Report of the Board of Public Works to the Governor of Ohio* (Columbus: Statesman Steam Press, 1856), 20; *The History of Clark County, Ohio [. . .]* (Chicago: W. H. Beers, 1881), 282.

41. *St. Clairsville Gazette,* Aug. 20, 1831.

42. *Ohio Republican* (Zanesville, OH), Oct. 8, 1836.

43. William G. Wolfe, *Stories of Guernsey County, Ohio, History of an Average Ohio County* (Cambridge, OH: Author, 1943), 220.

44. Ellis, *Fayette County,* 1:259; E. Howard Blackburn and William Welfley, *History of Bedford and Somerset Counties Pennsylvania [. . .],* 3 vols. (New York: Lewis Publishing, 1906), 2:216; Lewis Clark Walkinshaw, *Annals of Southwestern Pennsylvania,* 4 vols. (New York: Lewis Historical Publishing, 1939), 3:71.

45. Special Report of the Board of Public Works, Relative to the National Road, [Ohio] H. Doc. No. 21, Jan. 29, 1838; *Second Annual Report of the Board of Public Works,* 13.

46. National Road and Toll Gate Houses, Centerville, IN, Public Library Archives.

47. Hulbert, *Old National Road,* 107; *Sixth Annual Report of the Board of Public Works,* 22–23.

48. *Seventh Annual Report of the Board of Public Works,* 35; *Ninth Annual Report of the Board of Public Works,* 30; *Fifteenth Annual Report of the Board of Public Works, to the Fiftieth General Assembly of the State of Ohio* (Columbus: S. Medary, 1852), 31–33.

8. "YOU ARE SURE TO BE PASSED BY PETE BURDINE"

1. Wolfe, *Guernsey County,* 221; Schaff, *Etna and Kirkersville,* 74.

2. Earle R. Forrest, *History of Washington County Pennsylvania,* 2 vols. (Chicago: S. J. Clarke Publishing, 1926), 1:748; *Hagerstown Advertiser,* Sept. 2, 1818, Apr. 27, 1819; *Virginia Northwestern Gazette* (Wheeling, VA), Sept. 19, 1818.

3. Searight, *Old Pike,* 184; Forrest, *Washington County,* 1:743; Hulbert, *Old National Road,* 125–26.

4. Searight, *Old Pike,* 184; Forrest, *Washington County,* 1:744–45.

5. Jordan, *National Road,* 180–82; Forrest, *Washington County,* 1:748–49.

6. Forrest, *Washington County,* 1:749; Ellis, *Fayette County,* 260.

7. Jordan, *National Road,* 184–85.

8. Dorothy J. Clark, *Historically Speaking* (Evansville, IN: Whippoorwill Publications, 1981), 297.

9. "The Old National Pike," *Harper's New Monthly Magazine* (Nov. 1879): 804; Steigmair et al., *Allegany County,* 109; Brown, *Brown's Miscellaneous Writings,* 107; Johnson, "On and

about the National Road," 60; Seymour Dunbar, *A History of Travel in America*, 4 vols. (Indianapolis: Bobbs-Merrill, 1915), 2:734.

10. Stegmair et al., *Allegany County*, 109; Brown, *Brown's Miscellaneous Writings*, 108; Dunbar, *History of Travel in America*, 2:722–23; Johnson, "On and about the National Road," 60.

11. Searight, *Old Pike*, 148; Dunbar, *A History of Travel in America*, 2:722, 726; Wolfe, *Guernsey County*, 221; Prince, *Springfield and Clark County*, 219; Stegmair et al., *Allegany County*, 109; Clark, *Historically Speaking*, 298.

12. Jordan, *National Road*, 189; Searight, *Old Pike*, 147, 151.

13. John Lewis Peyton, *Over the Alleghenies and across the Prairies* (London: Simpkin, Marshall, 1870), 23; Brown, *Brown's Miscellaneous Writings*, 109; Wolfe, *Guernsey County*, 221; Jordan, *National Road*, 186–87.

14. Searight, *Old Pike*, 155.

15. Wolfe, *Guernsey County*, 221; Searight, *Old Pike*, 171–72.

16. Searight, *Old Pike*, 152–53.

17. Searight, *Old Pike*, 149.

18. Jordan, *National Road*, 189; *Ohio Republican* (Zanesville, OH), May 13, 1837.

19. *Indiana Journal* (Indianapolis, IN), July 12, 1839.

20. *Guernsey Times* (Cambridge, OH), Dec. 23, 1831.

21. *Wheeling Gazette*, in *Ohio State Journal* (Columbus, OH), Nov. 4, 1841.

22. *Springfield Republic*, in *Ohio State Journal* (Columbus, OH), July 6, 1842.

23. *Ohio Statesman* (Columbus, OH), Mar. 26, 1845; *Ohio State Journal* (Columbus, OH), Mar. 25, 1845.

24. *Guernsey Times* (Cambridge, OH), Jan. 13, 1832.

25. *Guernsey Times* (Cambridge, OH), Dec. 13, 1845.

26. *Ohio State Journal* (Columbus, OH), Apr. 23, 1839; *Ohio Statesman* (Columbus, OH), Apr. 23, 1839.

27. *Ohio Republican* (Zanesville, OH), Dec. 3, 1842; *Zanesville Aurora*, in *St. Clairsville Gazette*, Dec. 9, 1842.

28. *Guernsey Times* (Cambridge, OH), Mar. 14, 1835; *Zanesville Gazette* (Zanesville, OH), Mar. 31, 1847.

29. *Ohio Republican* (Zanesville, OH), Oct. 19, 1833; May 28, 1842.

30. *Uniontown Genius of Liberty*, June 20, 1820; *Uniontown Democrat*, in *St. Clairsville Gazette*, July 25, 1835.

31. *Brownsville American Telegraph*, Sept. 10, 1817, in Daniel Preston, ed., *The Papers of James Monroe: A Documentary History of the Presidential Tours of James Monroe, 1817, 1818, 1819* (Westport, CT: Greenwood Press, 2003), 470–72.

32. *Cumberland Allegany Freeman*, Oct. 20, 1817.

33. *Washington (PA) Reporter*, Mar. 28, 1825; Dunbar, *History of Travel in America*, 2:737; Searight, *Old Pike*, 176; Schlosnagle, *Garrett County*, 139.

34. Searight, *Old Pike*, 167; *Zanesville (OH) Gazette*, Nov. 2, 1836.

35. Thomas and Williams, *Allegany County,* 193

36. Marie B. Hecht, *John Quincy Adams: A Personal History of an Independent Man* (New York: Macmillan, 1972), 604; Schaff, *Etna and Kirkersville,* 79; Hadden, *History of Uniontown,* 774; *Washington (PA) Examiner,* Nov. 25, 1843.

37. Schlereth, *Roadscape,* 72; Burns, "National Road in Indiana," 234.

38. Miller, "Romance of the National Pike," 30.

39. Jordan, *National Road,* 329–30, 365.

40. *Virginia Northwestern Gazette,* May 14, 1818, in Winegerter, *History of Greater Wheeling,* 151; Stegmair et al., *Allegany County,* 113; *Richmond (IN) Palladium,* Oct. 8, 1842; *Ohio State Journal,* Oct. 11, 1842.

41. *Washington (PA) Reporter,* May 30, June 6, 20, 1825; Ellis, *Fayette County,* 433–34.

42. Miller, "Romance of the National Pike," 30; McFarland, *Washington and Washington County,* 217–18; Stegmair et al., *Allegany County,* 112.

43. Schlosnagle, *Garrett County,* 145; Brown, *Brown's Miscellaneous Writings,* 111; Ellis, *Fayette County,* 609–10; Jordan, *National Road,* 257; Wolfe, *Guernsey County,* 231; Travis, *Clay County,* 36–37; *Illinois Advocate and State Register* (Vandalia, IL), Nov. 2, 1838; May 10, 1839.

44. Searight, *Old Pike,* 192.

45. Parker, Story of an Old Road, Parker Papers, ISL; Searight, *Old Pike,* 223.

46. Parker, Story of an Old Road, Parker Papers, ISL; Heller, *Historic Henry County,* 190.

47. Beste, *Wabash,* 1:317–18; Burns, "National Road in Indiana," 229–30.

48. Entry for May 21, 1838, Jenks Diary, IHS.

49. Oliver, *Eight Months in Illinois,* 193–95.

50. Beste, *Wabash,* 1:316–17, 324–26.

51. *Uniontown Genius of Liberty,* Apr. 5, 1817; *Brownsville American Telegraph,* May 28, 1817; *Washington (PA) Reporter,* June 21, 1819; *Indiana Democrat,* June 14, 1837.

52. "Old National Pike," 802; Brown, *Brown's Miscellaneous Writings,* 112.

53. Wolfe, *Guernsey County,* 232; entry for Dec. 11, 1824, Owen Diary, in Hiatt, "William Owen Diary," 49; Buley, *Old Northwest,* 1:483; Jordan, *National Road,* 266.

54. Jordan, *National Road,* 266; Buley, *Old Northwest,* 1:483; entry for July 21, 1843, Sarah Henderson Diary, IHS; Fred Gustorf, ed., "Frontier Perils Told by an Early Illinois Visitor," *Journal of the Illinois State Historical Society* 55, no. 2 (Summer 1962): 154.

55. "Old National Pike," 802.

56. Brown, *Brown's Miscellaneous Writings,* 112; Thomas and Williams, *Allegany County,* 197; Wolfe, *Guernsey County,* 233; Beste, *Wabash,* 2:68–69, 70; Parker, Story of an Old Highway, Parker Papers, ISL.

57. Matilda Charlotte Fraser Houstoun, *Hesperos: or, Travels in the West,* 2 vols. (London: John W. Parker, 1850), 1:246–48, 255–56, 261–62.

58. Thomas and Williams, *Allegany County,* 197–97; Wolfe, *Guernsey County,* 232.

59. Searight, *Old Pike,* 225, 248; Thomas and Williams, *Allegany County,* 197; Wolfe, *Guernsey County,* 232.

60. William Faux, *Memorable Days in America Being a Journal of a Tour to the United States [. . .]* (London: W. Simpkin and R. Marshall, 1823), 173; Beste, *Wabash*, 1:320; Schlosnagle, *Garrett County*, 147; Wolfe, *Guernsey County*, 230.

61. Schlosnagle, *Garrett County*, 146–47; Searight, *Old Pike*, 229, 247, 268, 293.

62. Beste, *Wabash*, 2:69.

63. Searight, *Old Pike*, 206.

64. Searight, *Old Pike*, 205.

65. Faux, *Memorable Days*, 166.

66. Searight, *Old Pike*, 223–24; Ellis, *Fayette County*, 834–35.

9. "TRULY WORTHY OF A GREAT NATION"

1. James Hall, *Letters from the West: Containing Sketches of Scenery, Manners and Customs [. . .]* (London: Henry Colburn, 1828), 56; William Blaine, *An Excursion through the United States and Canada during the Years 1822–23, by an English Gentleman* (London: Baldwin, Cradock, and Joy, 1824), 85; Houstoun, *Hesperos*, 1:239.

2. Blaine, *An Excursion*, 87; John Lewis Peyton, *Over the Alleghanies and across the Prairies* (London: Simpkin, Marshall, 1870), 21; Godfrey T. Vigne, *Six Months in America*, 2 vols. (London: Whittaker, Treacher, 1832), 2:108; Houstoun, *Hesperos*, 1:243–44.

3. Peyton, *Over the Alleghanies*, 21; Joel W. Hiatt, ed., "The Diary of William Owen from Nov. 10, 1824 to Apr. 20, 1825," *Indiana Historical Society Publications* 4, no. 1 (Indianapolis: Bobbs-Merrill, 1906), 49; Houstoun, *Hesperos*, 1:240; Faux, *Memorable Days*, 167; entry for May 28, 1838, Jenks Diary, IHS.

4. Charles Fenno Hoffman, *Winter in the West*, 2 vols. (New York: Harper and Brothers, 1835), 1:39–40; Thomas Hamilton, *Men and Manners in America* (Edinburgh: William Blackwood, 1833), 161–62.

5. Hamilton, *Men and Manners*, 163; Blaine, *An Excursion*, 89; John Woods, *Two Years' Residence in the Settlement on the English Prairie in the Illinois Country, United States*, in *Early Western Travels*, ed. Reuben Gold Thwaites, 32 vols. (Cleveland: A. H. Clark, Co., 1904–7), 10:213; John P. Cockey to "Paul," Dec. 6, 1829, John P. Cockey Papers, 1829–33, OHS; Houstoun, *Hesperos*, 1:254–55.

6. Blaine, *An Excursion*, 86; Houstoun, *Hesperos*, 1:240; Woods, *Two Years' Residence*, 210; Vigne, *Six Months in America*, 2:108.

7. Houstoun, *Hesperos*, 1:245–46; Peyton, *Over the Alleghanies*, 21; Blaine, *An Excursion*, 86–87; Woods, *Two Years' Residence*, 208.

8. Peyton, *Over the Alleghanies*, 21; Blaine, *An Excursion*, 87–88.

9. Blaine, *An Excursion*, 85, 88, 91; entry for Nov. 1, 1838, Frederick W. Treadway Journal, Mss. 2639, Louisiana State Univ., Baton Rouge; Houstoun, *Hesperos*, 1:251.

10. Adlard Welby, *A Visit to North America and the English Settlements in Illinois* (London: Baldwin, Cradock, and Joy, 1821), 201, 204.

11. Hamilton, *Men and Manners,* 164–65.

12. Woods, *Two Years' Residence,* 215–16; Houstoun, *Hesperos,* 1:243–45.

13. Woods, *Two Years' Residence,* 212; Houstoun, *Hesperos,* 1:249–50, 255.

14. Houstoun, *Hesperos,* 1:261; Hamilton, *Men and Manners,* 165; Peyton, *Over the Alleghanies,* 28; Blaine, *An Excursion,* 89.

15. Hoffman, *A Winter in the West,* 1:52; Welby, *Visit to North America,* 204; Blaine, *Excursion,* 91; entry for Nov. 2, 1838, Treadway Journal, Mss. 2639, Louisiana State Univ., Baton Rouge.

16. Hall, Letters from the West, 54–55; Welby, *Visit to North America,* 202; T. S. Sears to John Pawling, July 31, 1847, T. S. Sears Letter, OHS.

17. Hamilton, *Men and Manners,* 163–64.

18. Searight, *Old Pike,* 259; Houstoun, *Hesperos,* 1:261.

19. Clifford M. Lewis, "The Wheeling Suspension Bridge," *West Virginia History* 23, no. 3 (Apr. 1972): 206–7; Cumberland Road East of the Ohio, H. Doc. No. 672, 24th Cong., 1st Sess. (May 17, 1836).

20. Cumberland Road East of the Ohio, H. Doc. No. 672, 24th Cong., 1st Sess. (May 17, 1836); Bridge at Wheeling, Virginia, H. Doc. No. 993, 25th Cong., 2nd Sess. (June 27, 1838).

21. Emory L. Kemp and Beverly B. Fluty, *The Wheeling Suspension Bridge: A Pictorial Heritage* (Charleston, WV: Pictorial Histories Publishing, 1999), 7, 19; Lewis, "Wheeling Suspension Bridge," 207–9, 211–14.

22. Lewis, "Wheeling Suspension Bridge," 217–26; Elizabeth B. Monroe, "Spanning the Commerce Clause: The Wheeling Bridge Case, 1850–1856," *American Journal of Legal History* 32, no. 3 (July 1988): 278–84.

23. Welby, *Visit to North America,* 205.

24. Joseph John Gurney, *A Journey to North America Described in Familiar Letters to Amelia Opie* (Norwich, England: Author, 1841), 28; entry for May 26, 1838, Jenks Diary, IHS; Faux, *Memorable Days,* 172, 176–77.

25. *New England Farmer,* June 10, 1840; Oliver, *Eight Months in Illinois,* 200–207.

26. William Cobbett, *A Year's Residence in the United States of America* (London: Author, 1828), 298–99; Gurney, *Journey to North America,* 28; entry for May 28, 1838, Jenks Diary, IHS.

27. Gurney, *Journey to North America,* 29; entry for May 28, 1838, Jenks Diary, IHS.

28. Oliver, *Eight Months in Illinois,* 205–6; *New England Farmer,* June 10, 1840.

29. *New England Farmer,* June 10, 1840; Oliver, *Eight Months in Illinois,* 199.

30. Gustorf, "Frontier Perils," 152; Edmund Flagg, *The Far West: A Tour beyond the Mountains [. . .],* 2 vols. (New York: Harper and Brothers, 1838), 1:248; Oliver, *Eight Months in Illinois,* 186–87.

31. Entries for Sept. 21–22, 1835, Alfred Brunson Diary, in Alfred Brunson, "A Methodist Circuit Rider's Horseback Tour from Pennsylvania to Wisconsin, 1835," *Wisconsin Historical Collections* 15 (1900): 270; entry for May 26, 1838, Jenks Diary, IHS.

32. Entry for Sept. 25, 1835, Brunson Diary, in Brunson, "Methodist Circuit Rider's Tour," 271; Peter Hessong to parents, May 21, 1838, Peter Hessong letter, IHS; *New England Farmer,* June 10, 1840; Oliver, *Eight Months in Illinois,* 197, 206.

10. "IT KICKED UP A DUST"

1. J. L. Ringwalt, *Development of Transportation Systems in the United States* (Philadelphia: Author, 1888), 31; Peyton, "Surveying and Building the Road," in Raitz, *National Road,* 136–37; William H. Koontz, ed., *History of Bedford and Somerset Counties Pennsylvania,* 3 vols. (New York: Lewis Publishing, 1906), 2:213–14; Forrest, *Washington County,* 1:749.

2. Searight, *Old Pike,* 164.

3. Winifred Gallagher, *How the Post Office Created America* (New York: Penguin Press, 2016), 91, 93; Jordan, *National Road,* 277.

4. Jordan, *National Road,* 279–80; *Zanesville Gazette,* Jan. 24, 1838; Interruption of the Mail at Wheeling, H. Doc. No. 137, 29th Cong., 1st Sess. (Feb. 24, 1846).

5. Condition of Cumberland Road, H. Doc. No. 269, 20th Cong., 1st Sess. (May 10, 1828); *Washington (PA) Examiner,* Aug. 6, 1831; *Ohio Statesman,* Feb. 26, 1847.

6. *Ohio Statesman,* Sept. 19, 1835.

7. Gallagher, *Post Office,* 71–72; James W. Milgram, *The Express Mail of 1836–1839: To Provide a Faster Mail Service between the North and the South* (Chicago: Collectors Club of Chicago, 1971), 22.

8. Milgram, *Express Mail of 1836,* 30, 64–67; Jordan, *National Road,* 281–83.

9. *Zanesville Gazette,* July 5, Sept. 13, 1837.

10. *Illinois State Register* (Vandalia, IL), Dec. 22, 1837.

11. Hill, *Licking County,* 482; Thomas and Williams, *History of Allegany County,* 186; Ellis, *Fayette County,* 259–60.

12. Burns, "National Road in Indiana," 227; Jordan, *National Road,* 283–85.

13. *Cumberland Civilian,* in *Indiana Journal,* Aug. 29, 1834; Stegmair, et al., *Allegany County,* 112; Lowdermilk, *History of Cumberland,* 334–35.

14. *Guernsey Times,* June 25, 1836.

15. *Ohio State Journal,* Aug. 9, 1837.

16. *Ohio State Journal,* Sept. 22, Nov. 17, 1837; *Ohio Statesman,* Sept. 27, 1837; Alfred E. Lee, *History of the City of Columbus, Capital of Ohio,* 2 vols. (New York: Munsell & Co., 1892), 1:351.

17. *Wabash Enquirer* (Terre Haute, IN), in *Indiana Journal,* Mar. 2, 1839.

18. *Uniontown Genius of Liberty,* July 20, 1819.

19. Oliver, *Eight Months in Illinois,* 198–99. Paris could be a reference to Fayette Township, located northwest of Terre Haute, which had originally been named Paris Township. It could also refer to Paris, Illinois, a community some thirty miles northwest of Terre Haute.

20. Perrin, *History of Effingham County,* 231–32.

21. Searight, *Old Pike,* 339–40; Jordan, *National Road,* 285–86.

22. Searight, *Old Pike,* 341–42.

23. *Uniontown Genius of Liberty,* in *Zanesville Aurora,* Jan. 22, 1841; *Washington (PA) Examiner,* Jan. 9, 1841; *Washington (PA) Reporter,* in *Ohio State Journal,* Jan. 12, 1841; Searight, *Old Pike,* 188–89.

24. *Uniontown Genius of Liberty,* in *Zanesville Aurora,* Jan. 22, 1841; *Washington Examiner,* in *Ohio Statesman,* Jan. 16, 1841.

25. *Washington (PA) Reporter,* in *Ohio State Journal,* Jan. 12, 1841; *Ohio Statesman,* Jan. 11, 1841.

26. Searight, *Old Pike,* 343, 350, 352; Jordan, *National Road,* 286–87; *Ohio State Journal,* June 8, 1841.

27. *Uniontown Genius of Liberty,* Sept. 1, 1842.

11. "A PECULIAR CLASS OF MEN"

1. Norman B. Wilkinson, "The Conestoga Wagon," *Historic Pennsylvania Leaflet,* no. 5 (Harrisburg: Pennsylvania Historical and Museum Commission, 1951), 2; Forrest, *Washington County* 1:740.

2. Wilkinson, "Conestoga Wagon," 2–3; Dunbar, *History of Travel in America,* 2:727.

3. Wilkinson, "Conestoga Wagon," 2–3; Searight, *Old Pike,* 118–19.

4. Dunbar, *History of Travel in America,* 2:727–28; Miller, "Romance of the National Pike," 24–25.

5. Thomas and Williams, *Allegany County Maryland,* 1:194; Searight, *Old Pike,* 119; *Washington Examiner,* May 20, 1843.

6. Searight, *Old Pike,* 110–11, 129; Lee, *History of Columbus,* 1:327.

7. Searight, *Old Pike,* 110; Wilkinson, "Conestoga Wagon," 41.

8. Wolfe, *Guernsey County,* 224; Searight, *Old Pike,* 133, 137.

9. Searight, *Old Pike,* 144–45; Jordan, *National Road,* 230–31.

10. Wilkinson, "Conestoga Wagon," 3; Jordan, *National Road,* 222.

11. Forrest, *Washington County,* 1:739; Jordan, *National Road,* 221.

12. Searight, *Old Pike,* 111.

13. Searight, *Old Pike,* 119; Lee, *History of Columbus,* 2:327; Forrest, *Washington County,* 739; Rene Bache, "Building a Thousand-Mile Boulevard," *Technical World Magazine* (Dec. 1910): 428.

14. Schneider, *Y Bridge City,* 102–3; Clark, *Historically Speaking,* 301; Searight, *Old Pike,* 110, 119; Thomas and Williams, *Allegany County,* 194.

15. Searight, *Old Pike,* 110, 121.

16. Searight, *Old Pike,* 120, 121.

17. Jordan, *National Road,* 220.

18. McFarland, *Washington and Washington County,* 217; William Henry Perrin, *History of Crawford and Clark Counties, Illinois* (Chicago: O. L. Baskin & Co., 1883), 273.

19. Searight, *Old Pike,* 111, 122–23, 136; Jordan, *National Road,* 218.

20. Jordan, *National Road,* 229–30; Searight, *Old Pike,* 142–43; *St. Clairsville Gazette* (1835), quoted in Hulbert, *Old National Road,* 131.

21. Jordan, *National Road,* 217; Schneider, *Y Bridge City,* 103; Searight, *Old Pike,* 115.

22. Jordan, *National Road,* 228; Thomas and Williams, *Allegany County,* 186–87.

23. Jordan, *National Road,* 217–18.

24. Searight, *Old Pike,* 143–44.

25. Hulbert, *Old National Road,* 129, 164–65; Miller, "Romance of the National Pike," 23–24; Wolfe, *Stories of Guernsey County,* 233.

26. Miller, "Romance of the National Pike," 25; Jordan, *National Road,* 223; Dunbar, *History of Travel in America,* 2:729.

27. Dunbar, *History of Travel in America,* 2:729–30; Miller, "Romance of the National Pike," 25–26.

28. Miller, "Romance of the National Pike," 26; Dunbar, *History of Travel in America,* 730; Clark, *Historically Speaking,* 301.

29. Miller, "Romance of the National Pike," 26–27; Searight, *Old Pike,* 142.

30. Forrest, *Washington County,* 743.

12. "A CONTINUAL STREAM"

1. Hiatt, "William Owen Diary," 49; Blaine, *Excursion,* 90; Peyton, *Over the Alleghenies,* 27.

2. Jordan, *National Road,* 235–36; Benjamin S. Parker, Story of an Old Highway, MSS, Benjamin S. Parker Papers, ISL.

3. Jordan, *National Road,* 236, 237–38; Parker, Story of an Old Highway, MSS, Parker Papers, ISL.

4. Jordan, *National Road,* 235, 238; *Cumberland Mountaineer,* in *Ohio State Journal,* Dec. 28, 1848. Walkinshaw, *Annals of Southwestern Pennsylvania,* 3:70.

5. Jordan, *National Road,* 235–36, 238, 241; Schaff, *A Sketch of Etna and Kirkersville,* 78; Searight, *Old Pike,* 121.

6. Parker, Story of an Old Highway, MSS, Parker Papers, ISL; Paul C. Heinlein, "Cattle Driving from the Ohio Country, 1800–1850," *Agricultural History* 28 (1954): 87–88; Robert Leslie Jones, "The Beef Cattle Industry in Ohio Prior to the Civil War," *Ohio Historical Quarterly* 64 (1955): 294.

7. William Renick, *Memoirs, Correspondence and Reminiscences* (Circleville, OH: Union-Herald Book and Job Printing House, 1880), 12; John C. Hudson, *Making the Corn Belt: A Geographical History of Middle-Western Agriculture* (Bloomington: Indiana Univ. Press, 1994), 68; Heinlein, "Cattle Driving," 83.

8. Renick, *Memoirs,* 14; Hudson, *Making the Corn Belt,* 83.

9. Heinlein, "Cattle Driving," 90; I. F. King, "The Coming and Going of Ohio Droving," *Ohio Archaeological and Historical Society Publications* 27 (1908): 248.

10. Oliver, *Eight Months in Illinois,* 105–6.

11. Oliver, *Eight Months in Illinois,* 106–7; Jones, "Beef Cattle Industry," 299.

12. Heinlein, "Cattle Driving," 92; Jordan, *National Road,* 243; King, "Ohio Droving," 250–51.

13. King, "Ohio Droving," 250.

14. Heinlein, "Cattle Driving," 87–88.

15. Jordan, *National Road,* 244.

16. King, "Ohio Droving," 251–52; Jordan, *National Road,* 244.

17. Jones, "The Beef Cattle Industry," 299; Henry Bushnell, *The History of Granville Licking County, Ohio* (Columbus: Press of Hann and Adair, 1889), 145.

18. King, "Ohio Droving," 252; Jordan, *National Road*, 244–45.

19. Mary Vose Harris, ed., "The Autobiography of Benjamin Franklin Harris," *Transactions of the Illinois State Historical Society for the Year 1923* (Springfield: Phillips Brothers, 1923), 77–78.

20. Jordan, *National Road*, 244; Heinlein, "Cattle Driving," 92–93; King, "Ohio Droving," 250.

21. Jordan, *National Road*, 245.

22. Jordan, *National Road*, 245–46; Utter, *Frontier State*, 165–66; Report of the Superintendent of the National Road, to the General Assembly of Ohio, 1835.

23. Jordan, *National Road*, 247–50; Schaff, *Etna and Kirkersville*, 78.

24. Parker, Story of an Old Highway, MSS, Parker Papers, ISL; Charles B. Johnson, "On and about the National Road in the Early Fifties," *Transactions of the Illinois State Historical Society for the Year 1922* (Springfield: Board of Trustees of the Illinois State Historical Library, 1922), 61–62.

25. Searight, *Old Pike*, 121; Stegmair et al., *Allegany County*, 108–9.

26. *Washington (PA) Examiner*, Aug. 5, Nov. 5, 1825.

27. Hiatt, "William Owen Diary," 50; Peyton, *Over the Alleghenies*, 26; *Indiana Democrat*, May 25, 1839; *St. Clairsville Gazette*, May 25, 1839.

28. Hulbert, *Old National Road*. For a good summary of this subject, see Gregory S. Rose, "Extending the Road West," in Raitz, *National Road*, esp. 170–76.

29. Rose, "Extending the Road West," 171.

30. Parker, Story of an Old Highway, MSS, Parker Papers, ISL; entry for May 25, 1838; Jenks Diary, IHS; *St. Clairsville Gazette*, May 25, 1839.

31. *Richmond Palladium*, Oct. 11, 1834; May 21, 1836; Oct. 24, 1840.

32. Johnson, "On and about the National Road," 60–61.

33. Parker, Story of an Old Highway, MSS, Parker Papers, ISL; Miller, "Romance of the National Pike," 13; Peyton, *Over the Alleghenies*, 26; Hoffman, *A Winter in the West*, 45.

34. Hoffman, *A Winter in the West*, 44–45; Parker, Story of an Old Highway, MSS, Parker Papers, ISL; *Guernsey Times*, Oct. 19, 1833.

35. Hiatt, "William Owen Diary," 49; Parker, Story of an Old Highway, MSS, Parker Papers, ISL; LeFever and Treaster, *Through the Archways of Time*, 16; Oliver, *Eight Months in Illinois*, 200.

36. Peyton, *Over the Alleghenies*, 26–27; entries for May 12, 22, 1841, Jane Voorhees Diary, in "Journal of Jane Voorhees Lewis," 86, 87; The Old National Road, MSS, Charles F. and Rhoda M. Coffin Collection, Earlham College.

37. Forrest, *Washington County*, 757–60; Crumrine, *Washington County*, 753–54, 770, 975–76; *Washington (PA) Examiner*, Sept. 16, Nov. 28, 1819.

38. Peter C. Boyd, *History the Town of Triadelphia on Its 125th Anniversary* (Triadelphia, WV: Author, 1954), 7.

39. *St. Clairsville Gazette*, Feb. 20, 1830.

40. *Biographical and Historical Memoirs of Muskingum County, Ohio [. . .]* (Chicago: Goodspeed Publishing, 1892), 297–99.

41. *Ohio Republican,* Sept. 21, 1833.

42. Hill, *Licking County,* 402, 475, 480, 496.

43. *The History of Clark County, Ohio [. . .]* (Chicago: W. H. Bears & Co., 1881), 645, 646, 647, 709.

44. Blakey et al., *Then and Now,* 10; Burns, "National Road in Indiana," 224; Parker, *Story of an Old Highway,* MSS, Parker Papers, ISL; Dan Poole, *A Town with Two Names* (Milton, IN: Kids at Heart Publishing, 2012), 3; Robert Dawson, "Dublin's Beginnings," in *Dublin 1830–1980* (Dublin, IN: Print Press, 1980), 2–4.

45. *History of Henry County, Indiana [. . .]* (Chicago: Inter-state Publishing, 1884), 613–14, 790; George Hazard, *Hazard's History of Henry County Indiana 1822–1906* (New Castle, IN: Author, 1906), 929, 937, 959; Ronald L. Baker and Marvin Carmony, *Indiana Place Names* (Bloomington: Indiana Univ. Press, 1975), 121.

46. Burns, "National Road in Indiana," 224; *History of Henry County,* 862–63; Hazard, *Henry County,* 936–37.

47. Burns, "National Road in Indiana," 224; Jordan, *National Road,* 374.

48. Burns, "National Road in Indiana," 224; David J. Bodenhamer and Robert G. Barrows, *The Encyclopedia of Indianapolis* (Bloomington: Indiana Univ. Press, 1994), 350, 486, 1306; Schlereth, *Roadscape,* 64; Rosalie Lewis, *Cumberland Reflections 1831–1988* (Nappanee, IN: Evangel Press, 1988), 4.

49. Burns, "National Road in Indiana," 224–25; *History of Hendricks County, Indiana [. . .]* (Chicago: Inter-state Publishing, 1885), 592, 635–36.

50. Jesse W. Weik, *Weik's History of Putnam County Indiana* (Indianapolis: B. F. Bowen, 1910), 181; *Biographical and Historical Record of Putnam County, Indiana* (Chicago: Lewis Publishing, 1887), 235; *Indiana Democrat,* Aug. 27, 1831.

51. Burns, "National Road in Indiana," 225; Travis, *Clay County,* 113–15, 154, 162.

52. Perrin, *Crawford and Clark Counties,* 305, 309, 343–44, 404–5; H. C. Bell, *History of Clark County* (Chicago: Middle West Publishing, 1907), 665–66.

53. *Illinois Advocate and State Register,* July 26, 1834.

54. Perrin, *History of Effingham County,* 151, 177–80, 218–19, 251–53.

AFTERWORD

1. Forrest, *Washington County,* 1:760–61; Miller, "Romance of the National Pike," 34; Arch Butler Hulbert, "The Old National Road," *Ohio Archeological and Historical Society Publications* 9 (1901): 491.

2. Rideing, "Old National Pike," 801; J. Hope Sutor, *Past and Present of the City of Zanesville and Muskingum County Ohio* (Chicago: Clark Publishing, 1905), 69; Koontz, *Bedford and Somerset Counties,* 2:216.

3. Wolfe, *Guernsey County,* 238–40; *Guernsey Times,* Feb. 22, 1833.

4. Theodore Sky, *The National Road and the Difficult Path to Sustainable National Investment* (Newark: Univ. of Delaware Press, 2011), 153, 155.

5. Glenn A. Harper, "Preserving the National Road Landscape," in Raitz, *National Road*, 382.

6. Harper, "Preserving the National Road," 384; Bache, "Building a Thousand-Mile Boulevard," 431.

7. Albert Douglas, "Auto Trip over the Old National Road," *Ohio Archaeological and Historical Publications* 18 (1909): 504, 508–12.

8. Frederic L. Paxson, "The Highway Movement, 1916–1935," *American Historical Review* 51 (1946): 238–39.

9. Sky, *National Road*, 155.

10. Sky, *National Road*, 239–40; Michael Wallis and Michael S. Williamson, *The Lincoln Highway: Coast to Coast from Times Square to the Golden Gate* (New York: W. W. Norton, 2007), 3; Paxson, "Highway Movement," 239–40, 241.

11. Paxson, "Highway Movement," 241–42.

12. Sky, *National Road*, 153–54, 190; Harper, "Preserving the National Road Landscape," in Raitz, *National Road*, 385–86; David McCullough, *Truman* (New York: Simon and Schuster, 1992), 171; Charles Henry Davis, "The National Old Trails Road," *Travel Magazine* (May 1915): 34.

13. Sky, *National Road*, 154, 155; Paxson, "Highway Movement," 238, 242–43.

14. John Chynoweth Burnham, "The Gasoline Tax and the Automobile Revolution," *Mississippi Valley Historical Review* 48 (1961): 436, 437–41, 446, 453; Karl Raitz, "The US 40 Roadscape," in Raitz, *National Road*, 239.

15. Sky, *National Road*, 158; Paxson, "Highway Movement," 243–49; John A. Jakle, "Travelers' Impressions of the National Road," in Raitz, *National Road*, 239.

16. For an excellent account of the First Transcontinental Motor Train, see Pete Davies, *American Road: The Story of an Epic Transcontinental Journey at the Dawn of the Motor Age* (New York: Henry Holt, 2002); for Eisenhower's story of the convoy, see Dwight D. Eisenhower, *At Ease: Stories I Tell to Friends* (Garden City, NY: Doubleday, 1967), 155–68.

17. Davies, *American Road*, 216.

18. Sky, *National Road*, 158–60; Paxson, "Highway Movement," 245–46.

19. Peyton, "Surveying and Building the Road," in Raitz, *National Road*, 158; Jordan, *National Road*, 388.

20. Sky, *National Road*, 162–63; Raitz, "The US 40 Roadscape," in Raitz, *National Road*, 289–90.

21. Raitz, "US 40 Roadscape," 300–311; Jordan, *National Road*, 394.

22. Richard H. Schwein, "Interstate 70 Landscape," in Raitz, *National Road*, 322–23; Sky, *National Road*, 170–71.

23. Schein, "Interstate 70 Landscape," in Raitz, *National Road*, 324.

24. For further perspectives see Schein, "Interstate 70 Landscape," in Raitz, *National Road*.

25. Douglas, "Auto Trip," 512.

Bibliography

MANUSCRIPT MATERIAL

Centerville, IN, Public Library Archives
    National Road and tollgate houses
Historic National Road Interpretive Center, Vandalia, IL
    Greenup, William C., to T. S. Brown, June 20, 1833
    Shriver, Joseph, Notebook of the Survey of the Cumberland Road between Terre Haute, Indiana and St. Louis, Missouri
Indiana Historical Society, Indianapolis
    Henderson, Sarah, diary
    Hessong, Peter, letter
    Jenks, M. H., travel diary
Indiana State Library, Indianapolis
    Parker, Benjamin S., papers
Licking County Courthouse Annex, Newark, OH
    Licking County Common Pleas Court, journal, 1847–1849
Louisiana State University, Baton Rouge
    Treadway, Frederick W., journal
Maryland Historical Society, Baltimore
    Mr. Pigman's report on the National Road
    Shriver Family Papers
National Archives and Records Administration, Washington, DC
    Record Group 77, Records of the Chief of Engineers
        Administrative and scientific reports of superintendents and Lesser Officials of the Cumberland Road, 1833–1840
        Correspondence of engineers in charge of repairs of the Cumberland Road, East of the Ohio, 1832–1833
        Correspondence and other records pertaining to the Cumberland Road, 1810–1824

Journal kept by Elie Williams during examination of route for Cumberland Road in 1806

Letters received by the Engineer Department relating to the Cumberland Road, 1829–1834

Letters sent by the Office of the Chief of Engineers relating to internal improvements, 1824–1830

Ohio Historical Society, Columbus

Cockey, John P., letter

Records of the Ohio Board of Public Works

Sears, T. S., letter

Pennsylvania State Archives, Harrisburg

Record Group 12, Department of Highways

National Road Reference File, 1806–1935, Hunter Collection

Western Reserve Historical Society, Cleveland

Shriver, David, Jr., papers, 1811–1852

NEWSPAPERS

Allegany Freedman (Cumberland, MD)

Brownsville (PA) American Telegraph

Columbus Gazette

Columbus Sentinel

Columbus Western Hemisphere

Cumberland Maryland Advocate

Cumberland Phoenix-Civilian

Guernsey Times (Cambridge, OH)

Hagerstown Advertiser

Illinois Advocate (Vandalia, IL)

Illinois Advocate and State Register (Vandalia, IL)

Illinois State Register and People's Advocate (Vandalia, IL)

Indiana Democrat (Indianapolis, IN)

Indiana Journal (Indianapolis, IN)

Indianapolis Sentinel

Indiana State Gazette (Indianapolis, IN)

New England Farmer

Ohio Monitor (Columbus, OH)

Ohio State Journal (Columbus, OH)

Ohio Statesman (Columbus, OH)

Richmond (IN) Palladium

Springfield (OH) Republic

St. Clairsville (OH) Gazette
Uniontown Genius of Liberty
Wabash Courier (Terre Haute, IN)
Wabash Enquirer (Terre Haute, IN)
Washington (PA) Examiner
Washington (PA) Reporter
Wheeling Gazette
Wheeling Times
Zanesville Aurora
Zanesville Courier
Zanesville Gazette

CONGRESSIONAL DOCUMENTS

Bridge at Wheeling, Virginia, H. Doc. No. 993, 25th Cong., 2nd Sess. (June 27, 1838).
Condition of the Cumberland Road, H. Doc. No. 269, 20th Cong., 1st Sess. (May 10, 1828).
Continuation of the Cumberland Road, H. Doc. No. 59, 21st Cong., 1st Sess. (Feb. 12, 1830).
Cumberland Road, Exec. Doc. No. 220, 9th Cong., 2nd Sess. (Jan. 31, 1807).
Cumberland Road, Exec. Doc. No. 243, 10th Cong., 1st Sess. (Feb. 19, 1808).
Cumberland Road, Exec. Doc. No. 258, 10th Cong., 2nd Sess. (Dec. 13, 1808).
Cumberland Road, H. Doc. No. 12, 21st Cong., 2nd Sess. (Dec. 21, 1830).
Cumberland Road, H. Doc. No. 39, 21st Cong., 2nd Sess. (Dec. 21, 1830).
Cumberland Road, H. Doc. No. 263, 10th Cong., 2nd Sess. (Feb. 16, 1809).
Cumberland Road, H. Doc. No. 410, 21st Cong., 1st Sess. (May 24, 1830).
Cumberland Road, H. Doc. No. 211, 29th Cong., 1st Sess. (Feb. 10, 1846).
Cumberland Road, H. Misc. Doc. No. 486, 16th Cong., 1st Sess. (Mar. 10, 1820).
Cumberland Road, Misc. Doc. No. 311, 12th Cong., 1st Sess. (Feb. 3, 1812).
Cumberland Road, Misc. Doc. No. 317, 12th Cong., 1st Sess. (Apr. 14, 1812).
Cumberland Road, Misc. Doc. No. 339, 12th Cong., 2nd Sess. (Mar. 2, 1813).
Cumberland Road, Misc. Doc. No. 356, 13th Cong., 2nd Sess. (Jan. 19, 1814).
Cumberland Road, Misc. Doc. No. 379, 13th Cong., 3rd Sess. (Jan. 2, 1815).
Cumberland Road, Misc. Doc. No. 403, 14th Cong., 1st Sess. (Mar. 11, 1816).
Cumberland Road and Ohio River, H. Doc. No. 52, 24th Cong., 2nd Sess. (Dec. 30, 1836).
Cumberland Road East of the Ohio, H. Doc. No. 350, 23rd Cong., 1st Sess. (Apr. 18, 1834).
Cumberland Road East of Ohio, H. Doc. No. 56, 23rd Cong., 2nd Sess. (Jan. 5, 1835).
Cumberland Road East of the Ohio, H. Doc. No. 672, 24th Cong., 1st Sess. (May 17, 1836).
Cumberland Road—Indiana and Illinois, H. Doc. No. 26, 24th Cong., 1st Sess. (Dec. 24, 1835).
Documents in Relation to the Construction of the Cumberland Road in the States of Ohio
    and Indiana, S. Doc. No. 37, 21st Cong., 1st Sess. (Feb. 22, 1830).
Document Relating to the Completion of the Cumberland Road in the State of Illinois, S.
    Doc. No. 314, 27th Cong., 2nd Sess. (Feb. 4, 1842).

Gratiot, C. to W. Hendricks, Jan. 28, 1836, S. Doc. No. 114, 24th Cong., 1st Sess. (Feb. 2, 1836).

Inspection Cumberland Road and Its Concerns, H. Doc. No. 417, 23rd Cong., 1st Sess. (May 14, 1834).

Interruption of the Mail at Wheeling, H. Doc. No. 137, 29th Cong., 1st Sess. (Feb. 24, 1846).

Letter from the Secretary of the Treasury, Transmitting a Report of the Commissioners, Appointed to View and Inspect the Cumberland Road, H. Doc. No. 27, 17th Cong., 1st Sess. (Jan. 15, 1822).

Letter from the Secretary of War, Transmitting a Report of the Chief Engineer in Relation to the Road through Ohio, Indiana, and Illinois, H. Doc. No. 18, 19th Cong., 2nd Sess. (Dec. 20, 1826).

Letter from the Secretary of War, Transmitting a Copy of the Last Annual Report of the Superintendent of the Cumberland Road, H. Doc. No. 14, 20th Cong., 2nd Sess. (Dec. 11, 1828).

Letter from the Secretary of War, Transmitting Reports and Drawing Relative to the National Road, H. Doc. No. 74, 19th Cong., 2nd Sess. (Feb. 3, 1827).

Message from the President of the United States, with Report on the Condition of the Cumberland Road in Illinois and Indiana, S. Doc. No. 19, 24th Cong., 1st Sess. (Dec. 22, 1835).

Message from the President of the United States, Transmitting a Report from the War Department on the Condition of the Cumberland Road in Indiana and Illinois, H. Doc. No. 26, 24th Cong., 1st Sess. (Dec. 24, 1835).

Message from the President of the United States to the Two Houses of Congress, at the Commencement of the Second Session of the Twenty-Seventh Congress, S. Doc. No. 1, 27th Cong., 2nd Sess. (Dec. 7, 1841).

National Road in Indiana, H. Doc. No. 36, 21st Cong., 2nd Sess. (Jan. 10, 1831).

National Road—Springfield, Ohio, to Richmond, Indiana, H. Doc. No. 62, 24th Cong., 1st Sess. (Jan. 13, 1836).

National Road West of the Ohio, H. Doc. No. 230, 24th Cong., 1st Sess. (Apr. 20, 1836).

Progress Made in Making Roads by Authority of the United States, Misc. Doc. No. 443, 15th Cong., 1st Sess. (Jan. 23, 1818).

Repairs of the Cumberland Road East of the Ohio, H. Doc. No. 15, 23rd Cong., 2nd Sess. (Dec. 10, 1834).

Report of the Committee on Roads and Canals, S. Doc. No. 160, 26th Cong., 1st Sess. (Feb. 10, 1840).

Report from the Secretary of War, in Compliance with a Resolution of the Senate, Transmitting Reports from the Superintendent of the Cumberland Road, for 1829 and 1830, S. Doc. No. 17, 21st Cong., 2nd Sess. (Dec. 31, 1830).

Report from the Secretary of War, in Compliance with a Resolution of the Senate of the 12th Instant, Showing the Progress Made in Opening the Cumberland Road Continued through Indiana, S. Doc. No. 27, 21st Cong., 1st Sess. (Jan. 15, 1830).

Report from the Secretary of War, in Compliance with a Resolution of the Senate of the 14th Instant, Transmitting a Report of the Agent Appointed to Inspect the Cumberland Road, S. Doc. No. 45, 23rd Cong., 1st Sess. (Jan. 17, 1834).

Report from the Secretary of War, in Obedience to a Resolution of the Senate of the 16th of January, 1835, Relative to the Construction of a Bridge over the Wabash River at the Crossing of the Cumberland Road, S. Doc. No. 10, 24th Cong., 1st Sess. (Dec. 10, 1835).

Report of the Secretary of War, in Compliance with a Resolution of the Senate, of the Eighth Instant, Transmitting a Report of the Commissioner for Locating the Continuation of the Cumberland Road, under Act of March 3, 1825, S. Doc. No. 99, 20th Cong., 1st Sess. (Feb. 12, 1828).

Report of the Secretary of War, in Compliance with a Resolution of the Senate, Relative to the Progress Made in the Construction and Repair of the Cumberland Road, &c., S. Doc. No. 43, 22nd Cong., 2nd Sess. (Jan. 17, 1833).

Road from Zanesville, Ohio, to St. Louis, Missouri, H. Doc. No. 113, 20th Cong., 2nd Sess. (Feb. 6, 1829).

Suspended Operations—Public Works, H. Doc. No. 41, 26th Cong., 2nd Sess. (Jan. 4, 1840).

Message from the President of the United States to the Two Houses of Congress, at the Commencement of the Third Session of the Twenty-Seventh Congress, H. Doc. No. 2, 27th Cong., 3rd Sess. (Dec. 7, 1842).

Report of the Commissioner on Roads and Canals, S. Doc. No. 324, 28th Cong., 1st Sess. (April 30, 1844).

Report of the Commissioner on Roads and Canals, S. Doc. No. 41, 28th Cong., 2nd Sess. (Jan. 15, 1845).

STATE DOCUMENTS

MARYLAND

First Semiannual Report of Jonathan Huddleson, Superintendent of National Road within the Limits of Maryland, 1842.

Report of the Superintendent of the National Road in the State of Maryland, 1836.

Report of the Superintendent of the National Road, with Abstract of Tolls, Received from 12th Oct. 1836, to 1st Oct. 1837.

Seventh and Eighth Semi-annual Reports of T. Thistle, Superintendent of the National Road within the Limits of the State of Maryland, 1843.

OHIO

Acts of a General Nature Passed by the General Assembly of the State of Ohio, vols. 11–13 (1843–45).

Annual Report of the Board of Public Works, to the General Assembly of the State of Ohio, 1836–55.

Report of the Board of Commissioners, Appointed under the Act of March 6, 1845, Entitled "an act to appoint Commissioners to examine the books, accounts and proceedings of the Board of Public Works, and for other purposes," Doc. No. 1 (Jan. 20, 1847).

Report of the Board of Public Works, in Relation to the Rate of Toll Charged on the National Road, Doc. No. 30 (Dec. 31, 1839).

Report of the Commissioners Appointed under the Act of March 6, 1845, Entitled "an act to appoint Commissioners to examine the books, accounts and proceedings of the Board of Public Works, and for other purposes" (Dec. 26, 1845).

Report of the Superintendent of the National Road, to the General Assembly of Ohio, 1835.

Special Commissioners' Report. Special Report to the Auditor of State, in reply to a resolution of the House passed Dec. 18, 1846, Doc. No. 24 (Jan. 2, 1847).

Special Report of the Board of Public Works, Relating to the Management of the National Road, in Answer to a Resolution of the House (Feb. 3, 1841).

Special Report of the Board of Public Works, Relative to the Lessees of the National Road (Feb. 18, 1856).

Special Report of the Board of Public Works, Relative to the National Road, Doc. No. 21 (Jan. 29, 1838).

Special Report of the Board of Public Works, Transmitting the Report of the Superintendent of the National Road, Doc. No. 42 (Dec. 30, 1839).

Special Report of the Board of Public Works to the Ohio House of Representatives, 1836.

PUBLISHED PRIMARY SOURCES

Adams, Henry. *The Writings of Albert Gallatin.* 3 vols. 1879. Reprint, New York: Antiquarian Press, 1960.

Bergh, Albert Ellery, ed. *The Writings of Thomas Jefferson.* 20 vols. Washington, DC: Jefferson Memorial Association, 1904–7.

Beste, J. Richard. *The Wabash: Adventures of an English Gentleman's Family in the Interior of America.* 2 vols. London: Hurst and Hackett, 1855.

Blaine, William. *An Excursion through the United States and Canada during the Years 1822–23.* London: Baldwin, Cradock, and Joy, 1824.

Brunson, Alfred. "A Methodist Circuit Rider's Horseback Tour from Pennsylvania to Wisconsin, 1835." *Wisconsin Historical Collections* 15 (1900).

Cobbett, William. *A Year's Residence in the United States of America.* London: Author, 1828.

Douglas, Albert. "Auto Trip over the Old National Road." *Ohio Archaeological and Historical Publications* 18 (1909).

Faux, William. *Memorable Days in America Being a Journal of a Tour to the United States [. . .].* London: W. Simpkin and R. Marshall, 1823.

Gurney, Joseph John. *A Journey in North America, Described in Familiar Letters to Amelia Opie.* Norwich: Josiah Fletcher, 1841.

Gustorf, Fred, ed. "Frontier Perils Told by an Early Illinois Visitor." *Journal of the Illinois State Historical Society* 55, no. 2 (Summer 1962).

Hall, James. *Letters from the West [. . .].* London: Henry Colburn, 1828.

Hamilton, Thomas. *Men and Manners in America.* Edinburgh: William Blackwood, 1833.

Harris, Mary Vose, ed. "The Autobiography of Benjamin Franklin Harris." *Transactions of the Illinois State Historical Society.* Springfield: Phillips Brothers, 1923.

Hiatt, Joel W., ed. "The Diary of William Owen from November 10, 1824 to April 20, 1825." *Indiana Historical Society Publications* 4, no. 1 (1906).

Hoffman, Charles Fenno. *Winter in the West.* New York: Harper and Brothers, 1835.

Houstoun, Matilda Charlotte Fraser. *Hesperos: or, Travels in the West.* 2 vols. London: John W. Parker, 1850.

Hulbert, Archer Butler, ed. *Washington and the West Being George Washington's Diary of September, 1784 [. . .].* New York: Century, 1905.

Ierley, Merritt, ed. *Traveling the National Road: Across the Centuries on America's First Highway.* Woodstock, NY: Overlook Press, 1990.

Lewis, Jane Voorhees. "The Journal of Jane Voorhees Lewis." *Proceedings of the New Jersey Historical Society* 65 (1947).

Long, Stephen H. *Account of an Expedition from Pittsburgh to the Rocky Mountains.* Philadelphia: H. C. Carey and I. Lea Chestnut, 1823.

McCord, Shirley S., comp. *Travel Accounts of Indiana, 1679–1961.* Indianapolis: Indiana Historical Bureau, 1970.

Oliver, William. *Eight Months in Illinois with Information to Immigrants.* 1843. Reprint, Chicago: Walter M. Hill, 1924.

Peyton, John Lewis. *Over the Alleghanies and Across the Prairies. Personal Recollections of the Far West One and Twenty Years Ago.* London: Simpkin, Marshall, 1870.

Preston, Daniel, and Marlena C. DeLong. *The Papers of James Monroe A Documentary History of the Presidential Tours of James Monroe, 1817, 1818, 1819.* Westport, CT: Greenwood Press, 2003.

Richardson, James D., ed. *A Compilation of the Messages and Papers of the Presidents.* 11 vols. Washington, DC: Bureau of National Literature, 1913.

Thwaites, Reuben Gold, ed. *Early Western Travels, 1748–1846.* 32 vols. Cleveland: Arthur H. Clark, 1904–7.

"Uria Brown's Journal." *Maryland Historical Magazine* 10 (1915).

Welby, Adlard. *A Visit to North America and the English Settlements in Illinois.* London: J. Drury, 1821.

Woods, John. *Two Years' Residence in the Settlement on the English Prairie, in the Illinois Country, United States [. . .].* London: Longman, Hurst, Rees, Orme, and Brown, 1822.

SECONDARY SOURCES

LOCAL, COUNTY, AND REGIONAL HISTORIES

Beers, W. H. *History of Clark County, Ohio [. . .].* Chicago: W. H. Beers, 1881.

Bell, H. C. *Clark County.* Chicago: Middle West Publishing, 1907.

Biographical and Historical Record of Putnam County, Indiana. Chicago: Lewis Publishing, 1887.

Blackburn, E. Howard, and William H. Welfley. *History of Bedford and Somerset Counties Pennsylvania [. . .].* 3 vols. New York: Lewis Publishing, 1906.

Bodenhamer, David J., and Robert G. Barrows. *The Encyclopedia of Indianapolis.* Bloomington: Indiana Univ. Press, 1994.

Boyd, Peter C. *History of Triadelphia on Its 125th Anniversary.* Triadelphia, WV: Author, 1954.

Bradsby, H. C. *History of Vigo County, Indiana, with Biographical Selections.* Chicago: S. B. Nelson, 1891.

Bushnell, Henry. *The History of Granville Licking County, Ohio.* Columbus: Press of Hann and Adair, 1889.

Clark, Dorothy J. *Historically Speaking.* Evansville, IN: Whippoorwill Publications, 1981.

Crumrine, Boyd. *History of Washington County, Pennsylvania, with Biographical Sketches of many of its Prominent Men.* Philadelphia: L. H. Everts, 1992.

Cumberland County Historical and Genealogical Societies of Illinois. *Cumberland County History.* Greenup, IL: Cumberland County Historical and Genealogical Societies of Illinois, 1968.

Dublin, 1830–1980. Dublin, IN: Prinit Press, 1980.

Ellis, Franklin. *History of Fayette County, Pennsylvania, with Biographical Sketches of Many of Its Pioneers and Prominent Men.* Philadelphia: L. H. Everts, 1882.

Everhart, J. F. *History of Muskingum County, Ohio, with Illustrations and Biographical Sketches of Prominent Men and Pioneers.* N.p.: J. F. Everhart, 1882.

Forrest, Earle R. *History of Washington County Pennsylvania.* Chicago: S. J. Clarke Publishing, 1926.

Fox, Henry Clay, ed. *Memoirs of Wayne County and the City of Richmond Indiana.* Madison, WI: Western Historical Association, 1912.

Hadden, James. *A History of Uniontown the County Seat of Fayette County Pennsylvania.* Akron, OH: New Werner, 1913.

Hazzard, George. *Hazzard's History of Henry County Indiana, 1822–1906.* New Castle, IN: Author, 1906.

Heller, Herbert L. *Historic Henry County, 1820–1849.* 5 vols. New Castle, IN: Courier-Times Inc., 1981.

Hill, N. N., Jr. *History of Licking County, O [. . .].* Newark, OH: A. A. Graham & Co., 1881.

The History of Clark County, Ohio [. . .]. Chicago: W. H. Beers, 1881.

History of Dayton, Ohio, with Portraits and Biographical Sketches of Some of Its Pioneer and Prominent Citizens. Dayton: United Brethren Publishing House, 1889.

History of Hendricks County, Indiana [. . .]. Chicago: Inter-state Publishing, 1885.

History of Henry County, Indiana [. . .]. Chicago: Inter-state Publishing, 1884.

History of Wayne County, Indiana. 2 vols. Chicago: Inter-state Publishing, 1884.

Koontz, William H., *History of Bedford and Somerset Counties Pennsylvania.* 3 vols. New York: Lewis Publishing, 1906.

LaFever, Carolyn, and Beth Treaster. *Through the Archways of Time: Centerville, Indiana Celebrates 200 Years*. Greensburg, IN: Winters Publishing, 2014.

Lee, Alfred E. *History of the City of Columbus Capital of Ohio*. 2 vols. New York: Munsell, 1892.

Lewis, Rosalie. *Cumberland Reflections, 1831–1988*. Nappanee, IN: Evangel Press, 1988.

Lewis, Thomas William. *History of Southeastern Ohio and the Muskingum Valley, 1788–1928*. 3 vols. Chicago: S. J. Clarke Publishing, 1928.

———. *Zanesville and Muskingum County Ohio [. . .]*. 2 vols. Chicago: S. J. Clarke Publishing, 1927.

Lowdermilk, Will H. *History of Cumberland (Maryland), from the Time of the Indian Town, Caiuctuccc in 1728, up to the Present Day*. 1878. Reprint, Baltimore: Regional Publishing, 1976.

McFarland, Joseph F. *Washington and Washington County Pennsylvania and Representative Citizens*. Chicago: Richmond-Arnold Publishing, 1910.

Oakey, C. C. *Greater Terre Haute and Vigo County Closing the First Century's History of City and County*. 2 vols. Chicago: Lewis Publishing, 1908.

Perrin, William Henry, ed. *History of Crawford and Clark Counties, Illinois*. Chicago: O. L. Baskin, 1883.

———. *History of Effingham County, Illinois*. Chicago: O. L. Baskin, 1883.

Poole, Dan. *A Town with Two Names*. Milton, IN: Kids at Heart Publishing, 2012.

Prince, Benjamin F. *A Standard History of Springfield and Clark County, Ohio*. 2 vols. Chicago: American Historical Society, 1922.

Richman, George J. *History of Hancock County Indiana*. Indianapolis: Federal Publishing, 1916.

Ross, Robert W., and John J. Bullington, eds. *Historical Encyclopedia of Illinois and History of Fayette County*. Chicago: Munsell Publishing, 1910.

Sarchet, Cyrus P. B. *History of Guernsey County Ohio*. Indianapolis: B. F. Bowen, 1911.

Schaff, Morris. *A Sketch of Etna and Kirkersville*. Buffalo: Houghton, Mifflin, 1905.

Scharf, J. Thomas. *History of Western Maryland [. . .]*. 1882. Reprint, Baltimore: Regional Publishing, 1968.

Schlosnagle, Stephen. *Garrett County: A History of Maryland's Tableland*. Parsons, WV: McClain Publishing, 1978.

Schneider, Norris F. *Y Bridge City: The Story of Zanesville and Muskingum County, Ohio*. Cleveland: World Publishing, 1950.

Stegmaier, Harry I., David M. Dean, Gordon E. Kershaw, John B. Wiseman. *Allegany County: A History*. Parsons, WV: McClain Printing, 1976.

Sutor, J. Hope. *Past and Present of Zanesville and Muskingum County, Ohio*. Chicago: S. J. Clarke Publishing, 1905.

Thomas, James W., and T. J. C. Williams. *History of Allegany County Maryland [. . .]*. 1923. Reprint, Baltimore: Regional Publishing, 1969.

Travis, William. *A History of Clay County Indiana [. . .]*. New York: Lewis Publishing, 1909.

Walkinshaw, Lewis Clark. *Annals of Southwestern Pennsylvania*. 4 vols. New York: Lewis Historical Publishing, 1939.

Weik, Jesse W. *Weik's History of Putnam County Indiana*. Indianapolis: B. F. Bowen, 1910.

Winegerter, Charles A. *History of Greater Wheeling and Vicinity*. Chicago: Lewis Publishing, 1912.

Wolfe, William G. *Stories of Guernsey County, Ohio: History of an Average Ohio County*. Cambridge, OH: Author, 1943.

ADDITIONAL SECONDARY SOURCES

Ambler, Charles H. *George Washington and the West*. New York: Russell and Russell, 1936.

Ammon, Harry. *James Monroe: The Quest for National Identity*. New York: McGraw-Hill, 1971.

Bache, Rene. "Building a Thousand-Mile Boulevard." *Technical World Magazine* (Dec. 1910).

Barnes, L. Diane. "Urban Rivalry in the Upper Ohio Valley: Wheeling and Pittsburgh in the Nineteenth Century." *Pennsylvania Magazine of History and Biography* 123, no. 3 (July 1997).

Bond, Beverly W. *The Foundations of Ohio*. Vol. 1, *The History of the State of Ohio*. 5 vols., edited by Carl Wittke. Columbus: Ohio State Archaeological and Historical Society, 1941.

Brown, Jacob. *Brown's Miscellaneous Writings upon a Great Variety of Subjects*. Cumberland, MD: J. J. Miller, 1896.

Buley, R. Carlyle. *The Old Northwest: Pioneer Period, 1815–1840*. 2 vols. Bloomington: Indiana Univ. Press, 1951.

Burnham, John Chynoweth. "The Gasoline Tax and the Automobile Revolution." *Mississippi Valley Historical Review* 48 (1961).

Burns, Lee. "The National Road in Indiana." *Indiana Historical Society Publications* 7, no. 4 (1919).

Chambers, Smiley N. "Internal Improvements in Indiana. No. II—The National Road." *Indiana Magazine of History* 3 (1907).

Chernow, Ron. *Washington: A Life*. New York: Penguin Press, 2010.

Colten, K. Craig. "Adapting the Road to New Transport Technology." In *The National Road*, edited by Karl Raitz. Baltimore: Johns Hopkins Univ. Press, 1996.

Cunningham, Noble E., Jr. *The Presidency of James Monroe*. Lawrence: Univ. Press of Kansas, 1996.

Davies, Pete. *American Road: The Story of an Epic Transcontinental Journey at the Dawn of the Motor Age*. New York: Henry Holt, 2002.

Davis, Charles Henry. "The Old National Trails Road." *Travel Magazine*. (May 1915).

Dunbar, Seymour. *A History of Travel in America*. 4 vols. Indianapolis: Bobbs-Merrill, 1915.

Dungan, Nicholas. *Gallatin: America's Swiss Founding Father*. New York: New York Univ. Press, 2010.

Esarey, Logan. *History of Indiana from Its Exploration to 1922*. 4 vols. Dayton, OH: Historical Publishing Company, 1924.

Gallagher, Winifred. *How the Post Office Created America*. New York: Penguin Press, 2016.

Gerken, Cyndie L. *Marking the Miles along the National Road through Ohio: A Survey of Old Stone Mile Markers on Ohio's National Road*. Zanesville: Muskingum Valley Archaeological Survey, 2015.

Hale, William Bayard. "The Old National Road." *Century Magazine* 83, no. 2 (Dec. 1911).

Hardin, Thomas L. "The National Road in Illinois." *Journal of the Illinois State Historical Society* 60, no. 1 (Spring 1967).

Hargreaves, Mary W. M. *The Presidency of John Quincy Adams.* Lawrence: Univ. Press of Kansas, 1985.

Harper, Glenn A. "Preserving the National Road Landscape." In *The National Road,* ed. Karl Raitz. Baltimore: Johns Hopkins Univ. Press, 1996.

Hecht, Marie B. *John Quincy Adams: A Personal History of an Independent Man.* New York: Macmillan, 1972.

Heidler, David S., and Jeanne T. Heidler. *Henry Clay: The Essential American.* New York: Random House, 2010.

Heinlein, Paul C. "Cattle Driving from the Ohio Country, 1800–1850." *Agricultural History* 28 (1954).

Henry, W. E. "Some Elements of Indiana's Population or Roads West and Their Early Travelers." *Indiana Historical Society Publications* 4, no. 6 (1908).

Holley, James. "The Constitution, Parties and the Cumberland Road, 1801–1822." MA thesis, Univ. of Iowa, 1965.

Holt, Michael F. *The Rise and Fall of the American Whig Party: Jacksonian Politics and the Onset of the Civil War.* New York: Oxford Univ. Press, 1999.

Howe, Daniel Walker. *What Hath God Wrought: The Transformation of America, 1815–1848.* New York: Oxford Univ. Press, 2007.

Hudson, John C. *Making the Corn Belt: A Geographical History of Middle-Western Agriculture.* Bloomington: Indiana Univ. Press, 1994.

Jakle, John A. "Travelers' Impressions of the National Road." In *The National Road,* ed. Karl Raitz. Baltimore: Johns Hopkins Univ. Press, 1996.

Johnson, Charles B. "On and about the National Road in the Early Fifties." *Transactions of the Illinois State Historical Society for the Year 1922.* Springfield: Illinois State Library, 1923.

Jones, Robert Leslie. "The Beef Cattle Industry in Ohio Prior to the Civil War." *Ohio Historical Quarterly* 64 (1955).

Jordan, Philip D. *The National Road.* Indianapolis: Bobbs-Merrill, 1948.

Kemp, Emory L., and Beverly B. Fluty. *The Wheeling Suspension Bridge: A Pictorial Heritage.* Charleston, WV: Pictorial Histories Publishing, 1999.

King, Rev. I. F. "The Coming and Going of Ohio Droving." *Ohio Archeological and Historical Society Publications* 17 (1908).

Knepper, George W. *Ohio and Its People.* Kent, OH: Kent State Univ. Press, 1997.

Lacock, John Kennedy. "Braddock Road." *Pennsylvania Magazine of History and Biography* 37, no. 149 (Apr. 1914).

Larson, John Lauritz. "'Bind the Republic Together': The National Union and the Struggle for a System of Internal Improvements." *Journal of American History* 74, no. 2 (Sept. 1987).

Lewis, Clifford M. "The Wheeling Suspension Bridge." *West Virginia History* 23, no. 3 (Apr. 1972).

Malone, Dumas. *Jefferson the President Second Term, 1805–1809.* Vol. 5, *Jefferson and His Time.* Boston: Little, Brown, 1974.

Martzolff, Clement L. "Zane's Trace." *Ohio Archaeological and Historical Publications* 13 (1904).

Milgram, James W. *The Express Mail of 1836–1839: To Provide a Faster Mail Service between the North and the South.* Chicago: Collectors Club of Chicago, 1971.

Miller, Mrs. Carroll. "The Romance of the National Pike." *Western Pennsylvania Historical Magazine* 10, no. 1 (Jan. 1927).

Monroe, Elizabeth B. "Spanning the Commerce Clause: The Wheeling Bridge Case, 1850–1856." *American Journal of Legal History* 32, no. 3 (July 1988).

Niven, John. *John C. Calhoun and the Price of Union: A Biography.* Baton Rouge: Louisiana State Univ. Press, 1988

"The Old National Pike." *Harper's New Monthly Magazine* 59, no. 354 (Nov. 1879).

Paxson, Frederic L. "The Highway Movement, 1916–1935." *American Historical Review* 51 (1946).

Peyton, Billy Joe. "Surveying and Building the Road." In *The National Road,* ed. Karl Raitz. Baltimore: Johns Hopkins Univ. Press, 1996.

Remini, Robert, V. *Andrew Jackson and the Course of American Freedom, 1822–1832.* New York: Harper and Row, 1981.

———. *Henry Clay: Statesman for the Union.* New York: W. W. Norton, 1991.

Ringwalt, J. L. *Development of Transportation Systems in the United States.* Philadelphia: Author, 1888.

Scheiber, Harry N. *Ohio Canal Era: A Case Study of Government and the Economy, 1820–1861.* Athens: Ohio Univ. Press, 1969.

Schlereth, Thomas J. *A Roadscape of the American Experience.* Indianapolis: Indiana Historical Society, 1985.

Schneider, Norris F. *The National Road: Main Street of America.* Columbus: Ohio Historical Society, 1975.

Schwein, Richard H. "The Interstate 70 Landscape." In *The National Road,* ed. Karl Raitz. Baltimore: Johns Hopkins Univ. Press, 1996.

Searight, Thomas B. *The Old Pike: A History of the National Road with Incidents, Accidents, and Anecdotes Thereon.* 1894. Reprint, Bowie, MD: Heritage Books, 1990.

Shank, William H. *Historic Bridges of Pennsylvania.* York, PA: American Canal and Transportation Center, 1974.

———. *Three Hundred Years with the Pennsylvania Traveler.* York, PA: American Canal and Transportation Center, 1974.

Sky, Theodore. *The National Road and the Difficult Path to Sustainable National Investment.* Newark: Univ. of Delaware Press, 2011.

Smith, Catherine Blaskovich. "The Terminus of the Cumberland Road on the Ohio." *West Virginia History* 14, no. 3 (Apr. 1953).

Then and Now: The National Road and Its People. N.p., n.d. Pamphlet in archives of the Centerville, Indiana, Library.

Thomas, Emory. *Robert E. Lee: A Biography.* New York: W. W. Norton, 1995.

Traub, James. *John Quincy Adams: Militant Spirit.* New York: Basic Books, 2016.

Unger, Harlow Giles. *The Last Founding Father: James Monroe and a Nation's Call to Great-ness.* Philadelphia: Da Capo Press, 2009.

Utter, William T. *The Frontier State.* Vol. 2, *The History of the State of Ohio.* 5 vols., edited by Carl Wittke. Columbus: Ohio State Archaeological and Historical Society, 1942.

Walkinshaw, Lewis Clark. *Annals of Southwestern Pennsylvania.* 4 vols. New York: Lewis Historical Publishing, 1939.

Wallace, Michael, and Michael S. Williamson. *The Lincoln Highway: Coast to Coast from Times Square to the Golden Gate.* New York: W. W. Norton, 2007.

Wayland, John W. "Washington West of the Blue Ridge." *Virginia Magazine of History and Biography* 48, no. 3 (July 1940).

Wilkinson, Norman B. *The Conestoga Wagon, Historic Pennsylvania.* No. 5. Harrisburg: Pennsylvania Historical and Museum Commission, 1951.

Wiltse, Charles M. *John C. Calhoun: Nationalist, 1782–1828.* Indianapolis: Bobbs-Merrill, 1944.

Index

Lewisville, IN, 152
Lexington, KY, 70
Lick Creek, 61
Licking County, OH, 41, 46, 151–52
Licking River, 11, 49, 87
Lincoln, Abraham, 101
Lincoln, Jesse, 33
Lincoln Highway, 159, 160
Lincoln Highway Association, 157–58
Lind, Jenny, 103
Linnville, OH, 151
Littell, A. L., 124–25
Little Darby Creek, 50
Little Meadows, PA, 4
Little Wabash River, 62–63
Little Youghiogheny River, 6, 20; bridge over, 28, 33, 162
Lloyd's Hill, 97
Logan (Mingo chief), 9
Long, Stephen H., 61
Lord Dunmore's War, 9
Loudon, PA, 134
Loudon whip, 134
Louisiana Purchase, x, 1, 8–9, 15
Louisiana Territory, 8
Luman, Samuel, 125

MacDonald, Thomas, 160
Macomb, Alexander, 39, 41
Macon, Nathaniel, 70
Madison, James, xii, 30, 32, 36–37
Madison County, OH, 142
Mad River, 51, 52
Manhattan, IN, 105, 153
Mansfield, Joseph K. F., 73–74
Manypenny, George W., 81, 82, 88
Marietta, OH, 146
Marion County, IN, 59, 79, 153
Marsh, Mifflin M., 133
Marsh, Roswell, 84
Marshall, IL, 154
Martinsburg, PA, 150
Martinsville, IL, 154
Maryland General Assembly, 73, 76–77, 80
Mason, Isaac, 19
Maysville, KY, 10, 70
McAdam, John Loudon, 39
McAdam roads, 39, 40, 73
McCartney, Nicholas, 109

McClure, John, 33, 99
McConnellstown, PA, 92
McDonald, Daniel, 85
McGiffen, Thomas, 30, 32
McGinnis, Hugh, 43
McIntire, John, 10, 11
McKean, Thompson, 32
McKennan, T. M. T., 135
McKinley, Henry, 22, 23, 24, 25
McLean, John, 122–23
McNeil, Archie, 95
McRee, William, 38, 45
Meridian Highway, 158
Miami County, OH, 65
Miami River, 46, 51
Midland Trail, 158
Miller, John, 32
Miller, William, 118
Milroy, John, 55, 56
Modesitt, Charles, 153
Monaghan, Thomas, 43
Monongahela River, 2, 20, 27, 99–100
Monroe, James, xii, 33, 37–38, 99–100
Monroeville, PA, 35
Moore, Daniel, 92
Moore, Henry, 93
Moore, Thomas, 17–20, 31
Moorefield, VA, 9
Moore & Stockton, 123
Morristown, OH, 11
Mt. Meridian, IN, 153
Mt. Vernon, VA, 5
Mulrine, William, 83–87
Murray, John, 9
Muskingum College, 151
Muskingum County, OH, 72
Muskingum River, 11, 72

Nash, Simeon, 84
National Highways Association, 158
National Interstate and Defense Highways Act, 161
National Old Trails Road, 158
National Road, 158; appropriations for, 14–15, 17, 21, 29, 33, 34, 35, 37, 38, 48, 55, 58, 59, 61, 73, 76, 156; books about, xi; bridges on, 27–29, 42–43, 49, 51, 52, 56, 61–62, 63, 75–76, 116–17, 161–62; celebrities travel over, 99–103; Congressional debates concerning, ix, 14–16, 36–37, 48, 69–70; corruption involving, 25,